The Center for South and Southeast Asia Studies of the University of California is the coordinating center for research, teaching programs, and special projects relating to the South and Southeast Asia areas on the nine campuses of the University. The Center is the largest such research and teaching organization in the United States, with more than 150 related faculty representing all disciplines within the social sciences, languages, and humanities.

The Center publishes a Monograph Series, an Occasional Papers Series, and sponsors a series published by the University of California Press. Manuscripts for these publications have been selected with the highest standards of academic excellence, with emphasis on those studies and literary works that are pioneers in their fields, and that provide fresh insights into the life and culture of the great civilizations of South and Southeast Asia.

RECENT PUBLICATIONS OF THE
CENTER FOR SOUTH AND SOUTHEAST ASIA STUDIES:

Surinder Mohan Bhardwaj
Hindu Places of Pilgrimage in India: A Study in Cultural Geography

Edward Conze
The Large Sutra on Perfect Wisdom

Rodney W. Jones
Urban Politics in India: Area, Power, and Policy in a Penetrated System

Tom G. Kessinger
Vilyatpur, 1848–1968: Social and Economic Change in a North Indian Village

Stanley Kochanek
Business and Politics in India

THE MYTH OF THE *LOKAMANYA*

*This volume is sponsored by the
Center for South and Southeast Asia Studies,
University of California, Berkeley*

THE MYTH OF THE *LOKAMANYA*

TILAK AND MASS POLITICS IN MAHARASHTRA

RICHARD I. CASHMAN

UNIVERSITY OF CALIFORNIA PRESS
BERKELEY · LOS ANGELES · LONDON

University of California Press
Berkeley and Los Angeles, California

University of California Press, Ltd.
London, England

Copyright © 1975 by
The Regents of the University of California

ISBN : 9780520303805

Library of Congress Catalog Card Number : 72-97734

Photosetting by
Thomson Press (India) Limited, New Delhi,

CONTENTS

Acknowledgments ... vii
Abbreviations ... viii
Introduction ... 1
I. The Traditions of Maharashtra ... 6
II. British Policy and Maratha Brahmans ... 17
III. The Making of a Protest Movement ... 45
IV. The Political Recruitment of God Ganapati ... 75
V. The Development of the Shivaji Tradition ... 98
VI. The Famine Campaign and the Deccan Peasantry ... 123
VII. Poona and Bombay ... 151
VIII. Tilak and the Bombay Proletariat ... 172
IX. The Legacy of Tilak ... 192
Conclusion: The *Lokamanya* as Myth ... 218
Appendix 1: Social Background of Some Prominent Figures of the Poona Brahman Elite, 1880–1920 ... 222
Appendix 2: Number of *Melas* in Some Important Towns of the Region for Selected Years, 1894–1910 ... 226
Appendix 3: Selections from the Songs of the *Sanmitra Samaj Mela* ... 227
Appendix 4: Active Members of the Council of the Bombay Presidency Association, 1885–1909 ... 229
Glossary ... 231
Index ... 233

MAPS

Towns Visited by the Sabha Agents	128
No-Rent Combinations Inspired by Sabha Agents	132

CHART

Representation of the Bhakti and Militant Traditions Intersected by the Variables of Asceticism and Eroticism	15

TABLES

Distribution of Chitpavan and Deshastha Brahmans in the Konkan and Deccan Districts of the Bombay Presidency, 1901	21
Community of Students Enrolled at Fergusson College, 1910 and 1935	22
Princely Donations to the Deccan Education Society, 1884–1910	102
Council Meetings of the Bombay Presidency Association	162
Geographical Distribution of Delegates at the Fifteenth and Seventeenth Bombay Provincial Conference (BPC) Poona, 1915	195
Occupations of Delegates at the Fifteenth and Seventeenth BPC, Poona, 1915	196
Managing Committee of the Poona *Sarvajanik Sabha*, 1916–21 Community	200
Congress Membership by Region, 1921; Lawyers Who Suspended Practice in 1920–21 by Region; Numbers of Charkas Recorded in 1921 by Region	209

ACKNOWLEDGMENTS

This study is based on a dissertation which was presented to Duke University in 1969. It was made possible by grants from the American Institute of Indian Studies and the Commonwealth Studies Center and the Program in Comparative Studies in Southern Asia of Duke University. In the preparation of a revised manuscript assistance was received from the University of Rochester and the University of New South Wales.

There are several personal debts to mention. Professor Robert I. Crane, my mentor, provided an initial stimulus and continuing encouragement. Professor N. R. Phatak, a prolific Marathi historian, and his son, B. N. Phatak, introduced me to important source material, made many helpful suggestions, and corrected many errors in the final draft. Many readers have commented on the manuscript: they include Rama Amritmahal, N. Gerald Barrier, Ralph Croizier, Ellen McDonald Gumperz, Max Harcourt, Stephen Henningham, Datta Kharbas, Ravinder Kumar, and Richard Tucker.

Aman Momin, my research assistant, assisted with Marathi sources and introduced me to many facets of Maharashtrian culture. The Editorial Committee of the *Indian Economic and Social History Review* permitted me to include Chapter IV, the substance of which appeared in their journal. Two maps and one diagram were prepared by Neville Dickson.

ABBREVIATIONS

BA	Bombay Archives
BG	Bombay Government
BPA	Bombay Presidency Association
BPC	Bombay Provincial Conference
BPS	Bombay *Prarthana Samaj*
BRNP	Report on Native Papers Published in the Bombay Presidency
DES	Deccan Education Society
DS	Deccan *Sabha*
GI	Government of India
IESHR	Indian Economic and Social History Review
INC	Indian National Congress
IOL	India Office Library
JAS	Journal of Asian Studies
MHFM	Office of the Maharashtra History of the Freedom Movement
NAI	National Archives of India
PSS } *QJPSS*	Quarterly Journal of the Poona Sarvajanik Sabha

SOURCE MATERIAL

BHFM	Source Material for a History of the Freedom Movement in India Collected from the Bombay Government Records
SA	South Asia

INTRODUCTION

I

Myth, in the popular usage, connotes a legend, a fictitious narrative, or an allegorical tale. A myth is usually regarded as a spurious representation of some past historical reality. In this book the word "myth" is used in the anthropological rather than the popular sense. It may be defined as the "large, controlling image" which is founded in man's experience,[1] and which forms an essential element of a group state of mind or consciousness. A myth reflects the manner in which a community conceives of itself and defines itself *vis-à-vis* the present, its past history, and future prospects. Whether a myth is based on reality or ignores or distorts reality, it is important because of its credibility to the intended audience. It is a powerful construct because it represents the sum of what a group wants to believe about itself.

Myth is strongest in the small preliterate archaic society, the traditional village, where the group is sufficiently cohesive, small and isolated, to nurture a common fund of myths to ward off any potential challenge to the collective mentality. By comparison, any large society, any nation, is faced with a plethora of myths, many of which are contradictory. The South Asian subcontinent is a prime example of this tendency, since India has freely assimilated and synthesized a wide variety of myths. The Great Tradition includes therianthropic deities along with gods in human form, the violent mother Durga-Kali side by side with the quietist Mahavira, and the potent Shiva, who is worshipped as a phallic symbol, together with the asceticism of the Upanishads. Scholars have attempted to detect some common themes, some vitalizing elements underlying the multitude of myths, such as *ahimsa* (non-violence), cyclical time, the "search for the real,"[2] and the narcissistic

---

[1] Henry A. Murray, "Introduction to the Issue of 'Myth and Mythmaking'," *Daedulus*, LXXXVIII, No. 2 (Spring, 1959), pp. 211–222.

[2] W. Norman Brown, *Man in the Universe: Some Continuities In Indian Thought* (Berkeley, 1966).

personality,[3] but for the most part Indian mythology has remained larger than the sum of all the interpretations.

In modern India the myth of the *Mahatma* (great soul) was one of the most powerful political myths. It was established to describe the career of India's foremost leader, Mohandas Karamchand Gandhi (1869–1948). The *Mahatma* concept underlined Gandhi's efforts to combine religion and politics, to bring morality into the sphere of politics. It also suggested his concern for non-violence, which was necessary to establish truly moral means to reach a spiritual end. Asceticism was another ingredient of the myth; in order to arrive at the most truthful positions Gandhi abstained from certain foods, liquor, and sexual activity.

The myth of the *Mahatma* was only one of the many political myths of modern India. For three decades prior to Gandhi's rise to political eminence, the myth of the *Lokamanya*, derived from the political career of Bal Gangadhar Tilak (1856–1920), was one of the most powerful political myths in India. *Lokamanya* (literally, one who is revered by by the people) stood for a more practical, pragmatic approach to politics and seemed to epitomize a more earthy and aggressive tradition. Tilak was a proud individual who valued physical strength and force and did not place much emphasis on asceticism.

It will be the task of this book to analyse the ingredients of the myth of the *Lokamanya*. How did the myth develop? Whom did it represent? What was the value of the myth for political mobilization? In a society which is undergoing rapid change, mythmaking, or the cross-fertilization of myths, is a significant activity. A leader defines his position in terms of the great epics, heroes, and values of the past. Biographers elaborate this interpretation and redefine it in terms of the later history of the society. Subsequent leaders modify or alter the leader's position to suit their own purposes. Critics of the original leader will question his authority and interpretation and attempt to establish counter-myths to expose the leader. This study will examine the creative role which myths can play in a colonial society, suggesting, in a small way, how modern Indians perceive themselves.

II

Lokamanya Tilak, the Maharashtrian leader, has been acclaimed as the first Indian nationalist to bridge the gap between the elitist Indian National Congress and the more traditional masses. It has been argued

[3]P. Spratt, *Hindu Culture and Personality: A Psycho-Analytic Study* (Bombay, 1966).

that Tilak achieved his success for several reasons. A forceful and charismatic personality enabled him to epitomize the struggle for Indian independence and develop cadres of supporters who looked to their leader for authority and inspiration. He linked the nationalist movement with religion and traditional heroes and succeeded in wooing orthodox leaders, peasants, and artisans to the cause. He was an educated Indian who valued such modern ends as industrial progress and the establishment of a nation state, and he made use of modern techniques of propaganda, such as the press. Tilak has been acclaimed as a leader who could tap the forces of modern, traditional, and charismatic authority.

In his own time Tilak was accorded the trappings of divinity in the popular mind. He was acclaimed as the *Lokamanya*, the leader revered by the people. Uncrowned king of the freedom movement, his deeds were likened to those of the Maratha hero Shivaji (1627–80). As a traditional king is semi-divine, it was a short step for Tilak to take on god-like qualities. His portrait was carried in the Ganapati festival along with Shivaji's, the saints of Maharashtra, and a host of gods, and his deeds were likened to the heroic struggles of the epics. To some artisans and peasants he was *Mahatma Bhagwan* Tilak (great soul god Tilak), god incarnate, to be revered and worshipped.[4] Tilak was, in other words, a politician whose career and achievements have been mythicized.

Historians have continued the process of the canonization of this "superhuman" politician. Tilak was the divine potter, the "Hercules & Prometheus of Modern India,"[5] who fashioned mass movements out of the shapeless clay of inertia. He was the master strategist who welded the diverse elements of Indian society in the common struggle against the British.[6] Specifically, he succeeded in "tapping and bringing together the hitherto ignored urban and peasant lower classes" into the elitist Congress movement.[7] A brilliant tactician, he combined

[4] Dhananjay Keer, *Lokamanya Tilak: Father of the Indian Freedom Struggle* (2d ed., Bombay, 1969), pp. 372–383. There are similar references in police reports and government documents. Sir George Clarke, Governor of Bombay (1907–13), noted in 1908 that Tilak was hailed as a Maharaja and an incarnation of Vishnu by the mill-hands of Bombay City. Sir George Clarke to Lord Morley, July 24, 1908, Morley Papers, MSS Eur. D 573/42E, IOL (India Office Library).
[5] S. L. Karandikar, *Lokamanya Bal Gangadhar Tilak : The Hercules & Prometheus of Modern India* (Poona, 1957).
[6] Ram Gopal, *Lokamanya Tilak: A Biography* (Bombay, 1956), pp. 90–91.
[7] Stanley A. Wolpert, *Tilak and Gokhale: Revolution and Reform in the Making of Modern India* (Berkeley, 1962), p. 68.

religion with politics, and tradition with modernity, and was thus able to bridge the gap between the westernized elites and the traditional masses. He was orthodox and yet in favour of reform; a spokesman of the Brahman community, he was revered also by the non-Brahman masses; he was an apologist for Hinduism, yet respected by people of other religions.

In the welter of accolades the real Tilak is obscured. As a superhuman individual there seem to be no limits to his achievements, his ability to accomplish miracles, to reconcile irreconcilables, and to overcome contradictions. He has been portrayed as a paragon of Hindu virtues by the Brahman historians of Poona and, more recently, has been acclaimed by a group of Soviet historians as the leader of the "democratic wing" of Maharashtra in the struggle against "feudal exploitation and national oppression."[8]

In order to examine the myth of the *Lokamanya*, to isolate the myth from political reality or, more correctly, to consider the myth as a component part of political reality, this study will concentrate on four mass movements initiated between 1893 and 1908: the Ganapati and the Shivaji festivals, a famine campaign, and an appeal to the urban proletariat of Bombay City. It will thus consider Tilak's appeals to religion, to an heroic leader of the past, to the Deccan peasantry, and to an urban proletariat. They have the advantage of focussing on the *Lokamanya* at specific points in time when he was involved in political action, and they provide the means of comparing public statements with actions and with claimed results. They offer the opportunity to analyse the political organization set up by Tilak and the lieutenants with whom he worked. The study will also examine, in Chapters II and III, the conflicts within Maharashtrian society and the circumstances which thrust Tilak into leadership.

It would be all too easy to write a study which could "debunk" the achievement of Tilak and suggest that the *Lokamanya* was a figment of the popular imagination. At this stage the author must confess an initial antipathy to Tilak and a preference for the moderate nationalist G. K. Gokhale. To the majority of western scholars Gokhale exemplifies the values of the academe, liberalism, scholarly integrity, and detachment from the rancour of professional politics. Tilak is disdained for his obvious relish for political infighting and is blamed for later Poona manifestations of regional chauvinism and Hindu revivalism.

---

[8] I. M. Reisner and N. M. Goldberg (eds.), *Tilak and the Struggle for Indian Freedom* (New Delhi, 1966), preface, p. 1.

However, in the course of working on Tilak, the writer's attitude has changed from antipathy to one of qualified sympathy for this man of action who understood the nature of power and the demands of leadership.

Chapter I

THE TRADITIONS OF MAHARASHTRA

Although Tilak was a national figure who epitomized the Indian struggle against the British in his day, he was primarily a Maharashtrian politician deeply imbued with the cultural traditions of the region. His influence at the national level was based on a sizeable local following achieved by the development of a style of politics in harmony with the region.

Maharashtrian culture has been fashioned by a number of distinctive forces. It has been shaped in the traditional towns and villages of the region rather than in the one modern city of the province, Bombay. Maharashtrians have never considered Bombay to be a Maharashtrian city in the way in which Bengalis have looked to Calcutta as the fulcrum of Bengali culture.[1] Bombay was and is a "small India. If you belong to Bombay that is a nationality in itself."[2] The Deccan towns have been sequestered from the coastal entrepôt cities by the rugged western *ghats* (mountains). The cultural values of Maharashtra have been fashioned in the more rustic, more conservative, and less industrial hinterland towns such as Poona.

Maharashtra possesses a relatively homogeneous population. The majority of the inhabitants come from the non-Brahman communities. The core of this group is the Maratha-Kunbi caste cluster which numbers forty per cent of the population and ranks with the Rajputs as one of the largest caste communities in India.[3] It is this group which produced Shivaji and many of the bhakti poet-saints and which has

[1] J. H. Broomfield, *Elite Conflict in a Plural Society: Twentieth Century Bengal* (Berkeley, 1968), p. 4.

[2] Arvind Mafatlal, quoted in Dom Moraes, "Bombay: Wealth, Shantytowns, Speakeasies, Intellectual Admen and Death on the Trains," *New York Times Magazine*, October 11, 1970, p. 143.

[3] Irawati Karve, *Hindu Society—An Interpretation* (Poona, 1961), pp. 19-20. The word Maratha is used in several senses: it signifies a particular caste community, the Maratha-Kunbi group, and is used also to refer to any inhabitant of Maharashtra. When used below it will refer to the Maratha-Kunbi caste cluster.

had a formative influence on the local culture. The support of many non-Brahman artisan castes, who number approximately one-quarter of the population and identify with the Marathas, has assured a non-Brahman political hegemony in recent times. The Brahmans, five per cent of the population, form a thin upper crust of society. The Depressed or Scheduled Castes, ten per cent of the total, form the third or lower tier of society. They were not effectively organized until the twentieth century. The Vaishya or trading element has always been small (two to three per cent) and weak, most likely because of the poor condition of the soil and the limited scope for capital formation savings. Its functions have been largely usurped by the Gujaratis and the Marwadis from regions to the north. The Muslim population, five per cent of the total, is poor and politically ineffective.

Because of their contribution to the bhakti movement and their participation in the Maratha armies, the Marathas have played an important role in shaping the regional culture and sense of identity. While they were not trained as soldiers (the Maratha army was recruited from farmers, shepherds, and artisans), the very success of the Maratha military endeavours established a claim to professional military or Kshatriya status. In due course Shivaji was reluctantly accepted as a Kshatriya at the time of his coronation. He was then declared to be a lineal descendant of the Rajput clan of Sisodia, a Kshatriya by birth as well as by achievement. Shivaji's connection with the Rajput Kshatriya tradition seems to suggest the weakness of the Kshatriya tradition in Maharashtra prior to the seventeenth century. There was even a "palpably absurd social theory," current at this time, that there was no ancient Kshatriya class of Maharashtra, that the caste had been annihilated by Parashurama.[4] The successes of Shivaji and his followers "discredited" this notion, and led to the foundation or the reassertion of the Kshatriya tradition in Maharashtra and to the popularization of Kshatriya values.

By the nineteenth century the tradition was sufficiently established for the Marathas to be acclaimed by one Englishman as one of the "martial races" of India, a distinction shared by the Sikhs, the Muslims, the Jats, the Pathans, and the Rajputs.[5] Another Englishman praised the performance of the Maratha soldier. Possessing a "short stature, a small but wiry frame," courage, and familiarity with the rugged

---

[4] Govind Sakharam Sardesai, *New History of the Marathas*, Vol. I, *Shivaji and His Line*, 1600–1707 (2d ed., Bombay, 1957), p. 216.
[5] Lieut.-General Sir George MacMunn, *The Martial Races of India* (London, 1933).

Deccan terrain, the Maratha warrior was renowned as an effective guerrilla, one who proved a thorn in the side of medieval Muslim rule.[6] The Maratha Kshatriya tradition is best personified by Shivaji, an adept horseman, a bold and daring general, who remains the romantic hero of the region to this day. The statue of the equestrian Shivaji, the lithe soldier-statesman, is one of the popular symbols of Maharashtra.

Although the Brahmans played an important part in shaping the regional culture, particularly during the eighteenth century when they were rulers, it is significant that their contribution was as priests, scholars, courtiers, and warriors. They thus strengthened rather than weakened the militant tradition of the region. The Brahman role reversal was recognized by the prominent Brahman essayist, *Vishnushastri* Vishnu Krishna Chiplunkar (1850–82), who applauded those Brahmans who became Kshatriyas: "Those people, who traditionally were priests, and who now are chiefly clerks, threw away, in that century [the eighteenth], their priestly functions and their pens and became Kshatriyas; some became kings, and some became soldiers. This was an unprecedented and remarkable change in which the people of Parashurama's land demonstrated their bravery all over the country."[7] Thus important leaders of both the Brahman and the Maratha communities have been attracted to Kshatriya values.

The Peshwas (prime ministers), the *de facto* Brahman rulers of the Maratha empire for a century, were the most visible symbols of Kshatriya Brahmans. Baji Rao I (1720–40) was a romantic figure, a "matchless cavalry leader" who ranked "next only to Shivaji in military genius."[8] Hardy and robust in constitution, Baji Rao led his troops into the thick of battle. The Maratha empire was greatly expanded under his leadership.

Madhavrao (1761–72) was a model Hindu king, a Kshatriya who remembered that he was also a Brahman. While the young Peshwa proved to be an able military leader, he also established a reputation for prudent, just, and wise rule. A devout ruler, he encouraged organized religion (introducing a large public celebration for Ganesha) and attempted to improve the moral life of his subjects by promoting social reform and by discouraging the consumption of liquor.[9] Unlike most

[6]Richard Temple et al., *Shivaji and the Rise of the Mahrattas* (Calcutta, 1953), p. 2.
[7]V. K. Chiplunkar, *Nibandhmala (Garland of Essays)* (3d ed., Poona, 1926), p. 992.
[8]Sardesai, *New History*, Vol. II, *The Expansion of the Maratha Power, 1707–1772* (2d ed., Bombay, 1958), pp. 194–195.
[9]A. C. Banerjee, *Peshwa Madhavrao I* (2d ed., Calcutta, 1968), pp. 191–192.

of the Peshwas, Madhavrao disapproved of the lavish expenditure of the court and kept a tight rein on expenses. He was the most puritanical of the Peshwas, preferring an unostentatious existence to the usual luxury and pleasures of courtly life. He was content with one wife, whereas Nana Phadnis had at least nine, and Baji Rao II had eleven. The wife of Madhavrao joined him on the funeral pyre when his life was cut short at the age of twenty-eight. According to Sardesai, he was the ideal Peshwa who combined the courage and skill of a Kshatriya with the devotion and decorum of a Brahman.[10]

Among the Peshwas the moderate and circumspect Madhavrao was an exception. Most of the Brahman rulers enjoyed the pleasures of court life, which included a retinue of dancing-girls and the earthy dance-drama, the tamasha, which was popularized in the Peshwa courts. Balaji, better known as Nana Saheb (1740–61), had "refined taste" and was fond of leading a "luxurious life" and of enjoying splendour and the fine arts. Baji Rao II (1796–1818), the last and most notorious Peshwa, literally fiddled his thumbs in Poona while the Maratha empire collapsed about him. He was sufficiently content with his regular "routine of baths and prayers, eating, drinking and making merry" to lose interest in the world about him.[11] He enjoyed the regular round of wine, lawnies (bawdy songs), and dancing-girls. In addition to his "vices," Baji Rao II, although a skillful rider and swordsman, lacked courage. He was the most ignominious of the Peshwas.[12]

According to the moderate nationalist, Mahadev Govind Ranade (1842–1901), Kshatriya forces coalesced with the bhakti movement to produce a sense of Maharashtrian identity which flowered at the time of Shivaji. From the twelfth century Maharashtra witnessed a literary and religious awakening which was fostered by the bhakti poet-saints. Coming chiefly from the lower echelons of society, the poet-saints developed a nationalist movement of heterodox and egalitarian character by preaching against "forms and ceremonies and class distinctions based on birth." In the late sixteenth and early seventeenth centuries Maharashtra was stirred by a political revolution which followed and to some extent was caused by the religious and social upheaval of several centuries. By integrating the various castes and

[10] *Ibid.*; Sardesai, II, 560–567.
[11] Sardesai, *New History*, Vol. III, *Sunset Over Maharashtra*, 1772–1848 (Bombay, 1948), p. 393.
[12] *Ibid.*; Pratul Chandra Gupta, *Baji Rao II and the East India Company*, 1796–1818 (2d ed., Bombay, 1964).

classes in his administration, Shivaji, the chief revolutionary, acted in accord with the national spirit proclaimed by the poet-saints.[13]

Ranade's work was a conscious effort to underline the importance of the Vaishnava bhakti movement in the formation of regional identity. He was attracted to the ideals and values of the poet-saints, to their pietism, asceticism, mysticism, and religious syncretism together with an emphasis on religious equality and a tradition of literary writing. While there were anti-intellectual strains in the bhakti tradition, it was not a movement which despised forms; it provided the direct inspiration for the flowering of Marathi literature in medieval times. The bhakti movement was given an intellectual focus in the late nineteenth century in the eclectic Bombay *Prarthana Samaj* (Prayer Society), a regional variation of the *Brahmo Samaj*. Ranade was an active member of the Bombay society.

In his writing Ranade tends to regard bhakti as the dominant tradition of the region. Kshatriya forces are subservient to and moulded by the devotional tradition. According to Ranade the Maratha peasant, "hardy and abstemious," is a child of the bhakti movement. Maratha nationalism was thus founded on a "Puritan enthusiasm."[14] Shivaji, the chief political architect, was influenced by pietism and guided by the dictates of bhakti.

Ranade's thesis is creditable in several respects. Shivaji and the bhakti saints were the two most formidable forces which shaped Maharashtrian culture. The bhakti movement provided the cultural and linguistic ingredients of Maratha nationalism. At the time of Shivaji the religious and political forces did, to some extent, coalesce. But the argument does not establish any true merging of the forces of bhakti with the martial spirit of the warrior class, or the dominance of the bhakti tradition in the region. Many Kshatriya values were antithetical to the bhakti movement. Military endeavours represent the antithesis of *ahimsa* and the worship of Vithal or Vithoba, the Maharashtrian variant of Vishnu. Shivaji's own deity was a Saivite goddess, Bhavani, a manifestation of Parvati, who sanctified military efforts. Bhavani represented "strength personified." The goddess made use of her power to slay demons.[15]

---

[13]M. G. Ranade, *Rise of the Maratha Power and Other Essays,* and K. T. Telang, *Gleanings from the Maratha Chronicles* (2d ed., Bombay, 1961), pp. 5–6.
[14]*Ibid.*, p. 28.
[15]N. K. Behere, *The Background of Maratha Renaissance in the 17th Century* (Bangalore, 1946), p. 164.

The differing bases of the two traditions can be illustrated by a comparison of Khandoba, the god of the shepherd community, with Vithal, the object of Maharashtrian bhakti worship. Khandoba, literally "swordsman father," is the guardian deity of the Deccan. He is worshipped at Jejuri in the form of a lingam. In the popular tradition he is pictured as a Kshatriya on horseback, brandishing a sword to thwart the demons. Khandoba is frequently associated with the sun—his flag, his steed, and his opponents are yellow—a symbol of strength and force. Khandoba has two wives and, in addition, enjoys the ministrations of mistresses from the shepherd community.[16] By comparison, Vithal is a "familiar philosopher, friend and guide," a symbol of spiritual love and devotion. Although he is flanked by his consort Rukhmini, he is regarded more as an "elder brother who is both a friendly guide and playmate" rather than a "sex-minded husband" or a "disciplinarian father."[17]

Unlike Bengal, where Vaishnavism developed some "left-handed" Tantric communities (though the "right-handed" tradition was the dominant one),[18] the bhakti saints of Maharashtra were yogic and considered sexual indulgence to be a hindrance to their mission. Jnaneshwar (thirteenth century) was a *Brahmachari* (one who has taken a vow of sexual abstinence); Tukaram (1608–50) and Eknath (1548?–99), although married, preferred spiritual union to physical pleasure. To such men politics was *maya*; they believed in the invisible kingdom of the spirit in which all men, Hindus and Muslims, Brahmans and Untouchables, were brothers.

From the time of Shivaji it was the fighting warrior who was the hero to be emulated as much as the saint in *samadhi*.[19] Strength and manliness, the arts of horsemanship and wrestling, were alternative values to devotion and renunciation. Soldiers, weary from the demands of war, preferred entertainment and pleasure to worship and withdrawal.

Unlike the militant tradition, the Vaishnava bhakti movement tended to be apolitical and ascetic. In fact, some writers, such as N. C. Kelkar, have questioned the contribution of the bhakti saints to the

---

[16]Rai Bahadur B. A. Gupte, *Hindu Holidays and Ceremonies with Dissertations on Origin, Folklore and Symbols* (2d ed., Calcutta, 1919), pp. 19–21.

[17]Behere, pp. 162–163.

[18]Edward C. Dimock, Jr., *The Place of the Hidden Moon* (Chicago, 1966).

[19]*Samadhi* refers here to a state of deep meditation or a devotional act of self-immolation. The word also refers to the place where an important figure is cremated. It is the usual Hindu custom to bury some of the remains there.

formation of Maratha nationalism.[20] In Kelkar's view, their teaching was negative and did not contribute to the political regeneration of the country. By concentrating on the devotional realm, the bhakti saints discouraged political activity. This is an extreme position, since the bhakti saints did contribute to the language and literature of the region and involved themselves in some movements of social reform; thus the militant and the devotional traditions rested on some common ground. Although a political activist, Tilak admired the commentary on the *Bhagavad Gita* produced by the thirteenth century saint Jnaneshwar. This work represented an attack on the renunciatory philosophy of Samkara, for Jnaneshwar believed the material world and man to be "natural expressions of Reality." But, true to the Vaishnava bhakti tradition, Jnaneshwar's emphasis was on individual salvation through devotional action, whereas Tilak preferred "social action for public welfare."[21]

There is evidence that Maratha nationality was made up of two parallel traditions, the Kshatriya and the bhakti. The diagram in this chapter suggests this relationship together with the intersecting variables of asceticism and eroticism. Whereas the Maharashtrian bhakti saints are close to the polarity of asceticism, the militant leaders range between the two extremes.

At the popular level the Kshatriya tradition might be likened to the little tradition of the region, for it seems more closely aligned to popular Hinduism, to figures of earth and the values of pleasure, humour, and, to some extent, eroticism. The popular Kshatriya gods, Khandoba and Bhavani, probably originated as local tribal gods. The militant tradition tends to be aligned rather to the Saivite gods of non-Brahman Maharashtra. The latter are far less wedded to asceticism than the gods of Brahmanic Hinduism. They condone the eating of fish and flesh.[22] This tradition also lacks the literary focus of the Vaishnava movement.

The Vaishnava movement produced what can loosely be called the high tradition of the region in that its tenets are closer to the great tradition of Brahmanical Hinduism. It has propagated the Brahmanical values of asceticism and renunciation and produced the early

---

[20]Quoted in Wilbur S. Deming, *Ramdas and the Ramdasis* (London, 1928), p. 16.
[21]D. MacKenzie Brown, "The Philosophy of Bal Gangadhar Tilak, *Karma* vs. *Jñāna* in the *Gītā Rahasya*," *JAS*, XVII, No. 2 (February, 1958), pp. 203–204.
[22]G. S. Ghurye, *Gods and Men* (Bombay, 1962), pp. 114–139; R. E. Enthoven, *The Tribes and Castes of Bombay*, 3 vols. (Bombay, 1922), III, 39–40.

literature of the region. However, in several senses, the Vaishnava movement differs from the great tradition: it was proclaimed chiefly by non-Brahmans, who have preferred the *prakrit* (vernacular language), Marathi, to Sanskrit.

The importance of the earthy Kshatriya culture is indicated by the popularity of certain institutions in the region. The tamasha, spurned by the upper classes, was and is a popular form of dance-drama developed in Maharashtra. It achieved recognition and official patronage at the Peshwa court.[23] The tamasha indicates the Maharashtrian propensity for humour, dancing, and eroticism.

The worship of the elephant-headed god Ganapati, who is more popular in Maharashtra than in any other region, seems to be another indication of the Maharashtrian bent for pleasure.[24] Ganapati[25] is a son of Shiva. Whereas the other sons of Shiva are warriors, Ganapati's status is ambiguous. Possessing a pot-belly and a rat as his vehicle, he resembles a figure of pleasure, but he is also a "guide of the soul," a symbol of wisdom. Legend depicts Ganesha as a wise man, but he is also a trickster, reminiscent of the youthful Krishna, who can use his talents to remove obstructions in the path of a devotee. According to Edmund Leach, there is an additional ambivalence in the god's sexual character, which is divided between a potent male and an effeminate eunuch. The Ganapati of myth is an "obese, effeminate, male," a "clumsy fellow" who "gets his way by ingenuity rather than by strength." Leach maintains that these mythological tales represent a "thinly masked theme of castration, mother-love." Ganapati is in part a symbol either of a eunuch or of sexual inadequacy.[26]

In medieval and modern Maharashtra Ganapati's status and personality have been enhanced together with a clarification of his ambiguous sexual role. He has been considered a potent figure who can remove obstacles and bring material success; he is the epitome of wisdom. Ganapati became the titular deity of the Peshwas, who presided over imperial expansion. By 1893 he was considered to be a more militant figure of strength who would protect the Hindu religion and frustrate its enemies. In a pamphlet of 1894 the writers declared

[23]Balwant Gargi, *Folk Theater of India* (Seattle, 1966), pp. 73–75.
[24]Although Ganapati is the titular deity of a minority of Maharashtrians, his annual festival is the most popular religious festival of the year.
[25]He is variously known as Ganapati, Gajanan, Ganesha, and Chintamani.
[26]Edmund R. Leach, "Pulleyar and the Lord Buddha: An Aspect of Religious Syncretism in Ceylon," *Psychoanalysis and Psychoanalytical Review*, XLIX, No. 2 (Summer, 1962), pp. 82–84, 88–91.

themselves to be the "proud soldiers of Ganapati" and stated that they could, with his godly assistance, "subdue the enemy and make them powerless."[27] Ganapati, here, is sufficiently powerful to render others impotent. In rural areas of Maharashtra Ganapati's sexual prowess has completed a full cycle from legendary times. He is considered to be a potent male, the trunk being a phallic symbol which may be worshipped and stroked by women desiring children.[28]

At the same time, Ganapati has retained his jovial and portly demeanour and is considered a friendly and sympathetic god who condones pleasure and fun. In the popular oral tradition he remains the prankster. The annual festival in Ganapati's honour is characterized by merriment, similar to the Holi festival of northern India, which includes dancing, drinking, and the use of obscene gestures among the small groups of devotees. It is a strikingly different atmosphere from the annual pilgrimage to honour Vithoba at Pandharpur, which involves serious devotional worship.[29]

It would be wrong to consider the Kshatriya element as the more popular tradition of the region. Both the militant and the devotional traditions have deep roots in rural Maharashtra. The peasant is familiar with the *abhangs* (verses) of Tukaram and the annual festival to honour Vithal and, at the same time, frequents the tamasha and the village wrestling pit. The two strains might be thought of as parallel traditions—militant and quietist, activist and intellectual, earthy and ascetic—which together incorporate the entirety of Maratha experience. In different ways they act as catalysts of regional consciousness since they cut across caste and class lines and provide symbols which are meaningful to the vast majority of regional society. But by virtue of its associations the militant tradition provided the more immediate and effective symbols for political mobilization in this region.

The precise relationship of the Kshatriya to the bhakti tradition has been an issue of controversy in modern Maharashtra. The debate centers around the role of the bhakti saint, Ramdas (1608–81). During Tilak's lifetime Ramdas was proclaimed the spiritual preceptor of Shivaji and was depicted as a figure who synthesized the bhakti and Kshatriya traditions. The Ramdas cult, first popularized by the

---

[27]BG, Judicial, 1894, Vol. 288, p. 317.
[28]Oral evidence of Datta S. Kharbas.
[29]I. Karve, "On the Road: A Maharashtrian Pilgrimage," *JAS*, XXII, No. 1 (November, 1962), pp. 13–29.

THE TRADITIONS OF MAHARASHTRA 15

historian V. K. Rajwade, was developed by two of Tilak's followers, Shankar Shrikrishna Deo and J. S. Karandikar, and until recently has been accepted by most historians of modern Maharashtra.

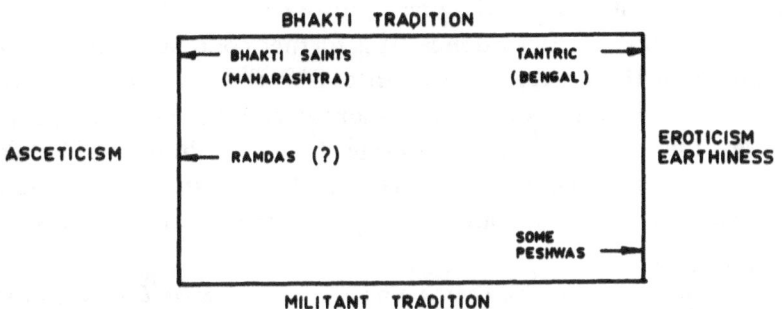

REPRESENTATION OF THE BHAKTI AND MILITANT TRADITIONS INTERSECTED BY THE VARIABLES OF ASCETICISM AND EROTICISM.

ARROW (—▶) REPRESENTS A TENDENCY TOWARD A POLARITY

According to the historians of the Rajwade school, Ramdas was an anomaly in the Vaishnavite tradition. Although a Brahman saint and a *Brahmachari,* Ramdas chose to worship Rama, a symbol of moral power, together with Hanuman, a figure of masculine strength whose "adamantine body" could gather up the whole world in his tail.[30] (Hanuman is the patron saint of wrestling.) Ramdas specifically rejected worship of the quietist Vithoba and encouraged Hindus to revere Rama and Hanuman, the symbols of a revitalized Hinduism in Maharashtra.[31]

In a popular drawing, Ramdas is depicted as a swarthy broad-chested man who valued strength and force.[32] He believed that true religion could flourish only when the Muslim rulers were driven out of Maharashtra. In one verse he compared the Muslim leader Aurangzeb to the wicked Ravana, the mythical king of Ceylon of the epic *Ramayana.* In order to prepare the populace for the struggle, Ramdas is reputed to have established more than a thousand *maths* (monasteries) throughout the country. Each monastery had a temple of Rama and Hanuman attached to it, and a wrestling pit where the monks learned the art of self-defence. Physical fitness, an essential element of spirituality, was

[30]Ghurye, p. 234.
[31]Behere, pp. 163–164.
[32]S. S. Apte, *Samarth Ramdas, Life and Mission* (Bombay, 1965), frontpiece.

promoted by stick, sword, and spear exercises together with wrestling.[33] Ramdas was also the popularizer of the phrase *Maharashtra Dharma,* interpreted as the call to return to the ancient theocratic state.

In a recently published biography of Ramdas,[34] Professor N. R. Phatak has disputed the major tenets of the Ramdas cult. In his opinion Ramdas was not a political figure, and the case for the militant monk is based on very scanty evidence. It is further contended that the view of Ramdas as the spiritual preceptor of Shivaji is without basis. While it is true that Ramdas established monasteries, the number was probably less than twenty rather than one thousand. Professor Phatak has effectively demythologized Ramdas and has questioned the merging of the two traditions of Maharashtra in the person of this monk.

[33] Behere, p. 160.
[34] N. R. Phatak, *Shri Ramdas, Vangmaya ani Karya (Shri Ramdas, Literature and Work)* (Bombay, 1963).

Chapter II
BRITISH POLICY AND MARATHA BRAHMANS

The Mahratta Brahmin has never been an attractive person.[1]

In a word the Poona Brahmin was on their brains. So deep rooted was their prejudice, so intense their hatred of Brahmins, and so convinced of the truth of the [conspiracy] theory ... that when ... clear evidence accumulated to prove up to the hilt that the theory was utterly without foundation, it was not believed.[2]

An elite performs a highly useful function for a colonial power. From its numbers are drawn bureaucrats to help in the task of administration and to interpret colonial rule to indigenous society, providing a model of the type of behaviour which the rulers hope might be emulated by other groups of the society. In return the elite hopes that it may be recognized as the legitimate spokesman of its society and may enjoy a continuing flow of benefits from the colonial power. In anticipation of some degree of present and future power, it learns a new style of behaviour, a process referred to as "anticipatory socialization." The colonial elite is thus a highly visible group delineated from its surroundings by its orientation to the new political idiom and the favoured treatment it receives at the hands of foreigners.[3]

If an elite is to be a successful purveyor of the new ideas, recruitment should be from groups which enjoy a high status in their society so that other communities may emulate their ways. When the British established hegemony in western India in 1818 it was natural for them to rely on the Brahmans of the Deccan, since they were the immediate

---

[1]Lord Elgin to Lord Hamilton, June 29, 1897, Elgin Papers, MSS Eur. F 84/15, India Office Library (IOL).

[2]*Mahratta,* October 21, 1894.

[3]T. B. Bottomore, *Elites and Society* (Middlesex, 1967); S. F. Nadel, "The Concept of Social Elites," *International Social Science Bulletin,* VIII, No. 3 (1956), pp. 413–424; John H. Broomfield, "The Regional Elites: A Theory of Modern Indian History," *IESHR,* III, No. 2 (September, 1966), pp. 279–291.

pre-British ruling elite. As the rulers of the Maratha empire of the eighteenth century, the Brahmans combined secular power with sacerdotal status and attained an authority scarcely rivalled in any other part of India. The Maratha Brahman also had the necessary administrative skills and aptitudes and was the logical subordinate to the British official. To ignore this powerful community and to build on any other foundation would have alienated this important group and hampered the spread of western culture, since Maratha society would have been less inclined to imitate a community of lower status. Elsewhere in the Bombay Presidency, the British were able to recruit from other elite communities, notably the Parsis of Bombay, but in the Deccan there was no other group to which the British could turn: the numerically dominant Maratha communities were educationally and politically backward and the Muslims of the Deccan were poor and insignificant.

The elite group of the Deccan was more homogeneous than the elites on which the British relied in other regions. It was drawn primarily from one community, the Maratha Brahmans, and was dominated by the members of one *jati* (sub-caste), the Chitpavans. The terms Poona, Deccan, or Mahratta Brahmans were usually synonyms for Chitpavan Brahmans or for those other Brahmans who had followed the Chitpavan example of combining political activity with the traditional pursuits of Brahmans.

The Chitpavans were a small community settled along the narrow coastal strip known as the Konkan. Possessing an intellectual tradition, political awareness, and ambition, they were able to acquire extensive political power under the rule of their castemen, the Peshwas, who effectively ruled the Maratha empire for a century prior to 1818. Their abilities and ambition, it has been suggested, were due to the overcrowded character of the Konkan and its inhospitable terrain which gave little scope to their talents.[4] Whether from ambition or necessity, the Chitpavan Brahmans migrated in large numbers throughout the eighteenth and nineteenth centuries from the Konkan to other areas, notably to the Deccan plateau east of the Konkan. They comprised approximately one-fifth of the Maratha Brahman community. More than half of the group were concentrated in the three districts of the presidency in 1901: in Ratnagiri and Kolaba, where they comprised about half of the Brahman population, and in Poona, where they numbered one-third.

[4] Irawati Karve, "Chitpavan Brahmins—An Ethnic Study" (unpublished M. A. thesis, University of Bombay, 1920), p. 17.

The Deshasthas, who hailed from the Deccan plateau, the Desh, accounted for three-fifths of the Maratha Brahman population. Although they considered themselves to be the traditional aristocrats of the region, superior to the Chitpavans, the Deshasthas could not rival Chitpavan modern-day progress in education, acquisition of wealth, and ability to secure positions in the colonial bureaucracy. But in the fields of banking, trading, and accountancy, the Deshasthas outstripped the Chitpavans. They constituted an important element of the village social and economic structure, as kulkarnis (accountants), banias (merchants), and deshmukhs (landed aristocrats), and of the business community of Poona City located at the Reay Market.[5]

The Brahmans, and Chitpavans in particular, recognized the advantages of recruitment in the service of the Raj and the benefits of learning the new style of administration and politics. Initially the response to western education was less enthusiastic than in Bengal, but by the 1870's the clamour for higher education was reflected in the attendance figures at Deccan College, the premier arts college of the Deccan.[6] Almost 90 per cent of the students were consistently from the Brahman communities.[7] This pattern of Brahmanical dominance was to be repeated in other colleges established in Poona and maintained well into the twentieth century. The Public Service Commission of 1886–87 indicated the extent to which Brahmans had profitted by this education to secure the majority of administrative positions held by Hindus: 211 of the 328 Hindus, 64.2 per cent, in the Bombay Uncovenanted Service were Brahmans. They ranked with the Parsis of Bombay City as the elite community on which the Bombay Government most relied.[8]

With the increasing opportunities for political power in the second

---

[5]Ellen E. McDonald and Craig M. Stark, "English Education, Nationalist Politics and Elite Groups in Maharashtra, 1885–1915," Occasional Paper No. 5, Center for South and Southeast Asia Studies, University of California (Berkeley, 1969), pp. 68–69, 73–74; Anil Seal, *The Emergence of Indian Nationalism: Competition and Collaboration in the Later Nineteenth Century* (Cambridge, 1968), p. 74.

[6]Average attendance figures at Deccan College, 1856–99:

1856–59 .. .. .. 31.5	1880–89	158.7
1860–69 .. .. .. 53.2	1890–99	145.0
1870–79 .. .. .. 90.2		

The decline in the last decade was due to the opening of Fergusson College in 1885. J. Nelson Fraser, *Deccan College: A Retrospect* (Poona, 1902), p. 35.

[7]McDonald and Stark, p. 17. Of the 1,271 students enrolled at Fergusson College, Poona, from 1885 to 1895, 1,105 (87 per cent), were Brahman; 560 students were identified as Chitpavan (44 per cent); and 277 were Deshastha (22 per cent).

[8]*Report of the Public Service Commission*, 1886–87 (Calcutta, 1888), p. 181.

half of the nineteenth century, owing to the extension of local self-government and to the greater proportions of Indians in the provincial service, the Brahman was further extending and consolidating his sway over Maratha society. The Brahmans dominated the elections to the Poona Municipal Corporation; they consistently returned a majority of the representatives.[9] They ruled Poona by default, since other Maharashtrian groups lacked the educational and property qualifications to make any impact on local government. Next to the Brahmans, non-Maharashtrian Hindus (Gujaratis, Rajasthanis, and South Indians) and Parsis were the most successful groups at the polls, returning 20-30 per cent of the popular representatives.[10] The election of a Parsi merchant, Dorabjee Padamjee, as president of the Poona Municipal Corporation from 1893 to 1905, by the non-official majority of the Corporation, suggests that the Brahmans of Poona were willing to co-operate with other communities.[11]

Many officials within the Bombay Government failed to notice such manifestations of Brahman liberality. (Sir) William Lee-Warner,[12] an influential official in the governments of Bombay and India, took on himself the task of leading a campaign to expose Brahman exclusivism and to show the extent to which Brahmans had capitalized on the increasing number of positions open to Indians in the post-mutiny years. In 1900 he wrote a minute to underline how from 1869 to 1899 the "thin line of European superior control" had been greatly reduced, and pointed out that the local administration in all branches below the Indian Civil Service was, outside Sind, "almost entirely in the hands of Brahmins." Lee-Warner produced statistics to demonstrate the increasing number of Brahmans in the Covenanted Civil Service, their dominance in the appointments of deputy collectors and

[9] In the ward elections of 1885, nine Brahmans, two Marwadis, two South Indians, one Muslim, one Parsi, and one Maratha were elected. In the ward and general elections of 1899, twelve Brahmans, two Marwadis, two South Indians, one Shimpi, one Maratha, one Gujarati, and one Parbhu were elected.

[10] Whereas Brahmans numbered approximately 5 per cent of the Poona City population, non-Maharashtrian Hindus and Parsis accounted for less than 4 per cent.

[11] By a reform of 1885, Poona City was permitted to elect two-thirds of its Corporation and to elect a non-official president. At this time most mofussil municipalities were saddled with an official chairman and could elect only half of their representatives.

[12] (Sir) William Lee-Warner (1846–1914) was appointed to the Bombay Civil Service in 1867. He was associated with the Bombay executive in the years 1887–93 when he held the post of Secretary in the Political and Judicial Departments. With his wide Indian experience and capacity for work, he was an important figure in the administration. After a brief spell in the Government of India, he returned to England. He was Secretary in the Political and Secret Departments, 1895–1903, and a member of the India Council, 1902–12.

DISTRIBUTION OF CHITPAVAN AND DESHASTHA BRAHMANS
IN THE KONKAN AND DECCAN DISTRICTS OF THE BOMBAY PRESIDENCY, 1901[a]

	Chitpavans	Per cent of Brahman Total	Deshasthas	Per cent of Brahman Total	Brahman Total
Thana	5,812	25.2	3,581	15.5	23,094
Kolaba	13,609	57.9	3,808	16.2	23,532
Ratnagiri	31,059	45.5	890	1.3	68,270
KONKAN	50,480	43.9	8,279	7.2	114,896
Khandesh	2,890	5.7	32,546	64.6	50,384
Nasik	3,191	11.5	20,525	75.6	27,493
Ahmednagar	1,694	5.1	27,342	82.5	33,146
Poona	13,742	27.3	30,119	59.9	50,274
Sholapur	1,820	6.2	24,165	82.3	29,351
Satara	8,229	18.0	30,019	67.9	45,669
DECCAN	31,566	13.6	164,716	69.6	236,317
TOTAL	82,046	23.3	172,995	49.3	351,213

DISTRIBUTION OF CHITPAVAN AND DESHASTHA
BRAHMANS IN THE BOMBAY PRESIDENCY, 1901

Konkan	50,480	43.9	8,279	7.2	114,896
Deccan	31,566	13.6	164,716	69.6	236,317
Karnatak	5,532	3.4	72,359	44.6	162,494
Kolhapur	5,092	15.9	20,278	63.4	32,726
Southern Maratha Country	10,924	35.0	18,376	56.9	32,317
Other Princely States	5,970	2.1	10,389	3.6	289,001
Bombay City	3,776	12.3	2,302	7.5	30,724
Others	265	0.2	1,459	1.0	154,503
TOTAL	113,605	10.8	298,158	28.3	1,052,978

[a]Calculated from 1901 *Census, Bombay*, IX, 192–272.

COMMUNITY OF STUDENTS ENROLLED
AT FERGUSSON COLLEGE, 1910 AND 1935

	1910	*Per cent*	1935	*Per cent*
BRAHMAN	526	86.2	759	63.3
Chitpavan	256		381	
Deshastha	197		260	
Karhada	57		55	
Saraswat	16		57	
NON-BRAHMAN	24	4.0	166	13.8
Prabhu	13		61	
Sonar	0		18	
Maratha	11		70	
Kunbi, Koli	0		17	
DEPRESSED	0	0.0	7	0.6
NON-MAHARASHTRIAN				
HINDU	36	5.8	124	10.3
Gujarati	6		74	
Sindhi	7		6	
Other	23		44	
OTHERS	24	4.0	144	12.0
Jain	0		69	
Lingayat	13		32	
Muslim	7		14	
Parsi	0		19	
Christian, Anglo-Indian	4		10	
TOTAL	610		1,200	

[a] P. M. Limaye, *History of the Deccan Education Society, 1880–1935* (Poona, 1935), Appendix 30, pp. 79–80.

mamlatdars (revenue officers), and the growing Brahmanical monopoly of educational advantages and patronage. He concluded, somewhat melodramatically, that "the representatives of a small minority" were "practically governing Bombay."[13]

Many officials in the Bombay Government were alarmed by this growing Brahmanical predominance. Lee-Warner, the self-appointed prophet of the dangers of antagonistic Brahmanism, warned that the experiment was a risky one which would eventually backfire against the rulers. This fear caused many Bombay Civilians to oppose the Ripon scheme to reform local government in the 1880's: Brahmans would be the chief beneficiaries from enlarged Indian participation and election to the municipalities. The direct result of the reforms, according to the Collector of Ahmednagar in 1881, "would be to give to the *Brahmin* his old supremacy and influence over prince and peasant— that is the patriot's duty as understood here, and if it is incompatible with loyalty to our rule, the prospect of seeing those who inculcate it borne to power on the shoulders of the people, and paralysing the executive on the Committee table, seems hardly encouraging."[14] The proposed reforms would amount to turning the clock back to 1818.

British attitudes toward Brahmans had long been conditioned by a positive fear of this community as the immediate pre-British rulers of the Deccan, and by a distaste for the priestly community, which they blamed for all that they disliked in Indian society. Their reliance on this community was born from the needs of administration and order rather than from any positive feelings toward Brahmans. Mountstuart Elphinstone (1819–27), the first governor of the Deccan, expressed what was to become a stereotype of the Maratha Brahman and his antipathy to British rule. His views were echoed in many an official document and popular account as proof of the Brahman mentality. Quoting two earlier administrators, Elphinstone categorized the Brahmans as an "intriguing, lying, corrupt, licentious and unprincipled race of people" who were now discontented and "only restrained by fear from being treasonable and oppressive," and added that he found them "superstitious and narrow in their attachment to

[13] W. Lee-Warner, "Note on Bombay Affairs," January 26, 1900, Lee-Warner Papers, MSS Eur. F92/1, IOL.

[14] Memorandum of J. King, Collector of Ahmednagar, to E. P. Robertson, Commissioner Central Division, December 23, 1881, Government of India (GI), Home, Public, A145–50, October, 1882.

caste to a degree not rivalled elsewhere."[15] The wily Brahman, inscrutable in his ways, unfathomable in his mind, disloyal in his feelings, clever and intelligent, was a familiar bogey to the British mind throughout the nineteenth century. Elphinstone hoped that by limiting social change and continuing the favoured status of Brahmans to some extent he might reconcile them to British rule—so far as this was possible.[16]

Others prophesied that the experiment was doomed to failure. In 1835 a member of the Bombay Government criticized the continuance of the government-supported Hindoo College of Poona, a Sanskrit institution maintained for the benefit of the Brahmans, on these grounds. The college, he maintained, "preserves and cherishes the old Brahmanical interest, which is anti-British in all its tendencies."[17] Many succeeding governors and officials were haunted by this vision, together with an awareness of the social and political power which the Brahmans still wielded over their society and which they might manipulate to foment unrest in other sections of society. The rulers were conscious also of what they considered to be a greater spirit of nationality among the Marathas, fostered by the visible reminders of former rule in the presence of the titular descendant of Shivaji at Kolhapur.[18] Many officials came to regard the Marathas, and the Maratha Brahmans especially, as the community most likely to pose a threat to the continuance of British rule. Hence they were intensely suspicious of and hypersensitive to political developments in the Bombay Deccan.

Equally strong was a feeling of antipathy toward the Brahman as the bearer of an alien and what was regarded as an inferior culture. It was the Maratha Brahman, with his attachment to caste and religion and his all-pervading power in Deccan society, who was held primarily responsible for the condition of his society. It was but a short extension of this idea to the usurper theory, which maintained that historically

[15]Hon. Mountstuart Elphinstone, "Report on the Territories Conquered from the Peshwa," quoted in George W. Forrest (ed.), *Selections from the Minutes and Other Official Writings of the Honourable Mountstuart Elphinstone, Governor of Bombay* (London, 1884), p. 260.

[16]Kenneth Ballhatchet, *Social Policy and Social Change in Western India*, 1817–1830 (London, 1957).

[17]Minute by R. Grant, November 22, 1835, quoted in R. V. Parulekar (ed.), *Selections from the Records of the Government of Bombay: Education*, Part I, 1819–1852 (Bombay, 1953), p. 121.

[18]Sir Richard Temple, *Minutes of His Excellency Sir Richard Temple, Bart., G. C. S. I., Governor of Bombay* (Bombay, 1879), II, 23–26.

the Brahmans of western India had gone beyond their sacerdotal calling at the time of the Peshwas: they had usurped power which, it was argued, rightly belonged to the non-Brahmans. Secure in this position, they had exploited it for selfish purposes and to the detriment of society as a whole. One English official, present at the Peshwa court before its demise, stated that the Brahmans, when in power, were "coolly unfeeling and systematically oppressive."[19]

This point of view was expressed also by the important official, James Grant Duff (1789–1858), whose three-volume *History of the Mahrattas*, published in 1826, was influential in shaping British attitudes toward the Marathas. Because it was the only significant history of the Maratha people at this time, and was based on original documents of the Maratha court which had burned in a fire of 1827, the work represented the standard British reference for the region. In this study Grant Duff made no attempt to hide his prejudices:

> The Brahmins are the priesthood, whose lives ought to be spent in worshipping and contemplating the divinity, and teaching, by precept and example, what is proper to be observed by the rest of mankind to enable them to gain the favour of the gods, and to attain a more exalted state in their transmigration. They ought to have no interference in worldly concerns; but they have long been the principal officers, civil and military, in all Hindoo states. Those Brahmins who strictly follow the tenets of their faith, and devote their lives to the study of what Hindoos conceive the divine ordinances, are held in great esteem; but otherwise, in the Mahratta country, there is no veneration for the Brahmin character.[20]

The popularity of this theory is indicated by its acceptance by the Presbyterian educator, the Reverend John Wilson, who did not dislike everything Brahmanical, but had some words of praise for the western-educated Brahmans of the 1870's. The Brahmanical Raj, Wilson argued, reflected "no credit on the Brahmanical order" for in becoming *de facto* kings they had acted contrary to the spirit of the law books and presumably out of "sheer love of grandeur and wealth." The low castes, he added, had suffered many indignities at the hands of the Peshwas and their agents.[21] The Victorian Englishman was able to find much evidence to support his belief in a continuing Brahmanical attempt to exploit the lower castes. The Brahman *khot* (village revenue officer) of the Konkan was considered to be one of the "worst of

---

[19] Forrest, *Selections* ..., p.260.
[20] James Grant Duff, *A History of the Mahrattas*, 3 vols. (4th ed., Calcutta, 1912), I, 8.
[21] John Wilson, *Indian Caste*, 2 vols. (Edinburgh, 1877), II, 45–46.

landlords" who tried to squeeze as much as he could from the underholder.[22] The attempts of the Brahman to secure his interests in the newly enfranchised municipalities was a further example. The Civilian frequently questioned whether the Brahman could act impartially and represent interests other than his own. The Collector of Satara opposed the municipal reforms of 1882 on the grounds that Brahmans were not always prepared to "sacrifice the interests of their own class for the good of the inferior and more numerous castes."[23] To the Civilian the view of a divided society, warring against itself, enabled him to see himself as the impartial arbitrator whose duty it was to protect the oppressed from the wiles of the oppressor, and thus to hold the balance in the society.

Combined with these attitudes was a distaste for the Brahman as the chief perpetuator of tradition. The orientation of the elite was thought to focus on the past glory of the Maratha empire rather than on the present. "The atmosphere of the Deccan," commented Lee-Warner in 1900, "with all its memories of the profitable rule of the Peshwa's Court, hangs heavy in the air."[24] The Brahman was considered to be both a barrier to modernization and an imperfect interpreter to his society of the aims and aspirations of British rule.

Lloyd and Susanne Rudolph have recently noted another factor which clouded the British perception of the Brahman. It was customary for imperialist spokesmen and conservative officials to draw a distinction between the "masculine" and "feminine" races of India. The "martial races" of India were considered to be the natural leaders of society since their physical prowess and military discipline seemed to approximate British public school notions of masculinity and leadership. By contrast, the Brahmans and the majority of Indians were regarded as cowardly, unathletic, and passive. Because of these "feminine" characteristics, they were unfit to rule.[25]

The British stereotype of the Brahman was enunciated in *Passage to India* by E. M. Forster. Professor Godbole, the symbol of Hindu and Brahmanical culture, was presented as cheerfully inept, disorganized, inefficient, and captive of an other-worldly philosophy. When con-

[22]*Gazetteer of the Bombay Presidency*, Vol. X, *Ratnagiri and Savantwadi* (Bombay, 1880), p. 241.
[23]W. R. Pratt, Collector of Satara, to the Bombay Government (BG), July 13, 1882, GI, Home, Public, A145-50, October, 1882.
[24]Lee-Warner, "Note on Bombay Affairs."
[25]Lloyd I. and Susanne Hoeber Rudolph, *The Modernity of Tradition: Political Development in India* (Chicago, 1967), pp. 162-167.

fronted with the question of whether Aziz, a Muslim, was guilty of an assault on Miss Quested, an Englishwoman, Godbole launched into a long a circuitous discourse which concluded with the homily that while good and evil were different they were "both of them aspects of my Lord." He later presided over a popular Hindu festival which was a "muddle," a "frustration of reason and form."[26] Godbole thus epitomized the inscrutable Brahman mind. It is significant that Godbole is a Chitpavan name and that Forster's work was not written until 1924, by which time the Chitpavans had established a reputation for political activism. Forster's Godbole underlined the British confusion when confronted by Brahmans who acted like Kshatriyas.

The emergence in the 1870's of a highly visible western-educated elite at Poona, organized in the *Sarvajanik Sabha* (Public Society), which involved itself in agitational politics, seemed to confirm the worst suspicions of many a Civilian. As in Bombay and Calcutta, the "westernized" Brahman leaders had formed a society in 1867, the Poona Association, which became the Poona *Sarvajanik Sabha* in 1870. Their aim was to press for wider Indian participation in the administration and greater benefits for the elite, and to represent the views of the non-vocal sections of Maratha society. They were concerned to place their own interests before the rulers and to interpret the conditions and needs of their society.

During the 1870's the *Sabha* established itself as one of the most vigorous and vocal political associations throughout India. Besides memorializing the government on a host of subjects, the *Sabha* experimented with novel styles of political activity which included a swadeshi campaign to revive and encourage indigenous industry, the establishment of a network of branch associations in the Deccan, and rural campaigns to investigate the nature of land tenure and the condition of the peasantry. In order to establish its representative character, the *Sabha* required new members to produce a *"mukhtiarnama* [power of attorney] signed by at least fifty adults authorizing him to speak and act on their behalf in all public matters." Thus the *Sabha* in 1871 could boast of 140 members and 17,000 constituents.[27]

The emergence of a western-educated elite in the 1870's coincided with considerable economic distress in the Deccan and seemed to demonstrate all the stereotyped notions of many of the rulers in regard

[26]E. M. Forster, *Passage to India* (New York, 1952), pp. 177–178, 285.
[27]S. R. Mehrotra, "The Poona Sarvajanik Sabha: The Early Phase (1870–1880)," *IESHR*, VI, No. 3 (September, 1969), p. 302.

to the loyalty of Brahmans. Whereas many officials could regard the emergence of a similar elite in Bombay with a degree of detachment which enabled them to consider it a constructive development, they viewed political activism in Poona as a resurgence of antagonistic Brahmanism.

The newly formed *Sarvajanik Sabha* went beyond the mendicant activities of other elite associations by involving itself in opposition to the revised land-revenue assessments of the early 1870's. Because of its campaign for reduced rates, the government suspected the hand of the *Sabha* when there was some withholding of payments in 1873.[28] The *Sabha* was active also when famine engulfed the Deccan in 1876–77. It sent a number of agents to assess the extent of the dearth and incorporated its findings in a series of "narratives" which severely censured the government for its inadequate attempts to grapple with the problem.[29]

At the same time, the Deccan press was critical of the British involvement in the Maratha-ruled state of Baroda, which led to the deposition of the Gaekwar in 1875.[30] Englishmen became increasingly alarmed at the "openly hostile tone of the native press" which, according to one official, was a product of the "herd of demi-semi-educated Brahmins, annually let loose on the country from the Government schools and colleges."[31] Both the British and the Brahmans were perplexed by the outbreak of agrarian distress in 1875, when the *rayats* (cultivators) of some thirty villages attacked the *sawkars* (moneylenders). Initially, the rulers suspected Brahman involvement in the outbreaks, but no such evidence was forthcoming. The *Sabha* did, however, present its views to the government as to the causes of the riots.[32]

The climax of this decade of unrest was the organizing of the dacoities by the Chitpavan, Vasudeo Balwant Phadke (1845–1883), in the first months of 1879. Since he wished to restore Maratha rule, Phadke engineered a series of daring raids in the Deccan which were of a

---

[28] James C. Masselos, "Liberal Consciousness, Leadership and Political Organisation in Bombay and Poona: 1867–1895" (unpublished Ph.D. dissertation, University of Bombay, 1964), pp. 392–396.

[29] *Ibid.*, pp. 488–493.

[30] S. Gopal, *British Policy in India,* 1858–1905 (Cambridge, 1965), pp. 105–109.

[31] *Bombay Gazette,* September 30, 1876. This was written by Major Jacob under the pseudonym of "Elephas."

[32] Ravinder Kumar, *Western India in the Nineteenth Century: A Study in the Social History of Maharashtra* (London, 1968), pp. 151–188; I. J. Catanach, "Agrarian Disturbances in Nineteenth Century India," *IESHR*, III, No. 1 (March, 1966), pp. 65–84; Masselos, pp. 402–403.

messianic character. The dacoits and their erstwhile leader eluded the police for several months. Before they were brought to task they succeeded in burning down several public buildings of Poona and in creating a state of panic in the Anglo-Indian press which drew parallels between the activities of Phadke and the guerrilla tactics of Shivaji, which had resulted in the downfall of Muslim rule in western India.[33]

The agitation of the 1870's, and Phadke's revolt in particular, led to a classic statement of the conspiracy theory by the then governor of Bombay, Sir Richard Temple.[34] In two secret letters in 1879, Temple maintained that the activities of Phadke were manifestations of a spirit of disaffection which had long existed in the Deccan. Hostility to an alien rule was sustained by the Marathas, and especially the Brahmans, by the remembrance of former rule: the mountains and the hill forts were visible reminders of the Maratha Raj. It was fortunate that the news of British weakness at the time of the first Afghan war, 1840–41, had been slow to reach the Deccan; otherwise there might have been even more trouble. The "conspiratorial class" managed, as it was, to foment a rising in the Southern Deccan and the Konkan in 1843–44. It was "truly providential," Temple maintained, that the events of 1857 caught the "disloyal classes" by surprise. They still managed, however, to promote a conspiracy among the Southern Maratha chiefs in 1858–59, which had for its object "nothing short of the reestablishment of the Mahratta Confederation." Phadke's revolt was therefore nothing new to the Deccan; it signified the continuing Brahmanical hostility to British rule which could be traced back to 1818. Temple concluded that the discontent of the 1870's arose not from any specific causes which could be "overtly alleged, probed and perhaps remedied" but from "causes, inevitably incidental to a foreign rule like ours," best summed up in the phrase "British rule *even* at its best."[35]

Temple went further to consider the conspiracy to be of a Chitpavan character. This community, he wrote, was "inspired with a national

[33] V. S. Joshi, *Vasudeo Balwant Phadke: First Indian Rebel against British Rule* (Bombay, 1959).

[34] Sir Richard Temple (1826–1902), Governor of Bombay, 1877–80, was an official with wide Indian experience. Some of his appointments, prior to 1877, included Chief Commissioner of the Central Provinces (1862–67), Financial Member to the Government of India (1868–74), and Lieutenant-governor of Bengal (1874–77).

[35] Sir Richard Temple to Lord Lytton, July 3 and 9, 1879, quoted in G. R. G. Hambly, "Mahratta Nationalism before Tilak: Two Unpublished Letters of Sir Richard Temple on the State of the Bombay Deccan, 1879," *Journal of the Royal Central Asian Society*, XLIX, No. 2 (April, 1962), pp. 144–160.

sentiment and with an ambition bounded only with the bounds of India itself." Although the Chitpavans had acquired "by force of merit" a dominant position in the administration of the country, nothing the rulers might do "by way of education, emolument, or advancement in the public service" could satisfy the Chitpavans. "They will never be satisfied," Temple maintained, "till they regain their ascendancy in the country, as they had it during the last century."[36]

Temple's analysis illustrates the manner in which a prominent British official tackled the issue of unrest in the Deccan. Disloyalty was not the product of western education, for, in the opinion of Temple, there was no significant difference between the mentality of the elite Brahmans of the *Sarvajanik Sabha* and those involved in more traditional spheres of activity. The diffusion of such sentiments was not "to be attributed to *our* education. In fact the Brahmins were educated *in a way before*. What we have done is to substitute one kind of education for another." Western education had two dissimilar effects. By inculcating modern ideas it attracted some Brahmans to the Raj. The men of the *Prarthana Samaj*, who worked for the reform of Hindu society, were examples of this class and were, Temple considered, sympathetic to British rule.[37] But at the same time western education made some Brahmans restless; by improving their political insight it gave "a sharp head to the lance of disloyalty." Temple regarded the educated Chitpavans as disloyal on the whole, and postulated some indirect connections between the activities of Phadke and the sympathies of the *Sarvajanik Sabha* members. Although there were no direct connections between the *Sabha* and the 1879 dacoities, "its wires are believed to be pulled by men tainted with the views described in this [Temple's] letter." Temple concluded that the British should rely on classes other than the educated Brahmans: the Maratha chiefs of the Deccan, the *rayats*, Brahmans engaged in banking and industry, and the educated of other castes and communities.[38]

Besides categorizing the educated Brahmans as tainted with disloyalty, Temple indirectly subscribed to the usurper theory by maintaining that Brahmans were intent on advancing their own interests at

[36]*Ibid.*
[37]Some of the prominent members of the Bombay *Prarthana Samaj (BPS)* were active also in the Poona *Sarvajanik Sabha (PSS)*. Ranade was a dominant figure in both societies. Temple's argument, that the *BPS* was a loyal institution while the *PSS* was not, is an example of the British inability to assess accurately the political situation.
[38]Temple to Lytton, July 3 and 9, 1879.

the expense of the peasantry. The land agitation of the *Sarvajanik Sabha,* a body which Temple narrowly described as an "association of Deccan landholders,"[39] was a case in point. The members of the *Sabha* were, in his view, more inclined to feel the burden of the land tax than the peasant proprietors, and "complaints" which often emanated from elite quarters did not "seem to find currency among the peasantry."[40] Thus Temple touched on what was to become an important dogma for the rulers: the elite was a class set apart from the masses, having no broad sympathy for the lower orders because it was bent on securing its own interests.

Temple's views of the Brahmans were neither startling nor original. In one form and another they had cropped up in the speeches and writings of many officials. They represented a common response of Englishmen to the Maratha Brahman. But it was not until the 1870's with the emergence of the elite as a visible group, that these theories were systematically developed and popularized in the Anglo-Indian press. The emerging elite provided convenient evidence of all that the British had suspected of the former ruling class.

The views of Temple found a shrill echo in the Anglo-Indian press. The *Bombay Gazette* made no secret of its distaste for the former ruling class of the Deccan, and declared that the western-educated Brahman elite was disloyal. "The foolish Brahmins of Poona." the *Gazette* editorialized, "have been educated by ourselves to a ridiculous conception of their own capacities and importance" and believe that they can repeat in the nineteenth century the events of two hundred years ago. The *Gazette* singled out the Brahman for all that the Englishman disliked in Indian society: he was lazy, dishonest, dirty, vain, unscientific, and disloyal. The work of an English district officer was "one long fight against his own clerks and subordinate officials."[41]

In the more sober language of government publications, officials from the 1870's turned to history to support their conviction that the Brahmans were and had been a conspiratorially inclined group determined to keep alive the memory of former rule, which was linked with antagonism to foreign rule. The Poona *Gazetteer,* published in 1885, catalogued evidence for this theory. Whereas the majority of the

---

[39]The *PSS* members had many interests other than land policy: specifically, efforts to secure greater Indian representation in the bureaucracy and wider participation in parliamentary-style institutions.
[40]Temple, *Minutes,* II, 156.
[41]*Bombay Gazette,* June 13, 1877, and May 15, 1879.

Poona populace accepted the changes of 1818, many Brahmans were discontented. Some were found plotting to murder the Europeans of Poona and Satara so as to re-establish the sovereignty of the Peshwas. Similarly, three Brahmans took advantage of the distress among the low-caste Koli (fishermen and water-carriers) community in 1844 to direct the movement against the British.[42]

The idea of a continuing memory of former rule was to be more fully developed in the books of Valentine Chirol, who popularized some of the prevailing British notions about Maratha Brahmans. While some of the Chitpavans were thought to be loyal, it was Chirol's opinion that the majority were tainted with the canker of disloyalty—a fatal flaw in the Brahman mentality which had been preserved since 1818. Chirol wrote in 1910:

Amongst Chitpavans are to be found many of the most enlightened and progressive Indians of our times and many have served the British *Raj* with unquestioned loyalty and integrity. But amongst many others—perhaps indeed amongst the great majority—there has undoubtedly been preserved for the last hundred years from the time of the downfall of the Peshwa dominion to the present day, an unbroken tradition of hatred towards British rule, an undying hope that it may someday be subverted and their own ascendancy restored.[43]

The unrest of the 1890's, spearheaded by Chitpavans, was considered to be a striking amplification of this view and a vivid instance of the correctness of earlier official predictions concerning Brahmans. This thesis has been so thoroughly documented by the British that it has been widely accepted by Indian and western historians as an explanation of the burgeoning agitation in Maharashtra of the 1890's.[44]

The conspiracy theory was an explanation which oversimplified the variety of Brahmanical responses to British rule. If some Brahmans had been disgruntled by the changes of 1818, and if some acted to destroy alien rule, this does not prove that the majority of Chitpavans had been conspirators or had harboured resentment to British rule from 1818. The British considered that the events of the 1890's demonstrated the validity of their assessment of the Chitpavan mentality, but this *ex post facto* argument does not establish the historical validity of the conspiracy theory.

[42]*Gazetteer of the Bombay Presidency*, Vol. XVIII, *Poona* (Bombay, 1885), II, 305–307.
[43]Valentine Chirol, *Indian Unrest* (London, 1910), p. 39.
[44]Hambly, in his introduction to the Temple letters, accepts the Temple view that the spasmodic outbreaks of violence throughout the nineteenth century were evidence that the memory for former rule was tenaciously retained by the Maratha Brahmans.

Another limitation of the explanation is that it raises more questions than it answers. If the Chitpavans were disgruntled by the 1818 changeover and resented British rule, why did it take them more than three generations to protest against it? Why, in fact, did protest movements emerge in the 1890's? Why not before or at some other time? Throughout the nineteenth century, when there was considerable unrest in both urban and rural India due to the adjustment to the new systems of law and government and to the new opportunities and changes these produced, Poona, the center of Brahmanism, was remarkably quiescent until the 1870's.[45] The anti-British revolts which did take place were few and far between, and their messianic character suggests that they were the improbable schemes of individuals rather than the concerted efforts of a "disloyal" community. The only Maratha Brahman to organize an effective anti-British movement was Nana Saheb, son of the last Peshwa, who had a personal grievance, the cancellation of his pension. As he was confined to northern India, his influence in Maharashtra in 1857 was limited.

It has been argued that the majority of Brahmans were too shrewd a class to involve themselves in such unlikely schemes, and were merely containing their hostility to foreign rule until the day when a more practical means could be found to achieve their ends.[46] But the only significant voice of protest, prior to the 1870's, was that of *Lokahitawadi, Sardar* Gopal Hari Deshmukh (1823–92),[47] who protested primarily not against the British but against Brahman indifference to modern ideas and the lethargy which had descended on Deccan society. The society he depicted was not one seething with dissent or reacting against British-induced change but one which had grown complacent and inward-looking. The British took over a society weary after more than a century of imperial rule. The creative streams which had produced

---

[45]Throughout the nineteenth century there were frequent manifestations of rural and urban distress in the Bombay Presidency. Some outbreaks assumed an anti-British character; others were conflicts within Indian society. It is all the more significant that Poona was relatively quiet and that the Brahman-organized revolts were few and ineffectual. *Source Material BHFM,* Vol. I, 1818–1885 (Bombay, 1957), Vol. II, 1885–1920 (Bombay, 1958) (*Source Material BHFM*); S. B. Chaudhuri, *Civil Disturbances during the British Rule in India* (Calcutta, 1955); S. Fuchs, *Rebellious Prophets: A Study of Messianic Movements in Indian Religions* (New York, 1965).

[46]Stanley A. Wolpert, *Tilak and Gokhale* ... (Berkeley, 1962), pp.4–9.

[47]Shripad Ramchandra Tikekar (ed.), *Lokahitavadici Shatapatre (Lokahitawadi's One Hundred Letters)* (Aundh, 1940). *Lokahitawadi* literally means "adviser of what is good for the people."

an impressive body of Marathi literature had dried up by the beginning of the nineteenth century.[48]

A further weakness of the theory is that it failed to recognize the dynamic character of elite-administration relations. It was widely believed by the British that, since the majority of the Chitpavans never made a serious attempt to work within the colonial framework, it was merely a matter of time before incipient rebellion would surface. Such a view divides the elite into two watertight compartments—the alienated majority and the co-operative minority—and fails to see other possibilities. It suggests that there were no worth-while conciliatory policies or effective means of rescuing the "conspiratorial" Brahmans. More significantly, it tends to exonerate the British from any important role in fomenting the unrest of the 1890's, for it assumes that the Brahmans were a lost cause intent on a dissenting role.

A recent study by McDonald and Stark underlines the diversity of the Poona Brahman elite of the late nineteenth century. Analysing the incomes of the guarantors of 1,271 students, enrolled at Fergusson College from 1885 to 1895, they find a very wide spread in the incomes of the Brahman guarantors. While 24 per cent of the 560 Chitpavan guarantors fall in the high-income bracket (800 rupees and above per annum), there are 39 per cent in the medium range (300–799 rupees), and 37 per cent in the low category (1–299 rupees). Surprisingly, these proportions are lower than those of the 277 Deshastha guarantors: 30 per cent of them fall in the high bracket, 40 per cent in the medium, and 30 per cent in the low. But in the medium income of all guarantors the Chitpavan figure of 612 rupees is much higher than the Deshastha 459 rupees. The study thus establishes the existence of a very wealthy Chitpavan minority, a group which probably benefited from the British presence. It also suggests that extremes of wealth and poverty were much greater in the Chitpavan community than in the Deshastha group.[49]

The British themselves were involved in a process of mythmaking. As a community in India, they constructed their own rationale and justification of the Raj. But this involved explaining why British rule was not palatable to a prominent regional elite. British myths about the history and purpose of the Raj necessitated interpretations and explanations of the reactions of Indian elites to British rule. In the

---

[48]Ramabai Ranade (ed.), *The Miscellaneous Writings of the Late Hon'ble Mr. Justice M. G. Ranade* (Bombay, 1915), pp. 12–56.

[49]McDonald and Stark, p. 35.

case of the Poona Brahmans, the British developed a version of nineteenth century history which was not acceptable to the Poona elite. The dialectic of British myth and elite counter-myth came to be an important element in the Poona synthesis of nationalism in the late nineteenth century.

Temple's reaction to the events of 1879 was an illustration of how some rulers denigrated the *Sarvajanik Sabha* and its leading spirit, Mahadev Govind Ranade (1842–1901). British preconceptions about Maratha Brahmans caused them to suspect the worst of the *Sabha* and to link its leaders with the dacoities of Phadke. If this opinion was expressed privately by Temple, it was widely publicized by the *Bombay Gazette* and was, *de facto,* the basis on which the Bombay Government acted. At the height of the dacoities, Ranade, a district judge, was transferred from Poona to the remote district town of Dhulia, an action which appeared to amount to "a concrete accusation that Ranade was in part responsible for the unrest."[50] Even with the arrest of the chief dacoit and the clear indication that the unrest of 1879 was organized by one individual, government suspicion of Ranade lingered, and he was not restored to the good graces of the Raj until two years later.[51] The *Sarvajanik Sabha* suffered a similar fall from favour.[52] The British reaction to the events of 1879 displayed their limited understanding of the Poona society and its leader. Ranade was a moderate leader who believed in the beneficence of the British connection. Even though he criticized the land and famine policies of the British and took part in the campaigns to discover the condition of the Deccan *rayat*, he was hardly, as some officials thought, a "Parnell of the Deccan,"[53] intent on embarrassing the rulers or seeking to weaken the fabric of the *Raj*. It was a consistent strain of British policy in times of political and economic stress in the Deccan to exaggerate the character of the unrest and to see more in the situation than existed.

With the accession of a new governor and a series of better harvests, a measure of confidence was restored between the Poona elite and the administration. The reinstatement of Ranade and the *Sabha* was a hopeful sign that the elite might look for better things from more liberal

[50]Richard P. Tucker, "The Proper Limits of Agitation," *JAS*, XXVIII, No. 2 (February, 1969), p. 349.
[51]*Ibid.*, p. 354. Ranade was reappointed in March, 1881, to his former position of First-Class Subordinate Judge of the Poona District Court.
[52]Masselos, p. 606.
[53]Tucker, p. 352.

statesmen, of whom Lord Ripon was the prime example in the 1880's. But the liberality of two Bombay governors of the 1880's only emphasized the capriciousness and the hasty measures conceived by the previous governor. Such changes created uncertainty among the elite, for it was possible that some future administrator, in time of stress, might again resort to the policies of Temple. The reasonableness of Ripon underscored the prevailing Civilian hostility to the Brahman community. The majority of the officials who interpreted and implemented the policies of the Bombay Government were strongly Brahmanphobe. The variety of government policy, both the change from one administration to another and the contradictory elements within each administration, acted as a stimulus to elite alienation.[54]

By their conciliatory policies Sir James Fergusson (1880–85)[55] and Lord Reay (1885–90)[56] did much to improve elite-administration relations. Fergusson, although a conservative, was a more prudent and pragmatic leader than Temple and believed in the ultimate reasonableness of elite politicians. He supported the Brahman-sponsored colleges established in the 1880's to further higher education.[57] Lord Reay was a liberal who went even further to gain the sympathy of the Brahman elite by his concessions to and recognition of the Poona politicians. While Fergusson was reluctant to implement the Ripon reforms of local government, one of the first acts of Lord Reay was

[54] The theses above are based on a sampling of the opinions of Bombay governors and officials from 1870 to 1920. Similar research on the period 1818–1870 may substantiate or disprove these hypotheses. Unlike the Punjab, which had a consistent conservative tradition in the nineteenth century, Bombay had a chequered pattern. Because the governor was a political appointee, an outsider imposed upon the Bombay Civil Service, he reflected the views of the British political party in power rather than local official opinion. However, as a newcomer, the governor had to lean heavily upon the accumulated knowledge of bureaucrats who had spent most of their working lives in the Bombay Presidency. While the prevailing Civilian attitude toward Brahmans was one of hostility, there were some exceptions. The most notable was Sir William Wedderburn, who became an active supporter of the Congress.

[55] Sir James Fergusson (1832–1907), sixth baronet of Kilkerran, educated at Rugby, University College, Oxford, served in the Crimean War, Conservative member for Ayrshire, 1854, Under Secretary of State for India, 1866–67, Governor of South Australia, 1868–73, Governor of New Zealand, 1873–75.

[56] Donald James Mackay (1839–1921), eleventh Baron Reay, educated at Leyden University, member of the States General, Netherlands, 1871–75, naturalized in England, 1877, elevated to the peerage, 1881.

[57] Fergusson supported the Brahman-sponsored New English School and the Deccan Education Society (DES), to which he made a donation of 1,250 rupees. The college established by the DES, Fergusson College, was named after him. P. M. Limaye, *History of the Deccan Education Society*, 1880–1935 (Poona, 1935), p. 57.

to confer an advanced constitution on the Poona municipality, which enabled it to elect two-thirds of its representatives and select its own president. This marked the Poona municipality as the most advanced in the presidency outside of Bombay City.[58] Lord Reay's known sympathy for the Indian National Congress enhanced his reputation as a governor who understood the needs of the elite. At a time when many Englishmen were having doubts as to the efficacy of an Indian body critical of the Raj, Reay declared his support for the Congress in a letter to the Bombay Muslim leader, Badruddin Tyabji: "The Congress criticises the administration to which I belong & the administration of course *must* welcome any criticism which leads to improvement & eradication of abuses. *Good* administration is of course 'republicae suprema salus.' That has always been my view & I am paid & *sent* here to make *administration* better and stronger. My relations to the Congress are those of a stage manager to a stage critic."[59]

But even in the 1880's there were developments which disturbed the Poona elite. The Bombay Government formulated the principle in 1881 that an effort should be made in future "to secure a due admixture of the various races and castes" in the service of the administration.[60] In practice this policy was easier to formulate than to implement: it remained virtually a dead letter in the Marathi-language districts (primarily the Central and Southern divisions) since the non-Brahman castes and non-Hindu communities were not sufficiently educated to take advantage of the policy. It was reported as late as 1910 that the Brahmans of these districts continued "to secure by far the largest proportion of Government posts in all Departments and in all grades of the service."[61] Nevertheless, the important principle had been formulated, and was to be reaffirmed from time to time, that the government should make every effort to encourage counter-elites so as to diversify the provincial service.

One of the first attempts to implement this policy was made by the Education Department in 1885. As Brahmans had long secured most of the free studentships to government high schools, obtaining two-thirds of those available for the presidency and four-fifths of those for

---

[58]Sir William Wilson Hunter, *Bombay, 1885 to 1890: A Study in Indian Administration* (London, 1892), pp. 432–433.
[59]Lord Reay to Badruddin Tyabji, September 8, 1888, Tyabji Papers, Reel 3, National Archives of India (NAI).
[60]L. Robertson, Secretary BG to GI, September 17, 1910, Home, Special file No. 283-1, "Employment of Brahmins in Government Service," in the records of MHFM.
[61]*Ibid.*

the Deccan, it was considered necessary to encourage some of the other communities.[62] To rectify this situation it was proposed in 1885 that half of the free scholarships should be reserved for Muslims and the "backward" Hindu castes. This statement of policy prompted a hostile rejoinder from Poona. To reserve studentships for non-Brahman communities amounted to a policy of "singling out Brahmans and setting them against other classes." The policy was a departure from the principle of "strict neutrality" hitherto maintained by the Bombay Government.[63] To reserve posts was to make caste a criterion of judgement. It was contended by the Poona Brahmans that they were not opposed to the "elevation" of the "backward" communities providing it was gradual: they supported the Deccan Association founded in 1885 to provide scholarships for Maratha students to attend high schools and colleges.[64] The Poona Brahman was primarily opposed to what he considered was excessive favouritism toward one community at the expense of another, what was later described as the "hot-house growth of one caste."[65] The aim of such a policy was to weaken the Brahman community.

The British did not accept the Brahman argument. It was their contention that scholarships based on merit perpetuated the Brahman monopoly. Because the lower castes lacked money, education, and the incentive for self-improvement, it was considered necessary for the state to take action to ensure "fair play by all classes"[66] and to make certain that the strong would not perpetually dominate the weak. To the British, the Brahman opposition to reserved studentships smacked of tokenism, for it was unlikely that the gradual progress of non-Brahman education, through the Deccan Association, would have much impact on the Brahman education monopoly for a long time to come.

In practice the policy of reserving studentships was difficult to implement, partly because of Brahman hostility but chiefly because of the government's inability to find a sufficient number of low-caste

[62]W. Lee-Warner to the *PSS*, November 3, 1885, quoted in *QJPSS*, VIII, No. 3 (January, 1886), p. 33. Of the 6,565 students in the government high schools, 3,986 were Brahman; of the 524 receiving free or partially free education, 318 were Brahman.
[63]*PSS* to BG, October 29, 1885, quoted in the above, p. 31.
[64]*Mahratta*, February 1, 1885.
[65]*Ibid.*, October 6, 1901. This was the *Mahratta's* reaction to the decision of the Maharaja of Kolhapur to reserve 50 per cent of the posts in the Kolhapur administration for members of the "backward" castes. See Chap. V.
[66]W. Lee-Warner to the *PSS*, November 3, 1885.

Hindus and Muslims to assist. The Director of Public Instruction complained, in 1900, that he was unable to find one suitable Muslim candidate for a college scholarship in the province of Sind. On inquiry, he discovered that this was due to the apathy of the Muslim community.[67] Despite a variety of attempts, the Government of Bombay did not succeed in weakening the position of the Maratha Brahman or in frustrating his attempt to secure more power in the municipalities of the late nineteenth century. It is significant that the Brahman position in the 1890's was one of strength rather than of weakness: he was both consolidating his position in the services and institutions of the province, and at the same time effectively warding off those who wished to curtail the Brahman hegemony. It was the very strength of the Brahman position which made him eager to defend his position, sensitive to any change, and willing to contest any effort to diminish his authority.

British policy and attitudes had a salient effect on the Poona Brahmans. A feeling of uncertainty was created among the elite, for the newly western-educated Brahmans were perplexed by changes in their society and the demands of modernization. Contact with western thought made them ponder as to why the once-powerful Maratha empire had dissolved into competing factions. It occurred when the Poona elite was attempting to work out its own myths, its attitudes toward the past, its explanation of the present, and its blueprint for the future. The British contributed to this confusion both by encouraging the Brahmans to participate in the new arenas of politics and by chastising them on critical occasions. The vacillations of policy within the Bombay Government added to this uncertainty and helped to create a suspicion in the minds of educated Brahmans that the days of previleged political position might be numbered. Official hostility towards Brahmans provided them with a greater sense of identity and acted as a stimulus for them to unite and organize some form of protest.

One of the principal issues of contention in Poona in the 1870's was the degree to which Brahmans could incorporate modern values at the expense of the traditional. Western education created a considerable gulf between the elite and its society. The gulf was particularly notice-

---

[67]"Memorandum of Mr. Giles, Director of Public Instruction," May 1, 1900, enclosure to Lord Northcote to Lord Hamilton, May 10, 1900, Hamilton Correspondence, MSS Eur. F 123/27. This memorandum was a rejoinder to Lee-Warner's "Note on Bombay Affairs."

able among the Brahman students who had been educated in the more cosmopolitan and liberal atmosphere of Bombay and returned to Poona for employment.[68] It was the view of some of the younger graduates, such as *Vishnushastri* Chiplunkar,[69] that Ranade and others among the older graduates who advocated such radical ideas as widow remarriage and a liberal brand of Hinduism, had become intoxicated by the new learning and were heedlessly abandoning traditional values. The generation conflict is best represented in the Chiplunkar family, in the fierce criticism which *Vishnushastri* levelled against his father, *Krishnashastri* Hari Chiplunkar (1824–1878), a prominent social reformer and an advocate of widow remarriage. In his magazine, *Nibandhmala, Vishnushastri,* stating the counter-thesis to his father's generation, which, in his view, prized the new and despised the old, argued that the traditional was in many ways superior to the modern. *Vishnushastri* unabashedly praised Indian religion and the role of the Brahmans in formulating it. The Peshwa period of Maratha history was seen as the glorious occasion when Brahmans took on the mantle of Kshatriyas.

Vishnushastri lashed out at all who were critical of Brahmans and disparaged traditional culture. *Lokahitawadi,* who had earlier railed against Brahman indifference to modern culture and depicted the Brahmans as steeped in useless learning, was ridiculed for his uncritical acceptance of western comparisons and his failure to realize that the rulers did not live up to their precepts. *Vishnushastri* attacked the missionaries with equal vigour. It was their aim to belittle tradition and assail the Hindu religion. Similarly, Chiplunkar attacked *Mahatma* Jotiba Govind Phule (1827–1890), the pioneer of the non-Brahman movement in western India, who wrote a series of trenchant attacks on Brahmans. He was critical also of the adherents of the *Prarthana Samaj,* who were critical of orthodox Hinduism. It was *Vishnushastri*'s self-proclaimed mission to remind the elite that they should not uncritically accept western norms and values, for "as the English are not gods, similarly we are not demons or animals." "Both of us," he continued, "have virtues and follies."[70]

[68] Ranade and Gokhale, for instance, both attended Elphinstone College in Bombay.

[69] It is a common practice in Maharashtra to give titles to political leaders. The most prominent are rewarded with titles such as *Lokamanya* or *Lokahitawadi* because of their popularity or their wisdom. Others acquire names such as *Balasaheb* or *Annasaheb,* which are really "nicknames," since they have no meaning. Such names are italicized in the text to distinguish them from proper names.

[70] S. Padhye and S. R. Tikekar, *Ajkalca Maharashtra (Maharashtra of Yesterday and Today)* (Bombay, 1935), p. 143.

The debate on educational and social reform was exacerbated by the growing number of college students and the inability of the British administration to absorb the graduates. The Director of Public Instruction noted in the 1870's that the public service was clogged with a surfeit of graduates.[71] The position was to worsen in the following decades, since it was not until the 1880's that the educational bulge made itself felt.[72] It has frequently been pointed out that the excess number of graduates caused unrest and stimulated nationalism in the late nineteenth century,[73] but the situation was worse in the Deccan, for the occupational biases of Brahmans fitted them for little else than public service and the professions. The Parsis and the Hindu mercantile communities of Bombay were less likely to be affected; their more diversified mercantile and manufacturing interests provided alternative employment.

A third factor which may have caused uncertainty in the nineteenth century was changes in the systems of land tenure. Ravinder Kumar and I. J. Catanach have described the social dislocation which culminated in the Deccan riots of 1875 and led to remedial land legislation which began with the Deccan Agriculturalists' Relief Act of 1879.[74] There was also considerable experimentation in the system of land tenure in the Konkan, known as *khoti*, where the government attempted to regularize the system of tenure and the relationship of the *khot* to his underholders. Many of the *khoti* tenures dated from Peshwa times, when the Maratha rulers appointed officials to a village to collect its revenue and to assist and protect its cultivators. The extent of the *khot's* proprietory rights was the subject of disputes throughout the

[71]*Report of the Director of Public Instruction in the Bombay Presidency for the year* 1877–78, Appendix D, 81.

[72]Enrollments were as follows:

	Deccan College	Fergusson College	Total
1860	36		36
1870	80		80
1880	123		123
1885	210	99	309
1890	103	240	343
1895	135	294	429
1900	193	243	436

[73]Bruce T. McCully, *English Education and the Origins of Indian Nationalism* (New York, 1940).

[74]I. J. Catanach, *Rural Credit in Western India, 1875–1930: Rural Credit and the Cooperative Movement in the Bombay Presidency* (Berkeley, 1970); Kumar, *Western India*.

nineteenth century: the government persistently viewed the *khot* as a mere "revenue farmer" and denied his claims to "full proprietory rights." The upshot of the debate and legislation on the subject was that many of the *khots* became involved in long and expensive litigation with the administration. The Tilak family was concerned with such legislation for three or four decades after 1865.[75] It is significant that one of Tilak's first public acts was to petition the Bombay Government against the 1879 bill to amend the *khoti* settlement.[76] The bill was, however, passed in 1880.

It is difficult to assess the impact of land legislation other than to suggest some connections. Having family ties with rural Maharashtra, the elite Brahmans who migrated to the urban centers of Bombay and Poona were concerned with the land policies of the government, the rising assessments, and the steady deterioration of relations between the *rayat* and the *sawkar*. As the spokesmen for their society, they wished to interpret to the rulers their assessments of the rural situation, and to be recognized as the legitimate group within Indian society which was consulted on such questions.

There has not yet been sufficient quantitative research to clarify the connections between economic conditions and political protest. Did those involved in political agitation come from families which benefited from or were impoverished by the British connection? What was the correlation between high, medium, and low income Chitpavans (as defined by McDonald and Stark) and political persuasion?[77]

Whatever the cause of migration, a large number of Brahmans did migrate to Poona and enrolled in the elite colleges as a means of obtaining employment in the professions and the bureaucracy. As new immigrants to Poona, the first generation of the western-educated, they were a highly visible group, clearly delineated from their society. This elite, perplexed by the changes in Maratha society and those wrought by modernization, attempted to work out their relationship to tradition and to rediscover their links with the unlettered masses.

---

[75] N. C. Kelkar, *The Life and Times of Lokamanya Tilak*, trans. D. V. Divekar (Madras, 1928), p. 18.

[76] A petition from Ramchandra Mahadeo Gondhalekar and Bal Gangadhar Tilak, *Khots* of Dabhola, Dapoli Taluka, Ratnagiri District, October 15, 1879, GI, Revenue and Agriculture, B37-40, May, 1880.

[77] Appendix 1 presents qualitative material on the socio-economic background of some prominent figures of the Poona elite. The data is inconclusive, since it does not suggest any pattern of poverty or affluence.

At the same time, they were perplexed by the hostility of the administration to Brahmanical aspirations.

Brahmans responded to this identity crisis in a variety of ways. The Chitpavan-edited Bombay journal, *Native Opinion,* published a series of articles in the 1870's attempting to analyse why Brahmans were disliked by officials. Part of the blame, it suggested, lay with the Brahman community and its specialization in professional and clerical occupations. It was necessary for Brahmans to diversify their interests, to become involved in industry, trade, and farming. It would be wise for Brahmans, advised the *Native Opinion,* to emulate the Parsi community by engaging in business and abstaining from politics, in order to win the respect of the rulers.[78]

Others were more inclined to criticize the government. To answer the critics from the administration but also to reassure the elite, Ranade, the dominant figure in Poona politics, turned to history to demonstrate the essential unity of Maratha society and the extent to which the spirit of nationalism had pervaded Maratha society in previous centuries. Ranade argued that the foundation of the Maratha Raj in the late seventeenth century was "an upheaval of the whole population" which was "strongly bound together by common affinities of language, race, religion and literature, and seeking further solidarity by a common independent existence." Preceding and shaping Shivaji's political coup was a religious and literary revival, fostered by the bhakti poet-saints, that reached its peak in the fifteenth and sixteenth centuries. Coming chiefly from the lower echelons of society, the poet-saints developed a nationalist movement of heterodox and egalitarian character by preaching against "forms and ceremonies and class distinctions based on birth." By integrating the various castes and classes in his administration, Shivaji acted in accord with the national spirit proclaimed by these poet-saints.[79]

Ranade thus countered the usurper myth by two main arguments. The first was that a genuine spirit of nationalism had existed at the time of Shivaji and before—a spirit which united all the castes, creeds, and classes of the region. The second was that the interests of Brahmans and non-Brahmans, Hindus and Muslims, were essentially compatible, and that it was natural for the Poona Brahmans, as the most educated

---

[78] *Native Opinion,* July 15 and 22, August 12, 1877, and June 22, July 20, August 24, 1879.

[79] M. G. Ranade, *Rise of the Maratha Power...,* pp. 5–6.

class of their society, to lead and direct Maratha society. They were the heirs of Shivaji.

Another group questioned the value of answering the critics from the administration and appealing to the better natures of the rulers. It was the opinion of *Vishnushastri* that little was to be gained by mendicant tactics. He doubted whether the benefits of the colonial relationship were worth the price of national servility and the debasement of Indian religion and culture. In his later years he uttered an "undisguised nationalist protest."[80]

The British were partly responsible for this growing Brahman sense of alienation. By denying that the elite truly represented Maratha society, they denied it the legitimacy which was essential to a colonial elite. By considering the elite to be a dangerous and unreconciled class, they helped to provide it with a growing sense of identity and common grievances. By introducing policies which appeared to threaten the power, status and prospects of the Brahmans, they provided a powerful stimulus for a dissenting movement to emerge.

Myths played a considerable part in the emergence of protest movements in Maharashtra. The British were bound by their fear and dislike of the Brahman community and the manner in which they interpreted nineteenth century Maratha history. It is ironic that their belief in the reality of the conspiracy theory helped, in fact, to ensure that the Brahmans would become conspiratorial. The prophets contributed to the fulfillment of their own prophecy. It is not surprising that one of the first protest movements was to revolve around the interpretation of the historical role of Shivaji.

[80]Wolpert, pp. 10–11.

Chapter III

THE MAKING OF A PROTEST MOVEMENT

> The Hindus of the advanced party are showing a most truculent demeanour & are being urged on by the 'Mahratta.'[1]
>
> The present year, 1894, has come round to witness once more the demoralization of the Bombay administration.[2]

Elite fears and uncertainties concerning the future reached a climax during the governorship of Lord Harris (1890–95),[3] a Curzonian figure who had little sympathy for the western-educated group. Harris epitomized the growing official disregard for the aspirations of elite communities; he considered that individuals who took part in the Congress movement were not representative of Indian society. He was a provincial replica of the Viceroy, Lord Dufferin (1884–88), who denounced the Congress as a "microscopic minority."[4]

This helped to weaken the moderate stance of Ranade by demonstrating the inadequacy of mendicant tactics. It heightened the Brahman sense of alienation and strengthened those who argued that elite interests could be secured only by protest. Further, it provided Bal Gangadhar Tilak, an aspiring young politician, with the issues and opportunities to weld together a new group based on a more extreme formula.

As one of the younger leaders of Poona, Tilak was less tolerant of gradual political advance and more radical in his criticisms of the rulers than Ranade. As a disciple of *Vishnushastri* Chiplunkar, Tilak

---

[1] Lord Harris to Lord Elgin, September 14, 1894, Elgin Papers.
[2] *Mahratta*, October 21, 1894.
[3] George Robert Canning Harris (1851–1932), fourth Baron Harris, educated at Eton, and Christ Church, Oxford, Under Secretary for India, 1885–86, Under Secretary for War, 1888–89.
[4] A statement made in 1888. It will be argued that the Bombay elites were more concerned with the policies of the provincial administration than with those of the national government.

had less faith in the beneficence of British rule and was critical of the gaps between British precepts and practice. The British dislike of Brahmans and the disregard of the Congress in the late 1880's seemed to demonstrate the validity of Chiplunkar's more extreme message that radical self-help was a better solution than mendicancy.

The alternative was for the Congress to broaden the scope of its activities and form a mass political party. Tilak's program was based on several premises. Indians should demand rather than beg for concessions. The fruits of constitutional agitation had been meagre. "For the last twelve years we have been shouting ourselves hoarse," he wrote in 1896, "but our shouting has no more affected the Government than the sound of a gnat."[5] It was demoralizing for Indians to depend on the whims of the rulers for progress; they would do far better to help themselves and claim concessions as their right. If the elites and Congress were to become more effective, they must develop mass support. To add weight to its resolutions, it was imperative for the Congress to demonstrate its strength and to present demands to the government which came not only from the annual Congress gatherings but from "every province, district, city, in fact from every village."[6] In one sense Tilak agreed with Lord Dufferin that the Congress was a "microscopic minority," an appendage to Indian society. "It was foolish for the educated people," he wrote in 1896, "to consider themselves to be a class apart from the people." They could only "sink or swim with the people."[7] The solution was for the Congress to become more Indian, to discover links with the traditional society, and to find means of communicating with the unlettered masses.

Bal Gangadhar Tilak was born on July 23, 1856, in the Konkan village of Chikhalgaon. His great-grandfather, Keshavrav, chief administrator of Ratnagiri's Anjanvel Taluka in the later years of the Peshwas, was a versatile man in the tradition of the modern Brahmans of Maharashtra. He was a man of letters, a capable horseman, an unerring marksman, a swimmer, and a cook. Rather than serve the new masters of the region in 1818, Keshavrav retired to the ancestral village.

Since that time the Tilak family had had to support itself by less glamourous means. Bal's grandfather, Ramchandrapant, an official in the Survey Department, later became a sannyasi. His father,

[5] *Kesari*, January 21, 1896.
[6] *Ibid.*, November 22, 1892.
[7] *Ibid.*, September 8, 1896.

Gangadharpant (1820–77), was an elementary schoolteacher who rose to the position of Deputy Educational Inspector. Bal's father supplemented the family income by writing textbooks on arithmetic, grammar, and history.

While the Tilak family was comfortably placed, Bal was left a legacy of 5,000 rupees together with the small ancestral property when his father died in 1872;[8] the family coffers were depleted by misfortune and litigation. Gangadharpant's large investment in the Ratnagiri Saw Company, begun by the official, Arthur Travers Crawford, was wasted when the company quickly folded. The Tilak family was saddled by legal suits concerning their *khoti* tenure which began in 1865 and lasted for the next three to four decades. According to Tilak's close associate, N. C. Kelkar, Tilak could not maintain himself "with ease" until 1899, when he could live off the profits of the *Kesari*. Within two years Tilak was to be drawn into the expensive litigation of the Tai Maharaj adoption case which dogged him for the rest of his life. He spent 60,000 rupees on the case which was not decided in his favour until the last week of his life.[9]

Little is known about Tilak's relationships to his parents, both of whom died in his youth. His mother, a devoutly religious woman, died in Bal's tenth year and his father in his sixteenth year, shortly after Bal had taken a ten-year-old Chitpavan bride. Tilak's father was an orthodox and self-made man whose formal studies ended at the high-school level. Knowledgeable in Sanskrit and mathematics, he was respectfully known as Gangadhar Shastri.

Many stories from Tilak's childhood attest to his petulant and independent character, which was marked by precociousness and moodiness. Unlike Gandhi, who was a shy and diffident youth, Tilak had from early times a strong ego and a definite sense of his own identity.[10] Whereas Gandhi had an undistinguished high school and college record, the young Tilak was already making his mark among peers and teachers. At Deccan College he was the favourite pupil of the mathematics teacher, Professor Chhatre. Frank and opinionated in discussions, Tilak was nicknamed "Blunt" by his fellow collegians.[11]

---

[8]D. V. Tahmankar, *Lokamanya Tilak: Father of Indian Unrest and Maker of Modern India* (London, 1956), p. 11.
[9]*Mahratta*, August 8, 1920; N. C. Kelkar, *Life and Times of Lokamanya Tilak*, p. 18.
[10]Erik H. Erikson, *Gandhi's Truth: On the Origins of Militant Nonviolence* (New York, 1969).
[11]D. P. Karmarkar, *Bal Gangadhar Tilak: A Study* (Bombay, 1956), p. 25.

Although the young Tilak was moody and rebellious, the limited evidence available suggests that he could accept his father as a figure to be emulated. Tilak did not rebel against his father or the family religion; at Deccan College he dined in the orthodox common room and wore the appropriate silk dhoti. By preferring to study Sanskrit and mathematics Tilak was following in the footsteps of his father. There were many episodes of youthful rebellion against teachers and officials, but no recorded instances of hostility to his parents. This is not surprising, since his mother died before any youthful oedipal struggle could develop, and his father died before Bal entered Deccan College. Moreover, he was the only son in the Tilak family, the favourite who was pampered rather than punished. Bal's moody and headstrong traits may have resulted from his upbringing: as a child he was used to getting his own way and as an adolescent he was frustrated by the loss of this congenial status after the death of his parents.

When Tilak entered Deccan College he was a physical weakling suffering from indifferent health. To correct this condition he began a vigorous program of daily exercise which included gymnastics, wrestling, rowing, and swimming. The results are evident in all the pictures of Tilak, who appears as a man with a robust physique and leonine features. Unlike Gandhi, a small man with a saintly look, Tilak stands as a proud individualist, a man of action with a high forehead, piercing eyes, and bushy moustache. From that time on, Tilak's strong constitution enabled him to engage in vigorous political life and to achieve the (no mean) feat of swimming the Ganges, a quarter of a mile wide, at the age of forty-four.

Tilak had a loud and powerful speaking voice, but was never a master of the "subtle graces of the art of eloquence." His strength lay in direct argument and occasional vehemence which "swept the field like a wild hurricane or slashing sleet." In his writing he was "extremely pointed and pithy," and was "sternly logical, scornful of ornamentation, forceful and blunt, and mercilessly aggressive."[12] Tilak's writing and oratory were in harmony with the Kshatriya traditions of the region.

During the 1880's Tilak became involved in a series of nationalistic endeavours, notably in the formation of the New English School (1880) and the Deccan Education Society (1884) and the establishment of two newspapers, the English language *Mahratta* and the

---

[12] *Mahratta*, August 8, 1920.

Marathi language *Kesari* (Lion), both initiated in 1881. The founders included *Vishnushastri* Chiplunkar, Gopal Ganesh Agarkar (1856–95), first editor of the *Kesari,* Waman Shivram Apte (1858–92), first principal of Fergusson College, Mahadev Ballal Namjoshi (1853–96), and several others. Gopal Krishna Gokhale (1866–1915) joined the Deccan Education Society in 1886.

The school and the society were founded on the missionary principles of sacrifice and service, but within a few years serious differences had emerged concerning the interpretation of these ideas. The immediate bone of contention was whether life members of the society should obtain employment outside the society and should contribute such income to the coffers of the society. The quarrels culminated in the resignation of Tilak from the Deccan Education Society in 1890.

Because of the recent publication of relevant Tilak letters which throw light on his personality, it is worth retracing the steps of the controversy. In the initial years of the society the life members worked for the rather modest monthly income of 40 rupees (480 rupees a year). In cases of special hardship the Managing Board could allocate funds or provide a loan to a needy member. When the society received government support in 1886, it was able to increase the annual salaries of life members to 880 rupees. The monthly salary, approximately 75 rupees, represented an adequate if not extravagant income.

According to Agarkar, serious differences within the society dated from the time when "Mr. Tilak made a proposal for a loan of money to the A. [rya] B. [hushan] press and I objected to it."[13] The majority of the members disagreed with Agarkar and the loan was made to Tilak. Agarkar won a Pyrrhic victory when a motion was passed that no loan should be sanctioned without the unanimous approval of the members. This motion backfired on Agarkar, for it was applied to his ally, Gokhale, who was later denied a loan despite "great need."[14]

A second difference of opinion arose at the meeting of February 22, 1887, when Agarkar attempted to amend the bye-laws of the society to increase the monthly salaries of life members by five rupees, to approximately eighty rupees. Agarkar and Gokhale, both very poor, argued that the members should enjoy some of the fruits of the society's

---

[13]"Agarkar's minute on the internal situation of the Deccan Education Society in 1889," P. M. Limaye, *History of the Deccan Education Society,* 1880–1935 (Poona, 1935), p. 125.

[14]*Ibid.*

recent prosperity. In opposing the amendment Tilak contended that salaries should be limited to necessities in accordance with the principle of "jesuitical" poverty.[15]

A more divisive issue occurred in 1888 when the Maharaja Holkar of Indore donated a purse of 700 rupees to the society. The gift was received by Tilak and Agarkar in Poona. Agarkar deposited the amount with the treasurer of the society, Trimbak Rao. On the same day Agarkar learned that Holkar wished to obtain a number of high-school textbooks. Agarkar wrote to the Maharaja suggesting that two of his works might be appropriate for Holkar's purchase. In reply the Maharaja's aide-de-camp, B. A. Gupte, placed an order for six hundred books. The books were then sent to Indore together with a bill for 300 rupees.[16]

At this point the Maharaja decided to reapportion the purse of 700 rupees, already in the coffers of the society. In a letter sent to both Tilak and Agarkar, Gupte stated that the Maharaja would now like to donate 400 of the 700 rupees to Agarkar in appreciation of his book, and the remainder, 300 rupees, to the other members of the society.[17]

On receiving this letter Tilak acted quickly. He wrote to the treasurer, Trimbak Rao, to keep the whole sum intact and to make an entry in the account book that the sum had been handed over jointly by Tilak and Agarkar. He then drafted a letter to Gupte in which he reminded Holkar of the original purpose of the donation and added that "acting upon this understanding I communicated the fact to my friends and made over their respective portions to them." On the same day Tilak sent a draft of this letter to Agarkar suggesting that he might append his signature to it.[18]

Agarkar was furious at Tilak's "downright falsehoods" which "cut my heart as deeply as it was possible to do." In addition to the manipulation of the society's account books, there was the glaring untruth that the 700 rupees had already been distributed. Agarkar interpreted Tilak's letter as a thinly disguised attempt to deny him the 400 rupees which he would earn by the sweat of his brow.[19] The incidents clearly

[15]*Ibid.*, pp. 103–104; Dhananjay Keer, *Lokamanya Tilak* (2d ed., Bombay, 1969), p. 45.

[16]Limaye, pp. 105–106; Agarkar to Tilak, December 22–24, 1888, quoted in M. D. Vidwans (ed.), *Letters of Lokamanya Tilak* (Poona, 1966), pp. 240–242.

[17]B. A. Gupte to Agarkar and Tilak, December 21, 1888, quoted in Vidwans, pp. 238–239.

[18]Tilak to Trimbak Rao, Tilak to B. A. Gupte, Tilak to Agarkar, December 22, 1888, quoted in Vidwans, pp. 239–240.

[19]Agarkar to Tilak, December 22–24, 1888.

indicate Tilak's capacity to manipulate a situation to his own political advantage. He was willing to alter the society's books and to misrepresent a situation in a proposed official letter.

According to Gandhi, Tilak was an exponent of the position that "everything is fair in politics." Tilak challenged this interpretation of his credo by defining politics as a "game of worldly people and not of *sadhus* (saints) and by preferring the dictum of Shri Krishna, *"ye yatthaa maam prapadyamthe thaamsthatthaiva bhajaamyaham"* [I worship them the same way as they worship me],[20] to the maxim of the Buddha, *"akkhodhenajino kkhodham"* [Non-anger wins over anger].[21] By this argument Tilak identified the end as more important than the means. In the spirit of Lord Krishna, who valued any path which would lead to *moksha* (release), Tilak recognized the value of any political tactic, legal or illegal, which would achieve a worth-while political end. In this sense Tilak did not believe everything to be fair in politics; he was prepared to sanction any means which might lead to a justifiable result.

In this instance there were many ends which account for Tilak's provocative means. Tilak was angered by Agarkar's letter to Holkar, following the original donation, in which he could think of "individual *patronage so soon after our disclaiming, most emphatically all individual interests.*"[22] The incident seemed to underscore Tilak's apprehension that the members were becoming self-seeking and moving away from the original "jesuitical" principles. Agarkar's behaviour catered to Tilak's growing paranoia that important decisions were consummated behind his back.

Tilak's letter to Holkar was a clever tactic to force the Maharaja to face up to his change of heart. By stating that the money had already been distributed, Tilak was broadly hinting that Holkar should honour his original commitment and also reimburse Agarkar for the textbooks. While this course of action was economically sound, it was not one calculated to soothe the feelings of the sensitive Agarkar or to improve relationships in the society. Tilak could be overbearing

---

[20]This statement refers to Krishna's willingness to accept any of the major religious paths of *moksha* (devotion, asceticism, and knowledge). The end is more important than the path followed.

[21]Mahatma Gandhi, *Young India*, 1919–1922 (Madras, 1924), pp. 784–785, quoted in Stanley A. Wolpert, *Tilak and Gokhale* (Berkeley, 1962), pp.291–292; J. C. Masselos, "Gandhi and Tilak: A Study in Alternatives," in Sibnarayan Ray (ed.), *Gandhi, India and the World* (Philadelphia, 1970), pp. 81–98.

[22]Tilak to Agarkar, December 24, 1888, quoted in Vidwans, p. 245.

and insensitive, but he had the grace to admit some of his shortcomings in personal relationships. In his letter of resignation to the Deccan Education Society Tilak shouldered part of the blame when he confessed to having a temper: "The chief fault that I am aware of in me is my manner of expressing myself in strong and cutting language. I am, I think, never violent in the beginning but being a man of very strong feelings, I often fall into the error of giving sharp and stinging replies when aroused and of being unsparing in my criticism."[23]

Tilak's inability to get along with the dominant faction of the Poona Congress circle reinforced his concern to form a new party. In the late 1880's Tilak consistently found himself in a minority position in the decisions of the Deccan Education Society. His decision was due in part to thwarted political ambition: he increasingly found himself out of favour with the dominant figures of the Poona Congress party and passed over for a younger man, Gopal Krishna Gokhale, a protege of Ranade, who was selected for some of the key positions. Gokhale was appointed joint secretary of the Bombay Provincial Conference in 1888, a secretary of the Poona *Sarvajanik Sabha* in 1889, and became editor of its quarterly journal in 1890. Tilak doubtless resented this rising young star in the Poona political firmament, particularly as Gokhale was a relative newcomer to Poona. Gokhale had not joined the Deccan Education Society until 1886, whereas Tilak was one of the founding members of the New English School of 1880, the forerunner of the Deccan Education Society.

These personal rivalries reflected fundamental differences in attitudes toward religion and society. During the 1880's Tilak emerged as a more orthodox figure, more rooted and grounded in Hindu tradition than most of his colleagues. He was on opposite sides of the fence from Agarkar on most questions of social reform and particularly on the most controversial issue of the day, the Age of Consent Bill, a successful attempt to legislate change in Hindu society, to raise the marriageable age of consent for women from ten years to twelve years.

Ravinder Kumar has pointed out that, far from being a reactionary, Tilak was inspired by a "vision of a dynamic society as opposed to a static society," which included a commitment to "economic progress along the lines of the West."[24] In his belief in the inevitability of social change, Tilak differed little from the other liberal Brahmans of Poona.

---

[23]"Tilak's Statements of Reasons for his Resignation," December 15, 1890, Limaye, Appendix I, p. 28.
[24]Ravinder Kumar, *Western India*...(London, 1968), p. 310.

Although opposed to legislated change, Tilak was willing to sign a circular which suggested that girls should not marry until the age of sixteen and boys not until the age of twenty. Tilak believed that the liberal Brahmans should support such a reform.[25]

Tilak disagreed with his colleagues on two fundamental issues: the timetable of change and the primacy of political change over social reform. The politics of nationalism provided a practical sphere of action which would unite the country, whereas the movement of social reform would tend to divide or at least to expose the cleavages within Hindu society. Nationalism set up a tangible goal, whereas the lofty aims of the social reformers would take generations of struggle. Tilak believed that the cause of social reform might best be tackled when India was independent, for it was the British who were responsible for many social conflicts, such as communalism, and who were culpable for introducing social ills such as alcoholism.

Underlying these opinions was a different philosophy of social change. Tilak believed that the social reformers were attempting to reconstruct society from outside, "with a magic wand." Co-operating with the government and the missionaries, the reformers advocated drastic measures to root out social evils, reforms which would alienate Hindu society and frustrate their purposes. Only a program of gradual change—a compromise between the reformer's wishes and the society's expectations—would produce lasting results.[26]

Tilak's attitude toward social change can best be gauged from his attitude toward the caste system. While he believed that the divisions within Indian society, like those of any society, were "unnatural and artificial," and degrading to the Untouchables, Tilak considered them to be a fact of Indian life. The Buddhists had attempted to root out the system in ancient times and had failed. Tilak believed it important that the issue of self-government should not be harnessed to the goal of abolition of caste, which would take centuries to achieve.[27]

A society attempting to win its freedom needed structure, and, to Tilak, caste provided the most enduring core of Indian society. "Caste distinctions" were originally planned on the secular "principle of division of labour," and were based on mutual interdependence rather than on the modern practice of discrimination. At the second provincial

[25] Source Material BHFM, II, 201.
[26] N. G. Jog, Lokamanya Bal Gangadhar Tilak (Delhi, 1962), p. 33.
[27] Mahratta, March 21, 1920, quoted in S. L. Karandikar, Lokamanya...(Poona, 1957), pp. 627–628.

Industrial Conference, held at Poona in 1892, Tilak likened caste to the trade guilds of medieval Europe. If it were reformed and preserved from decay, the Indian institution might contribute to industrial development and improve the material and moral condition of the working classes.[28] Caste was thus considered to be a dynamic entity rather than, as one reform paper suggested, a system of "fossilised conservatism."[29] Tilak emphasized the traditional structure, not because he wished to defend or preserve it, but because it offered the most viable means of modernization.

While he was prepared to work within the social fabric, and at a gradual tempo in harmony with his society, Tilak remains something of a free spirit, ahead of his time, who could be more liberal than the social reformers. Thus in 1892 he agreed to undergo *prayascita* (penance) for the "sin" of accepting tea at a Poona mission house, but could ridicule the rationale for the orthodox custom. Arraigned before a religious court by the orthodox faction of Poona, Tilak silenced his critics by his knowledge of Hindu law and scripture and concluded that "there was no sin in taking tea, from anybody."[30] In other words, Tilak agreed to do penance only after he had established the morality of his own action and had vanquished the orthodox forces in their own court. This was in contrast to Ranade, who meekly submitted to the orthodox demand for penance. Tilak was a free agent, a law unto himself, who would bow neither to priest nor to reformer, neither to government nor to the elite, unless it suited his purposes.

Tilak's advanced social views and his sympathy for modern positions produced conflicts of interest and led to political inconsistencies throughout his career. Although he severely criticized the high school for girls, established in Poona in 1883, and denigrated female education, he enrolled his own daughter there.[31] Tilak was able to ridicule many caste customs, but he could not risk the ostracism which would result from active violation. Referring to the caste taboo against crossing the ocean, Tilak boasted to Motilal Ghose in 1916, "We, Mahratta Brahmans do not allow our religion to interfere with our politics," but, several years later, took *prayascita* following his 1919 trip to England.[32] In 1918, at a conference of the Depressed Classes, Tilak

[28]*Indian Spectator*, September 11, 1892; *Indu Prakash*, September 12, 1892; Kumar, pp. 310–311.

[29]*Kaiser-i-Hind*, September 11, 1892.

[30]Tahmankar, p. 52.

[31]N. R. Phatak, "Lokamanya Tilak," II, *Vividhdynanavistar* (March, 1924), p. 151.

[32]Ambica Prasad Wajapayi's reminiscences, quoted in S. V. Bapat (ed.), *Reminiscences of Lokamanya Tilak* (Poona, 1924), pp. 8–9.

declared that "if a God were to tolerate untouchability, I would not recognize him as God at all." Soon thereafter Tilak disappointed the leaders of the conference by refusing to sign a memorandum for the removal of untouchability.[33]

According to V. R. Shinde, a moving spirit behind the conference, Tilak's unwillingness to sign the memorandum was due partly to the opposition of his orthodox lieutenants.[34] The more liberal Tilak was shackled by their opinions, his own notions of gradual change, and his conservative constituency. The reform-minded Tilak, who could genuinely sympathize with a movement of social uplift, was circumscribed by the fear that reform movements would seriously hamper a unified political front.

Tilak's approach to religion was fashioned by his rationalist and activist outlook. In his two works, the *Orion or Researches into the Antiquity of the Vedas* and the *Gita Rahasya* (Secret Meaning of the Gita), he attempted a modern approach to the ancient texts. By utilizing calculations from Sanskrit texts, which were based on astronomy, Tilak explored the thesis, in the *Orion*, that the *Rig Veda* was composed as early as 4500 B.C. By reinterpreting the *Gita* Tilak tried to establish an objective analysis to replace what he considered to be the partial commentaries of Samkara, Ramanuja, and Madhva, each of whom wished to substantiate the dogmas of his own cult. In his interpretation Tilak was critical of Samkara's renunciatory philosophy and the notion that the world was illusory. He was more sympathetic to those traditions which regarded the material universe and man as "natural expressions of Reality."[35] Tilak preferred the doctrine of "Karma Yoga," which he believed to be the central idea of the *Gita*. "No one can expect Providence to protect one who sits with folded arms and throws his burden on others," wrote Tilak, for "God does not help the indolent."[36]

Tilak was always legalistic in his attitude toward religion. His approach to the Hindu tradition was "frequently analytic emphasizing praxis, the formal and behavioural side of religion." By contrast,

---

[33]G. P. Pradhan and A. K. Bhagwat, *Lokamanya Tilak: A Biography* (Bombay, 1958), p. 306, quoted in Eleanor Mae Zelliot, "Dr. Ambedkar and the Mahar Movement" (unpublished PhD. dissertation, University of Pennsylvania, 1969), pp. 147–148.

[34]*Ibid*; Keer, *Lokamanya Tilak*, pp. 394–395.

[35]D. MacKenzie Brown, *Journal of Asian Studies*, XVII, No. 2 (February, 1958), pp. 197–214.

[36]Bal Gangadhar Tilak, *Srimad Bhagavadgita Rahasya or Karma-Yoga-Sastra*, trans. Bhalchandra Sitaram Sukthankar, 2 vols. (Poona, 1935–36), pp. xxvi–xxvii.

Ranade and Gandhi were more attuned to emotional religion, the religion of the heart, bhakti. Thus the terms "orthodoxy" and "resuscitation of tradition" had different meanings for them.[37]

Part of Tilak's success as a politician was due to his ability to play a mixed role and speak in different social and religious terms to various groups. Thus, in 1891, when he was wooing the orthodox party, he spoke in traditional language; at other times he was a spokesman for reform and modernity. In 1893, following the communal riots, he was to speak in a Hindu voice, whereas at other times he wooed the non-Hindus. On many occasions he was the complete democrat, who wished to take the politics of the Congress to the humble villager; on other occasions he appeared to be an advocate of Brahmanical supremacy. It was part of Tilak's charisma that most of his followers did not see such remarks as inconsistent. Each group tended to appropriate the sayings which appealed to it. Even his biographers have selected the material which suited their predilections. Hence Tilak has been referred to variously as the defender of tradition,[38] as a centrist,[39] and as a social revolutionary.[40]

Tilak's desire to launch a new party was based on a combination of thwarted political ambition and a desire to provide an alternative to mendicancy, with the issue of social reform and religion providing the means of attaining political power. The particular question was the Age of Consent Bill introduced in 1890 by the Government of India at the promptings of the reformers. Tilak realized at this time that there was potentially more opposition to the bill than support. Although the reformers were better educated, more articulate, and well organized, they represented a fraction of Hindu opinion. The bulk of Indian society, from the shastris and moulvis to the middle and lower castes, were opposed to British-legislated change.

To appeal to such groups it was necessary to communicate to them in the language of tradition and to champion issues which concerned indigenous society. With this aim in mind, Tilak attempted in 1890 to make himself more acceptable in orthodox eyes. The change was noted by the police inspector, Mr. Brewin:

Up to this period of his life Tilak paid little attention to the customs of caste. Knowing, however, that he would want the support of all orthodox Brahmans

---

[37]Communication from Richard P. Tucker.
[38]N. C. Kelkar, *Life and Times of Lokamanya Tilak*, p. 207.
[39]S. L. Karandikar, p. 104.
[40]Tahmankar, p. 49.

in the struggle he was about to engage in, he determined to conform to all his caste usages, so that it might not be alleged against him that he was unfit to champion their cause. With this object in mind he proceeded to Allahabad and performed the ceremony of shaving his moustache and bathing in the Ganges. Having thus conformed to what he had long neglected, he returned to Poona and prepared for the struggle.[41]

Tilak's 1891 campaign struck deeper chords in Indian society than did the platform of the reformers. Although the reformers controlled the leading journals of the presidency,[42] there was more popular support for the orthodox position. The only sizeable meetings in favour of the bill were held in Bombay City; meetings held in Poona and throughout the mofussil were, with few exceptions, against the bill.[43] The bill tended to attract the backing of the educated leaders of Bombay and Poona, but it failed to enlist the sympathy of the more orthodox rank and file. Thus, while elitist societies such as *Anjuman-i-Islam* (Society of Islam) supported the bill, whole caste communities came out against it.[44] Opposition meetings were attended by an impressive array of shastris, moulvis, and pandits who frequently appeared on public platforms. At one such meeting in Bombay, the principal speaker was a shastri and the chairman was Maharaj Davakinandan, spiritual head of the *Vallabha Vaishnavas*.[45] The Poona shastris were equally active in opposition to the bill. A meeting of shastris in February, 1891, resolved that the bill would interfere with social practice ordained by religious authorities.[46] Hindu orthodoxy was supported in its cause by Muslim religious leaders: a meeting of a thousand moulvis and orthodox Muslims, held at Juma Masjid, also passed a resolution against the bill in February, 1891.[47]

[41]"Life of Bal Gangadhar Tilak," Police History Sheet 1897, p. 5, Political Despatches from Bombay, Political and Secret Department, 1899, Nos. 23–49, IOL.
[42]Journals which supported the bill included *Sudharak, Indu Prakash, Indian Spectator, Kaiser-i-Hind, Subodha Patrika, Rast Goftar*. The leading opposition papers were *Mahratta, Native Opinion, Kesari*, and *Gujarati*.
[43]Meetings to express opposition to the bill were held in the following mofussil towns: Ahmednagar, Panvel, Mahad, Revdanda, Satara, Ratnagiri, Belgaum, Sholapur, Thana, Dharwar, and Nasik. Bombay Presidency Police, Abstract of Intelligence (Bombay Police Abstracts), January to March, 1891, consulted at MHFM.
[44]The Nownath Brahmans, the Pushkarna Brahmans, and the Valmik Kayastha communities all held meetings to express opposition to the bill. Bombay Police Abstracts, January 31, 1891, para. 5; *Native Opinion*, February 12, 1891; *Indu Prakash*, March 16, 1891.
[45]*Gujarati*, November 9, 1890.
[46]*Mahratta*, February 22, 1891.
[47]Bombay Police Abstracts, February 28, 1891, para, 27.

The meetings in Poona dramatized the popular character of the opposition cause. From October, 1890, to April, 1891, the antilegislationists held three meetings in Poona City which drew from five thousand to ten thousand people each,[48] but the one meeting promoted by the reformers attracted only one or two hundred. Mindful of the orthodox opposition to the bill, and fearful of a recurrence of the rowdyism which had marred the Poona visit of Dayananda Saraswati in 1875, the reform party restricted admission to those who signed a petition in favour of the bill.[49] The meeting took place on February 25, 1891, at Kridabhuvan. As the hour of the meeting drew near, the crowd outside swelled to more than a thousand students and orthodox leaders who resented the fact that they could not attend the meeting. The ensuing riot was one of the most rowdy witnessed in Poona. After four hours, hardly a chair was left unturned or a lantern unbroken.[50] The reformers escaped with difficulty to a nearby house where they locked themselves up from the fury of the mob.

Several days after the riot, a telegram in the *Times of India* implied that Tilak had "got up" the mob, encouraged it in its rampage, and had made no attempt to disperse it or to assuage its fury.[51] Tilak's solicitors admitted his presence at the meeting, and offered an explanation of his behaviour:

Mr. Tilak had no connection with the mob or the mobbing that took place. It is true that the police jamadar [chief] asked him to tell the mob to disperse, but Mr. Tilak told the jamadar that he was in no way responsible for the action of the mob, and by interfering and undertaking on himself the duties of the police he would only expose himself to the great risk of personal injury. Mr. Tilak at the time thought that the request made to him to disperse the mob was part of a trick on the part of someone to make him appear responsible for the riotous proceedings.[52]

Tilak's editorials and activities during the controversy suggest, however, that if he did not openly advocate violence, he condoned violent tactics. His very presence at the Kridabhuvan encouraged the mob in their cries of "Victory to Tilak."[53] Tilak himself set the example,

---

[48] 5,000 attended a meeting at Tulsibag temple on October 26, 1890; 4,000 to 5,000 were at Shanwar *Wada* on February 8, 1891; and a meeting at the same place attracted 10,000 on March 29, 1891.
[49] *Mahratta*, March 1, 1891.
[50] *Ibid.*; *Indu Prakash*, March 2, 1891.
[51] *Times of India*, February 27, 1891.
[52] *Ibid.*, March 8, 1891.
[53] *Indu Prakash*, March 2, 1891.

followed by a number of orthodox leaders, by infiltrating the meeting.[54] After the riot, five persons were arrested for disorderly behaviour. One of them was Tilak's close personal friend *Wasukaka* Wasudeo Ganesh Joshi, who was later acquitted on the basis of inadequate evidence. The *Mahratta* laid the blame solidly at the feet of the reformers for excluding citizens from a public meeting and creating a spirit of excitement and frustration which culminated in violence. "If you call a man a brute or an ass," the *Mahratta* suggested, "you will have no ground to complain if you receive brutal treatment or a few kicks from him."[55]

Tilak's willingness to cultivate and work with the militant party of *Balasaheb* Balwant Ramchandra Natu (1855–1914) was a further indication that he condoned violence. The leader of some of the more turbulent elements of Poona, Natu had no qualms about the use of violence. *Balasaheb*, the elder of two brothers, came from a wealthy *sardar* family whose fortunes dated from the time when the family had betrayed the Peshwas to the British.[56] *Balasaheb* attempted to wipe this blot from the family name by his defence of orthodoxy, which ranged from funding pilgrims to Benares and preventing non-Hindus from entering the Parvati Hill temple, to supporting cow protection societies and railing against the social reformers. A man of limited education, he persistently opposed all "measures of progress" within the municipality.[57]

Natu had an even greater following outside the municipality, among uneducated spirits who preferred militant action to constitutional agitation. Typical of this group was his younger brother, *Tatyasaheb* Hari Ramchandra Natu, who was regarded by the Brahmans as a "sepoy," an idiomatic expression for a Brahman who preferred riding, shooting, and fencing to the customary pursuits of Brahmans. *Tatya* established a gymnasium to teach riding, drilling, and fencing, and numbered the Chapekar brothers, who assassinated two officials in 1897, among his clientele.[58]

---

[54]Keer, *Lokamanya Tilak*, pp. 65–66.
[55]*Mahratta*, March 1, 1891.
[56]The income of the Natu brothers was estimated in 1897 to be rupees 24, 997/2/4. Their estate included extensive property in Poona district, a *cal* (apartment building) in Bombay City, and shares in several industrial enterprises. GI, Home, Public, B111-16, October, 1897.
[57]"Life of Balwant Ramchandra Natu," Political Despatches from Bombay, Political and Secret Department, 1899, IOL; *Kesari*, December 29, 1914.
[58]GI, Home, Public, B111-16, October, 1897.

Balasaheb was the charismatic leader of the coterie which formed a type of vigilante group ready to harass any opponent of the traditional order. Although he stressed blind adherence to tradition, the emphasis on force and the practice of the martial arts created a new set of obligations among the members. While conforming to tradition, they constituted a new group outside the pale of caste society.

Bhau Rangari and Ganesh Narayan Ghotwadekar were the two other members of *Tatyasaheb*'s coterie. Bhau Rangari, whose real name was Bhau Lakshman Javle, was a Maratha whom the police considered an "extremely dangerous and troublesome man"; he was deprived of his license to hold arms in 1895 on account of his "bad reputation." He and Ghotwadekar were committed to the Poona Court of Sessions in 1894, after the Daruwalla bridge communal riot, when they were charged with being the ringleaders of the crowd attempting to aid rioters and obstruct the police. The charges were not sustained.[59]

Sardar Tatyasaheb Krishnaji Kashinath Khasgiwale was one of the more aristocratic supporters of the Natus. Khasgiwale epitomized the curious blend of the Natu party, which combined orthodox Hinduism with a militant style of politics tinged with social radicalism. As an orthodox Brahman, he was a member of the Poona Cow Protection Society, an opponent of social reform, and a delegate to a conference to preserve the ancient religion. But he was also alleged to be addicted to hashish, to drink liquor, and to eat meat, and was described by the police as a "dissolute and disreputable character." *Tatyasaheb* was a fair horseman who made a few rupees by training and selling horses; he and his family were practically penniless despite his status as a *sardar*.[60]

Tilak's rising political stock represented a serious threat to the Natu party. To the ultra-orthodox Natus, Tilak's views were too liberal and too modern. *Balasaheb* attempted to expose Tilak's liberalism and to question his authority when he attacked Tilak for accepting tea at a Poona mission house. The matter was settled in an ecclesiastical court; Tilak emerged victorious, exposing *Balasaheb*'s limited knowledge of scriptural injunctions, and reminding him that it was the Natu family who had contributed to the ruin of the Peshwas.[61]

The subsequent willingness of the Natu party to work with Tilak in

---

[59] GI, Home, Public, A142–55, February, 1895; Bombay Police Abstracts, June 24, 1895, para. 675.
[60] Bombay Police Abstracts, July 15, 1905, para. 737.
[61] Keer, *Lokamanya Tilak*, pp. 69–70.

the Ganapati and Shivaji festivals seems to be a clear indication of the political victory of Tilak and the eclipse of *Balasaheb* Natu. This also indicates that Tilak did not rule out violence and was willing to work with a militant group. It was part of his strength as a leader that he was willing to work with a variety of groups. Unlike Gandhi, Tilak tended to accept men as they were and made little attempt to mould them according to some ideal pattern.

During the Age of Consent controversy, Tilak secured support from diverse groups: the religious leaders of Poona and Bombay who were not usually involved in elite-style politics; the students who turned up in large numbers at the Kridabhuvan meeting and exhibited an interest in Tilak's program; the militant party of *Balasaheb* Natu; and prominent Brahmans in mofussil towns throughout the Deccan.[62] Although Tilak gained political prestige as a champion of tradition, he failed to establish a political base. He had not yet found ongoing issues to weld the diverse groups which had supported him in 1890 into a political force. He also had to discover how to bridge the gap between the interests of traditional leaders and the activities of the western-educated elite. He needed some means of communicating with a traditional society.

Prior to 1891, Tilak's reputation was staked on his bright journalistic career. His following in Poona was limited to a handful. The Chitpavan, Mahadev Ballal Namjoshi (1853–96), was a close associate and lieutenant since the 1880's. A selfmade man born of a poor family, Namjoshi became the editor of two journals in the 1870's, was associated with the formation of the New English School in 1880, and was an elected member of the Poona Municipality. He was an active fund-raiser who persuaded the chiefs of the Southern Maratha Country to contribute 50,000 rupees to Fergusson College. His chief interest was the promotion of Indian industry.[63]

Another associate was *Wasukaka* Wasudeo Ganesh Joshi (1856–1944), manager of the Chitrashala Press. *Wasukaka*, who failed to matriculate, came to Poona in the 1870's and helped *Vishnushastri* to publish *Nibandhmala* just as he was later to help Tilak to publish his journals. *Wasukaka* was both a useful man behind the scenes and a successful entrepreneur who travelled throughout the world. Among

---

[62] The mofussil meetings were not organized from Poona, but were spontaneous occurrences promoted by local leaders who are not listed in the police reports.

[63] *Times of India*, January 21, 1896; Limaye, Part II, pp. 210–211; *Mahratta*, January 19, 1896.

his achievements was the management of a circus tour to China and Japan in 1903. He enjoyed a long and fruitful life in politics, was active in Gandhi's satyagraha campaigns, and was imprisoned twice, one time for a period of six months at the age of seventy-six. *Wasukaka* came from a prominent money-lending family of the Satara district.[64]

Tilak's following was minute in comparison with those who worked with Ranade, the dominant figure in the *Sarvajanik Sabha*. Ranade was supported by a number of princes and *sardars* who acted as patrons for for the society, liberally contributed to its coffers, and provided an important link between the *Sabha* and traditional authority.[65] Ranade could also count on a large array of professors and government servants, who supported the *Sabha* as the premier elite association of the city and by virtue of its commitment to constitutional agitation. While the majority of members were Brahmans, the moderate and catholic stance of Ranade attracted a sizeable number of non-Brahmanical adherents including several important non-Brahman leaders, for example, Gangaram Bhau Mhaske, one of the guiding spirits of the Deccan Association.[66]

Tilak waged a vigourous campaign against the Age of Consent Bill, but it was passed in March, 1891. He was left a fledgeling politician without a following, an issue, or a continuing means of garnering support for his program. It was a frustrated politician who continued the fight against the act and took the battle to the Bombay Provincial Conference which met in Poona in May, 1891. A resolution criticising the government for not giving "due regard to public opinion expressed about the Age of Consent Bill" was passed. It represented a Pyrrhic victory for Tilak.[67]

Within two years the policies of the Bombay Government, coupled with the outbreak of communal unrest, produced the issues which rescued Tilak from the political wilderness. They created a sense of alienation out of which Tilak was able to fashion a following. They effectively undermined the position of Ranade and the moderate hegemony of the *Sarvajanik Sabha*.

Lord Harris, Governor of Bombay (1890–95), provided the cathartic

[64]Bombay Police Abstracts, 1898, para. 218; S. Chitrav, *Arvacin Caritrakosh (Modern Biographical Encyclopedia)* (Poona, 1949), pp. 302–303.
[65]See Chap. V. The two most important princes in the presidency, the Maharaja of Kolhapur and the Gaekwar of Baroda, supported the *PSS*.
[66]The Deccan Association was founded in January, 1884, by Ranade, William Wedderburn, and *Lokahitawadi* to promote education among the Maratha community.
[67]*Mahratta*, May 17, 1891.

symbol of elite unrest. Harris declared his heart to be with the unlettered masses, the humble village dwellers who could not write to the newspapers, or read them, and had only a "dumb way of showing what they want."[68] The needs of good government, he perceived, were not heroic undertakings but simple measures such as repairing irrigation tanks, keeping drinking water sweet, and providing a little elementary education. Harris was a paternalist who lacked broad understanding of or sympathy for the professional elite. His dislike for them is indicated by his reaction to the election of the Bombay Parsi, Dadabhai Naoroji, to the House of Commons in 1892. Publicly he congratulated Naoroji, but privately he wrote to the Secretary of State: "I am very disgusted at Dadabhai Naoroji getting elected to the House. Why England should elect natives I can't for the life of me see: they can't govern themselves. Why should they govern us? This man is of the priestly class, I believe, the class as a rule, I don't say that he does, who wash themselves night and morning in cow's urine."[69] His elite myopia was an unfortunate flaw for, as a sportsman of note who captained England in three Anglo-Australian "Test" cricket matches, he believed in the dictum of "fair play" and attempted to hold the balance between Hindu and Muslim, Brahman and non-Brahman. But his patronizing and tactless manner blinded the Indian elite to any redeeming features.

The Harris administration provided the immediate occasion for the revolt of the 1890's, the spark which ignited the protest movements. Following the liberal and conciliatory Lord Reay, the conservative and unsympathetic Lord Harris created a difficult adjustment for the elite. The spirit of the Harris administration was made manifest in the manner in which it broached the question of implementing the legislative council reforms of 1892. At this time, legislation passed in the British Parliament placed the onus upon the Viceroy and the provincial governors to introduce a measure of the elective element in the provincial legislative councils. Whereas Lord Reay welcomed the chance to extend the elective principle to the Poona Municipality in 1885, Harris was reluctant to implement the reforms, for he considered it "scarcely possible" to devise any scheme to obtain a "fair representation of all classes": to balance the divergent interests of town and country, to consider the traditional aristocracies and western-educated elites, and to include the many different castes and communities of the

[68] Harris to Kimberley, December 15, 1892, Harris Papers, MSS Eur. E 256, IOL.
[69] Harris to Cross, July 18, 1892, Harris Papers.

presidency.[70] Whereas every man had an opportunity in England to be elected to the House of Commons, Harris considered that each man would not have an equal chance in India. Harris, as a conservative, agreed with the dictum of Lord Salisbury that the "principle of election ... does not fit Eastern traditions or Eastern minds."[71] It was his opinion that by the existing system of nomination he was better able to select useful additions to the Council.[72]

With the passage of the 1892 bill, Harris was forced to devise some scheme of representation. By the first months of 1893 he had worked out a system by which eight electoral bodies were to each "elect" a representative for approval by the administration. The resulting eight enfranchised bodies, each with one seat, were the Bombay Municipal Corporation, the Fellows of the University, the Chamber of Commerce of Bombay, the Chamber of Commerce of Karachi, the *zamindars* (landlords) of Sind, the *sardars* of the Deccan, the municipalities of the Northern Division, and the local boards of the Southern Division. These constituted a considered attempt by the governor to balance the various interests of the presidency. As Harris pointed out to his superior, Lord Lansdowne, the scheme allowed four seats to the cities and four for the mofussil: three to the leading maritime city of Bombay (university, municipality, and chamber of commerce) and one to the second seaport of Karachi; and apportioned one rural seat to each of the four divisions of the presidency, Sind, the Northern, Central, and Southern divisions. Three seats were allowed to landed and traditional aristocracies (*zamindars, sardars,* and the local boards), two to trade (chambers of commerce), two to municipalities and modern elites (Bombay and Northern Division), and one to learning (the university).[73]

Harris was surprised at the hostile reaction to his proposals. The elites criticized the scheme on a number of grounds,[74] but chiefly because it slighted Poona and the Central Division. As the most advanced municipal city outside of Bombay, Poona City deserved a better fate than to be represented by 192 *sardars* of the Deccan.[75] It

[70]Harris to Lansdowne, May 4, 1892, Harris Papers.
[71]Lord Salisbury, House of Lords, March 6, 1890, 3 *Parliamentary Debates*, CCCXLII (1890), 98.
[72]Harris to Lansdowne, May 20, 1892, Harris Papers.
[73]*Ibid.,* April 9, 1893.
[74]The elites were disappointed by the limited character of the reforms and particularly by the small number of seats apportioned to Indians and the rules under which the council was to operate. *Mahratta,* February 12, 1892.
[75]The Central Division had a larger number of municipalities and local boards,

was considered unreasonable that the district boards of the educationally backward Southern Division should be given preference over the district and municipal institutions of the Central Division. It was considered unfair that the two chambers of commerce, dominated by European business, should be enfranchised. If business was to be represented, why were the two important and predominantly Indian bodies, the Bombay Mill-Owners' Association and the Bombay Native Piece-Goods Merchants' Association, overlooked? To designate two of the eight seats to the European business community appeared to be a deliberate attempt to water down the spirit of the legislation, which had been to increase Indian proportions in the council. In view of this fact, together with the privileged status previously granted to the Poona Municipality, the advanced state of opinion in Poona, and the sensitivity of Brahmans to such issues, it does seem, in retrospect, that Harris made a tactical mistake in devising a scheme so obviously unpalatable to the elites.[76]

When the proposals were published early in 1893, the Bombay Government was deluged by memorials referring to the administrative slight of Poona and the Central Division. The *Sarvajanik Sabha* protest found broad support in Bombay and formed the subject of a resolution passed at the annual meeting of the Bombay Provincial Conference.[77] Harris, in effect, was to admit the force of the argument by nominating three representatives of the Central Division to the council: Sardar Dorabjee Padamjee, the Parsi president of the Poona municipality, Ranade, and the English Agent for the *sardars*.

---

and a larger proportion of elected representatives in these institutions, than either the Northern or Southern Division:

Division	Number of municipalities	Number of elected representatives
Central	63	413
Northern	49	242
Southern	39	182
	Local boards	
Central	71	565
Northern	46	327
Southern	56	397

[76] Harris noted, in a letter to Lansdowne, that he intended to rotate the constituencies and to allow the municipalities of the Central Division to "elect" a representative in 1895. This private intention, which would have allayed elite criticism, was not made public. Harris to Lansdowne, July 31, 1893, Harris Papers.

[77] *Report of the Sixth Provincial Conference Held at Ahmedabad on the 1st, 2nd and 3rd November,* 1893 (Bombay, 1894), p. 13.

With the elected *sardar* the Central Division was amply represented with four members out of a council of twenty, a situation which even the *Mahratta* admitted was favourable to Poona and the Central Division.[78] If this concession mollified the elite, it failed to satisfy them. They wanted nothing less than to choose their own representative, who by virtue of election would be directly responsible to his constituents. One of the first acts of the next governor, Lord Sandhurst (1895–1900),[79] was to reverse the decision of Harris and to enfranchise the municipalities of the Central Division at the expense of the Karachi Chamber of Commerce. This was a significant decision, as it confirmed elite opinion that their protest was just and reasonable and that it was necessary to protest vigorously to secure their essential interests.

The reputation of Harris as an unsympathetic and paternalistic governor was enhanced by his reaction to the Bombay and Deccan riots of 1893–95. Communal conflict emerged with dramatic suddenness in Bombay City on August 11, 1893. By the time order was restored 80 people had been killed, 530 injured, and 1,505 arrested.

The Bombay riot was a manifestation of a larger malady which gripped much of India in the later 1880's.[80] Fed by a vaguely defined anxiety for the future and considerable fear of change and modernization,[81] the contagion of communalism rapidly enveloped the country. The Bombay outburst was directly connected with a riot which took place in July, 1893, at Prabhas Patan in the princely state of Junagadh, within the northern reaches of the Bombay Presidency. The Gujarati Hindus of Bombay City, alarmed by the desecration of Hindu temples in the sacred city of Somnath, Prabhas Patan, and by the deaths of eleven of their co-religionists, had held several meetings in the weeks prior to the Bombay riot to deplore the outrages and to raise funds for the Hindu victims.[82] The Muslims of Bombay responded in kind by

[78] *Mahratta*, July 22, 1893.
[79] William Mansfield, second Baron Sandhurst (1855–1921), educated at Rugby, entered the army, 1873, Under Secretary for War, 1886, 1892–94.
[80] GI, Home, Public, A345–64, September, 1894.
[81] Note the following Ganapati song of 1894:
  "Remember this, bow to the elephant-headed deity
  The Arya religion is superior, other religions will not help you
  The Ghodepir [Muslim *tabut*] is not worthy of your salutations
  Is the multitude of your gods found wanting?
  You will come to grief
  All that is ancient is not bad, all that is western is not good."
                    BG, Judicial, 1894, Vol. 287, pp. 252–253.
[82] R. H. Vincent to BG, September 9, 1893, BG, Judicial, 1893, Vol. 195, pp. 87–88; *Times of India*, July 31, 1893.

holding their own sectional meetings and by forming a committee to support those of their community who were injured or who faced trial.[83]

The emergence of communal organizations, notably societies to protect the cow, was another manifestation of communal tension and orthodox disquiet. The cow protection movement was a fundamentalist and revivalist movement, an attempt to cleave to one of the basic symbols of Hinduism at a time when many traditional ideas and customs were under attack. The roots of the movement were in Bihar and the North-West Frontier Provinces; missionaries from these regions attempted to found branch organizations in western India.

The Bombay *Gorakshak Mandali* (Cow Protection Society), founded in 1887, was a moderate body which showed few signs of activity from 1887 to 1892.[84] Its main concerns were the erection of *goshalas* (cow refuges) and the holding of an occasional bazaar with a procession through the city streets. The president of the society was the aristocratic Parsi mill-owner, (Sir) Dinshaw Petit, although most of the members were Gujarati Hindus.[85] In 1893 a second and more militant cow protection society known as the *Gaupalan Upadeshak Mandali* (Society for the Propagation of Cow Protection) was formed in Bombay City. Its president and guiding spirit was the Bhatia mill-owner, Lakhmidas Khimjee. The society launched a vigourous campaign to further its cause: it conducted noisy demonstrations, with "violent speeches and warlike songs," engaged six preachers to proselytize against cow slaughter, and formulated a project to send agents to Lanowli to buy horned cattle and thus intercept kine which would otherwise have been slaughtered in the Bombay market.[86]

It was in Bombay City, rather than in the Maharashtrian Deccan, that the most vigorous defence of the cow took place. A cow protection society, established in Poona in 1888, held infrequent meetings and was largely ineffective. Several societies were founded in Deccan towns during the years of communal tensions, 1893–95, notably at Hubli and Dharwar, but their activities were spasmodic, and they seem to have collapsed through lack of interest and funds.[87]

[83] Vincent to BG, September 9, 1893; *Times of India*, August 15, 1893.
[84] Bombay Police Abstracts, November 14, 1891, para. 1555, November 5, 1892, para. 1600.
[85] Of the 110 life-members of the Bombay *Gorakshak Mandali*, 11 were Parsis. The majority of the remainder were Gujarati Hindus. GI, Home, Public, B132–33, January, 1894.
[86] Bombay Police Abstracts, July 10, para. 1262, August 5, para. 1424, September 11, 1893, para. 1070.
[87] *Ibid.*, 1887–95.

There appear to be several reasons why it was the Gujarati Hindus of Bombay City rather than the Maharashtrians who took up the cause of the cow. The most obvious reason was that the Muslims of Maharashtra, numerically small, poor, and politically insignificant, posed no threat to the dominant Hindu majority. The Muslims of Bombay City were a larger and more vociferous community.[88] There is a deeper and more significant cultural difference between the two regions of Gujarat and Maharashtra which is reflected in their religion. The Gujarati has been nurtured by the Vaishnava and Jain puritan traditions with their emphasis on abstention from meat and alcohol. In Maharashtra the majority of the population, the non-Brahman Hindus, are Saivite and not committed to abstention, though meat-eating is usually confined to mutton.

According to the Acting Commissioner of Police, R. H. Vincent, the activities of the Bombay cow protection societies had materially contributed to the riot of 1893. His assessment of the causes laid the blame on the Hindu protectors of kine. "I have not the slightest hesitation," asserted Vincent, "in ascertaining the origin of ill-feeling between the two races to the anti-cow-killing agitation of the Hindus," particularly the Bhatias, Lohanas, and Gujaratis.[89] Vincent's strictures were widely publicized and amplified in the Anglo-Indian press, notably the *Times of India*, and were endorsed by several important officials, including H. A. Acworth, the Bombay Municipal Commissioner.

The *Mahratta* considered this a very jaundiced view. Cow protection was a time-honoured practice of Hindus which in no way interfered with the just and legal rights of Muslims. It was not the Hindus, the *Mahratta* pointed out, but the Muslims who had begun the riot when they emerged from the midday service at Juma Masjid and proceeded to attack neighbouring temples. The Hindus of Bombay had acted in self-defence. The blame lay with the Muslims and the Bombay police, who were "fully aware of the possibility of a disturbance" but had failed to take action to nip the riot in the bud.[90]

The moral which the *Mahratta* drew from the riot was that certain Anglo-Indian officials, such as Vincent, considered it the duty of government to "support Mahomedans against Hindus." Such a policy, the journal ominously warned, would be both "unjustifiable and

---

[88] The Muslims accounted for 20 per cent of the Bombay City population, whereas they represented approximately 5 per cent of the Deccan population.
[89] Vincent to BG, August 12, 1893, BG, Judicial, 1893, Vol. 194, p. 148.
[90] *Mahratta*, August 20, 1893.

impolitic," for "we, in the Deccan, never lived by the sufferance of the Mahomedans." The reaction of the Hindu mill-hands of Bombay indicated that this "spirit is not yet extinguished."[91] Tilak was not yet ready to point the accusing finger of partiality at the Bombay administration as a whole, merely to certain Anglo-Indian elements within the government.

The moderate leaders of Bombay and Poona reacted differently to the crisis. In their opinion the riot was an unfortunate outburst of the passions of the lower-class Hindus and Muslims for which no person or community was entirely to blame. At such a time it was important for the leaders of all communities to work together for communal harmony and to avoid words or actions which might fan the fires of communal unrest. To demonstrate their common purpose, the leaders of the Bombay Hindu and Muslim communities held a joint public meeting presided over by the governor. The leaders then paraded through the streets of the city in a show of unity.[92]

The assumption which underlay the moderate position was that the government, despite the questionable views of individual officers and of the Anglo-Indian press, was impartial and had handled the riot as well as could be expected. This view prevailed in the moderate-dominated Bombay Provincial Conferences of 1893 and 1894. Reviewing the riot, R. M. Sayani, the Muslim president of the 1893 conference, stated that the government was "strictly neutral" in such matters.[93] The view was echoed by Javerilal Yajnik, the Gujarati Brahman president of 1894, who stated that the British rulers had at heart "the interests of order and peace, progress and co-operation."[94]

Whereas the moderates joined in a common display of unity, Tilak emphasized the need for separate sectional deliberations. With this end in view he convened a meeting of seventy-five leading citizens of Poona. As the riot had been confined to the lower classes, it was necessary for the leaders of each section of society to meet with their respective communities in order to heal the communal breach. It was superfluous for the leaders of various communities to demonstrate their own concord; the riot had struck deeper roots in society.[95]

[91] *Ibid.*
[92] *Times of India,* August 17 and 18, 1893.
[93] *Report of the Sixth Provincial Conference,* p. 11.
[94] *Report of the Seventh Provincial Conference held at Bombay on the 2nd, 3rd and 4th November, 1894* (Bombay, 1895), p. 21.
[95] Bombay Police Abstracts, September 15, 1893, para. 1682; *Mahratta,* September 17, 1893.

A more significant reason for the meeting which was not publicly stated was the need to enunciate a Hindu view of the riot to counteract the Anglo-Indian view expressed by Vincent and the *Times of India.* Tilak referred to this need in a letter to the Bombay leader, Pherozeshah Mehta, soon after the riot:

> From the numerous letters that I have received from Bombay ... I find the view is approved in Bombay & the recent meeting of the Bombay *balyas* [domestic servants] shows that the Hindu public in Bombay is sadly in want of a bold leader who will organise a movement to assert their just & legal rights. I was quite surprised to see that Mr. Acworth was not contradicted at the meeting he convened by any of the Hindu leaders. You will, I am sure, agree with us in holding the view put forward by the *Times of India,* Mr. Acworth and Mr. Vincent is mischievous & that we must do all that we can to protest against it.[96]

The Hindu meeting, held in front of Shanwar *Wada* on September 10, 1893, was attended by more than 3,000 persons. The convenors, Tilak, Namjoshi, and *Balasaheb* Natu, had intended to embarrass the government, but they modified their aims at the last moment. Twenty-nine prominent figures from Bombay, including eighteen high court pleaders, wired their opposition to the meeting. Ranade, Bhandarkar, and some prominent Poona leaders voiced similar sentiments, arguing that such a meeting would excite further communal tensions. What was more important to Tilak,—for he was no respecter of names,—was that some of his 1891 supporters were opposed to the meeting.[97] Whatever the reason, Tilak decided that the time was not ripe to launch forth against the administration, and therefore the meeting was moderate in tone. The first resolution praised the Queen Empress, and the second thanked Lord Harris for "insisting upon mutual toleration and charity as the best means for keeping up their brotherly relations." The one note of criticism was directed to officials within the Bombay Government who saw cow protection as the cause of the riot.[98]

Events were now to assist Tilak. The Bombay riot proved a precursor to communal strife which reverberated throughout the Deccan for two years. Communal tension was a continuing factor in more than a dozen towns. Riots broke out in Yeola (Nasik district) in September,

---

[96]Tilak to Pherozeshah Mehta, August 26, 1893, Mehta Papers, NAI microfilm, Reel 1.
[97]N. R. Phatak, "Lokamanya Tilak," p. 225.
[98]Bombay Police Abstracts, September 15, 1893, para. 1682.

1893, and February, 1894, when four persons were killed; at Poona in September, 1894, one person being killed; and at Dhulia (Khandesh district) in September, 1895, when nine were killed.[99]

During the first months of 1894 Tilak became increasingly critical of the Bombay Government and of Lord Harris in particular. The governor, he argued, relied too closely on the opinions of local officials, who were notoriously anti-Brahman and anti-Hindu. Harris was not able to solve the immediate cause of the Deccan riots, the vexed problem of music before mosques, because he attempted to impose partial solutions which were unacceptable to Hindus.[100]

In expressing such opinions, Tilak anticipated the position of the moderates and the Poona Brahman elite as a whole. At first the moderates were reluctant to criticize the administration, praising Lord Harris for the manner in which he handled the Bombay riot, but by 1895 they had come round to Tilak's point of view. A November, 1894, resolution of the Poona *Sarvajanik Sabha,* drafted by Gokhale, criticized the inflexibility of district officials and their inability to understand past customs.[101] Several months later the journal of this society summed up the governorship of Lord Harris by stating that on the issue of the riots, the "question of questions," he had dismally failed. Harris lacked the necessary "tact, resourcefulness, and sympathy" to deal with the crisis. He had depended too closely on official opinion. While the policy of the government was "undoubtedly one of strict neutrality" the instinctive opinion of the official was to favour the Muslim, and by relying on governmental advice Lord Harris pursued a policy which was anti-Hindu.[102]

S. Krishnaswamy, in a monograph on the Bombay and Deccan riots, argues that the Poona Brahmans were responsible for the communal impasse which developed after 1893. In his opinion, Tilak's use of communal tactics, combined with the virulent tone of the vernacular press, inflamed sectional passions which hampered government attempts to resolve conflict situations. By blaming the Poona Brahman elite Krishnaswamy indirectly exonerates the Bombay administration.

---

[99] Bombay Government Resolution on the Yeola riots, February 15, 1894, BG, Judicial, 1894, Vol. 283, pp. 542–546; Bombay Police Abstracts, August 18, 1895, para. 1216.

[100] *Kesari,* February 13, 1894.

[101] "Memorial to the Government on Music Rules," November 29, 1894, *QJPSS,* XVII, No. 3 (January, 1895), p. 40.

[102] "Five Years's Administration of Lord Harris," April 4, 1895, *ibid.,* XVII, No. 4 (April, 1895), p. 36.

It is his contention that Harris did as much as could be expected to solve the problem of music before mosques. His analysis of British records suggests that there is no evidence that the rulers deliberately attempted to divide Hindus against Muslims or pursued a policy of favouritism toward Muslims.[103]

But documents only reflect the official mind in action. They do not establish how the official policy was translated into action, how it appeared at the local level, or how it was interpreted by the elites. If the records suggest that Harris attempted to be impartial, they do not indicate that he failed to communicate a sense of this impartiality to the elite, and that he failed, at a time of crisis, to reassure the elite that the administration was sympathetic to Brahmans and to Hindus. Harris was fair but in an aloof and paternalistic manner. Because of such attitudes, together with the governor's anti-Brahman reputation, Brahmans were sensitive to the manner in which he responded to the riots. While they praised his attitude toward the Bombay riot, they criticized his handling of the affair. A greater number of police might have prevented the riot. It was impolitic for the governor to refuse to meet with Lakhmidas Khimjee, president of the *Gaupalan Upadeshak Mandali*, in the week following the riot.[104]

But such criticisms were trivial compared with the condemnatory articles which appeared during the crisis in Yeola and Poona. For five months, September, 1893, to February, 1894, the small district town of Yeola (population 20,000) was beset with communal tension which finally erupted in February in a riot which cost four lives and resulted in the firing of four mosques and a temple. During this time local officials appeared helpless to reconcile the warring communities. Even the usually loyal Anglo-Indian press criticized the inability of the Harris government to resolve the conflict.[105]

A similar situation occurred in Poona, where local officials appeared equally inept at divining past customs and resolving the communal tensions which had existed for the best part of twelve months. It took the presence of the military to prevent a threatened riot in April, 1894. Two months later there was a serious scuffle when the Hindu processionists refused to stop playing music, as they had been ordered,

---

[103] S. Krishnaswamy, "The 1893 Riots in Bombay" (unpublished Ph.D dissertation, University of Chicago, 1965).

[104] *Mahratta*, August 20, 1893.

[105] *Gujarati*, February 25, 1894, lists the journals which criticized the handling of the Yeola riots.

outside the Madar Chala mosque. The Nagoba procession of August resulted in further infractions of the music-before-mosque rules and led to the arrest of several Hindus. At the same time the Muslim *Muharram* festival, in which Hindus and Muslims freely intermingled, was boycotted by Hindus.[106]

The Deccan riots marked a new low point in relations between the Bombay administration and the Poona Brahman elite. They failed to communicate with each other and to understand their differing points of view. Both failed to perceive the complex socio-economic factors which produced rioting, and both oversimplified the causes of communal unrest. Each party blamed the other for the impasse and interpreted the riots in terms of its own preoccupations.

The Bombay administration, contrary to Poona Brahman opinion, made a genuine effort to avoid the imbroglios of Yeola and Poona. Harried local officials held numerous inquiries and produced lengthy reports in a vain attempt to ascertain rules and customs which might satisfy both parties. Large-scale communal conflict was a novel development in the Deccan. The local administration had no adequate machinery, no set of precedents, and no adequate records of Hindu and Muslim customs to help resolve the situation. The problem was complicated by the bad relations between local officials and Hindu leaders and the limited co-operation between the two parties. The criticism of the Indian press added to the fund of myths and "inherited" suspicions with which the Poona Brahmans viewed the Bombay Government.

Most officials failed to recognise the complex causes of the riots, or to see them as a reaction to rapid modernization and British-introduced change; they found it more convenient to attribute the continuance of riots to the truculence of Poona Brahmans. The already established conspiracy myth provided a ready-made and convincing explanation for a phenomenon which the Englishman did not understand. The seditious Poona Brahman was a convenient whipping boy and figured prominently in official explanation of the riots. "The agitation of the Deccani Brahmans," in the opinion of the Acting Commissioner of the Central Division, was "directed in reality not against the Muhammedans but against the Government."[107]

[106]District Superintendent of Police to District Magistrate, Poona, September 21, 1894, BG, Judicial, 1894, Vol. 288, pp. 57–71.
[107]Acting Commissioner, Central Division to BG, October 2, 1894, BG, Judicial, 1894, Vol. 288, pp. 103–104.

The Poona Brahmans also oversimplified the causes of riots. They failed to appreciate the extent of the problem and to give the administration due credit for the efforts it made to solve the problem. The government provided a convenient explanation for all the ills which plagued the Deccan.

During 1894 Lord Harris became progressively more frustrated by the continuance of the riots and the crescendo of elite criticism. Following the Poona riot of September, 1894, Harris, in two public speeches, lambasted the "unscrupulous and designing critics" of the administration. Casting aside the reasonableness which had hitherto characterized his public statements, he lectured the Maratha Brahmans, and launched a tirade against those "indiscreet and thoughtless persons" who made the Deccan, over the previous year, a "byword throughout India for violence, disobedience and inconsiderateness."[108]

This represented the low watermark in relations between the Brahman elite and the government. The *Mahratta,* in response, published an article, "How History Repeats Itself!" in which it compared the year 1894 to the previous year of dissension, 1879. In both instances, British distaste for the Poona Brahmans overcame a policy of good sense and impartiality. In both instances, the Bombay Government panicked when confronted with what it thought to be the living phoenix of Poona Brahman intrigue and sedition. By its "unrighteous, unchristian and unstatesmanlike policy of repressing poor and innocent Brahmans" the Harris government matched the administration of Sir Richard Temple in its "demoralization."[109]

It was during the administration of Lord Harris that Brahman alienation from the British, which had been increasing since the 1870's, reached its peak. Harris seemed to epitomize the official hostility toward Brahmans and the futility of expecting favours from the rulers. Tilak stood most to gain from this situation. He was the leading and most trenchant critic of the administration. He was the journalist who seemed to capture best the Brahman sense of alienation. He was, above all, the politician who seemed to offer the most promising solution to the impasse which hàd developed between the elite and the governments—a more extreme program which would force the administration to heed Brahman aspirations. He was thus the first leader to attempt to organize mass movements of protest.

[108]*Gujarati,* October 14, 1894; *Mahratta,* October 21, 1894.
[109]*Mahratta,* October 21, 1894.

Chapter IV

THE POLITICAL RECRUITMENT OF GOD GANAPATI

> Why shouldn't we convert the large religious festivals into mass political rallies?[1]
>
> It seems to me that Mr. Tilak, Mr. Namjoshi and other leaders of what I would venture to call the Reactionary Party are trying to put the clock back by 100 years; and are behaving in a very silly way.[2]

In the year following the outbreak of communal violence in Bombay City, Tilak joined with the traditional leaders of Poona to reshape the annual festival in honour of the popular elephant-headed deity, Ganapati. By enlarging the scope of the festival, Tilak attempted to insert politics into a religious festival in order to bridge the gap between Brahmans and non-Brahmans, and between the Congress and the traditional masses. By effectively mobilizing support for the cause, Tilak hoped to answer those critics from the administration who denigrated the Brahman community.

The ambiguous nature of Ganapati made him an ideal symbol for the transitional leader who wished to play a mixed role. The god was a syncretistic figure, combining the elements of high Hinduism, asceticism and wisdom, with the values of village Hinduism, devotion and pleasure. Unlike the popular regional god Vithal, who was closely tied to the apolitical bhakti tradition, Ganapati had links with the three broad traditions of Indian philosophy: devotion, asceticism, and action. Since one part of his personality derived from Shiva, the potent warrior, Ganapati had the potential for a political career. As the "Overcomer of Obstacles" he was a useful symbol for a protest movement.

---

[1] *Kesari*, September 8, 1896
[2] H. M. Birdwood, Member of the Bombay Executive Council, Note of September 2, 1894, BG, Judicial, 1894, Vol. 287, p. 471.

Ganapati's political elevation was closely linked to the rising political stock of the Chitpavan community in modern times. With the accession of the Peshwas, Ganesha enjoyed official patronage, and in the reign of Madhavrao (1761–72) the celebration became a lavish public affair which lasted six days.[3] During the nineteenth century public celebrations continued to be held in the Maratha princely states such as Baroda and Gwalior.[4] As the titular deity of the Peshwas and important Chitpavan families, such as the Patwardhans, Ganapati benefited from the improved circumstances of the Chitpavan community in the eighteenth and nineteenth centuries. He continued to attract greatest allegiance in Poona and in the Chitpavan villages and towns of the Konkan and the Desh.[5]

Although non-Brahmans worshipped gods other than Ganapati, chiefly Khandoba, Bhairav, Hanuman, and Bhavani, they freely took part in the annual festival to Ganesha. An Italian savant, Count Gubernatis, who witnessed the Ganapati celebrations in Bombay City in 1885, referred to Ganesha as one of the more plebeian gods and gave the following description of the festival:

> I followed with the greatest curiosity crowds who carried in procession an infinite number of idols of the god Ganesh. Each little quarter of town, each family with its adherents, each little street corner I may almost say organises a procession of its own, and the poorest may be seen carrying on a simple plank their little idol of plaster or of papier mâché ... A crowd, more or less numerous, accompanies the idol, clapping hands and raising cries of joy, while a little orchestra generally precedes the idol.[6]

The public worship of Ganesha had long been popular in the Deccan. Since before the thirteenth century, an annual one-and-a-half day festival has been held in honour of the god. If it was primarily a private affair, it did have a group aspect. The immersion of clay images on the second day of the festival was a "neighbourhood and spontaneously emerging group event." Householders, carrying their clay images, joined in the march to a pond, river, or seashore for the final immersion ceremonies.[7] With the accession of the Peshwas, Ganesha enjoyed official patronage and the festival took on a group aspect.

The Poona festival, prior to 1893, seems primarily to have been a

[3] J. S. Karandikar, *Shriganeshotsavaci Sath Varse (Sixty Years of the Shri Ganesh Festival)* (Poona, 1956), p. 8.
[4] *Ibid.*
[5] G. S. Ghurye, *Gods and Men* (Bombay, 1962), pp. 114–139.
[6] *Bombay Gazette,* November 6, 1886.
[7] Ghurye, pp. 121–122.

private and domestic affair. The custom of family celebration was described by a resident of Budhwar *Peth* (ward):

A Ganapati is purchased in the bazaar by each family on the day previous to the Ganesh Chaturthi or even on that morning and then it is brought by the members of each family to their own houses. Some bring it home in procession with music. Others who cannot afford this carry them home on their heads. The Ganpati is then worshipped on the following day, the Ganesh Chaturthi, and is kept in the house for various periods up to but not later than the Anant Chaturthi corresponding this year to the 13th September. The Ganpattis are then taken to the river sometimes by single families and sometimes several families join in the procession.[8]

The description of another citizen, Coopuswamy Mudliar, suggests that the Poona celebration had some group aspects. It was the custom of his family to keep the image in their home for three to five days and then to join "with other members of the community" (presumably the South Indian Brahman community) and sometimes with neighbours in a procession.[9]

In order to reshape the festival, Tilak popularized a number of innovations in the 1894 festival. Large public images of the god were installed in *mandaps* (decorated pavilions). Each street, each *peth* or market, collected subscriptions for a *sarvajanik* (public) ganapati which became the object of collective worship for the unit involved. Another change was the consolidation of the group aspects of the festival. Whereas families or small groups had proceeded on the second, third, fifth, seventh, or tenth days to various sections of the river, all the *sarvajanik* ganapatis were now conveyed together on the tenth and final day to immerse the images in a united ceremony.

A more important change was the introduction of the *mela* movement of singing-parties which were attached to the public ganapatis. In many streets, *wadas* (compounds), or *peths*, a *mela*, composed of from twenty to several hundred singers, mostly boys and students, rehearsed verses in honour of the god and marched for weeks before the annual procession. Dressed in lavish costume,[10] sometimes in the garb of Shivaji's soldiers, armed with bamboo sticks decorated with coloured paper and emblems of Hinduism, practised in dancing, drilling, and

[8]Statement of Venkatesh Shastri, resident of Budhwar *Peth*, Poona, BG, Judicial, 1894, Vol. 287, pp. 439–440.
[9]Statement of Coopuswamy Visairangam Mudliar, resident of Rastia's *Peth*, Poona, BG, Judicial, 1894, Vol. 287, pp. 435–436.
[10]One newspaper estimated that each costume cost twenty-three rupees. *Indu Prakash*, September 9, 1895.

fencing, the *mela* was a colourful and ceremonious unit. According to the *Times of India,* these innovations were not entirely novel; *melas* had existed in one form or another in Deccan towns for two or three centuries. Bombay citizens were familiar with the dancing-parties of the *Bankotis* who annually paraded from house to house. What distinguished the ganapati *melas* from their prototypes was their "better organization and impromptu songs."[11]

Another important innovation was the insertion of topical political songs. The verses sung by the *melas* of 1894 exhorted Hindus to boycott the Muslim *Muharram* celebrations and make common cause in their own festival. A typical verse was:

Oh! why have you abandoned today the Hindu religion?
How have you forgotten Ganapati, Shiva and Maruti?
What have you gained by worshipping the *tabuts*?
What boon has Allah conferred upon you
That you have become Mussalmans today?
Do not be friendly to a religion which is alien
Do not give up your religion and be fallen.
Do not at all venerate the *tabuts,*
The cow is our mother, do not forget her.[12]

Another extract was:

Let us dance, O let us dance
Ganapati has seated himself on his vehicle and started in procession
You work hard to erect poles and make garlands, banners and flags
On this auspicious occasion do not sit quiet and become dispirited
Let us tie *shelas* [scarves] around the waist and having gaily dressed ourselves carry the shield and dagger jauntily
Disturbances have taken place in several places, and Hindus have been beaten
Let all of us with one accord exert ourselves to demand justice.[13]

The 1894 Ganapati festival was promoted as a counterpart to the *Muharram* procession. By copying certain aspects of the *Muharram*[14] and by urging Hindus to boycott the Muslim festival, the organizers hoped to wean away those Hindu artisans, musicians, and dancers who had freely participated in the *Muharram* in previous years.

The rationale for reorganizing a religious festival was elaborated in several editorials of the *Kesari.*[15] As the ancient Olympic festivals of the

[11] *Times of India,* September 2, 1895.
[12] BG, Judicial, 1894, Vol. 287, pp. 263–264.
[13] *Ibid.,* pp. 254–255.
[14] For instance, the formation of groups attached to a public image.
[15] *Kesari,* September 1 and 8, 1896. This was written two years after the reorganized Ganapati festival. The rhetoric of politization was not clearly enunciated until this time.

Greeks had been a means of spreading national culture, creating national cohesiveness, and providing pure and innocent enjoyment for the people, so festivals in India could serve the purpose of establishing a sense of national identity. Since Indian culture was primarily religious, a revival of [the Hindu] religion would provide an essential means of creating this spirit. It was incumbent on the educated people to recognize the potential of festivals to disseminate political and social ideals among the common people:

This work will not be as strenuous and expensive as the work of the Congress. The educated people can achieve results through these national festivals which it would be impossible for the Congress to achieve. Why shouldn't we convert the large religious festivals into mass political rallies? Will it not be possible for political activities to enter the humblest cottages of the villages through such means? Will it not be possible to make available to our illiterate countrymen in the villages the moral and religious education which you [the educated people] have obtained after strenuous efforts.[16]

It was wrong for the elite to ignore its society. It was futile for the educated leaders to anticipate political power without broader support:

Our ancestors have already prepared occasions when people get together. These are completely ignored by the educated people ... Instead of singing devotional songs in the *Prarthana Samaj*, it would be better if people, such as judges, would describe the importance of bhakti in the Ganapati festival hall. Instead of giving a lecture on Ramdas in an empty temple, why not explain chapters of the *Dasabodha* [written by Ramdas] in Ganapati's festival.[17]

Behind the rhetoric of politicization and the dissemination of nationalism was the more immediate and practical concern of protesting the alleged government partiality for Muslims, or conversely against the non-recognition of the Brahmans of the Deccan. By encouraging Hindus of all communities to join in a common quasi-political festival, Tilak was challenging the British thesis that Hindu society was divided and that the elite Brahmans were out of step with their society. It was thus Tilak's intention to expose the British "partiality" for Muslims.

The Brahmans of Poona and the Deccan were the chief beneficiaries of the revived interest in Ganesha. It was they who most respected the god and were most alienated by government policies. As a "threatened" group, whose authority and status were questioned, the

[16]*Kesari*, September 8, 1896.
[17]*Ibid*.

Brahmans stood to gain most from a Hindu show of strength. Tilak was aware that the Brahmans, because of their education and degree of alienation, provided the most likely recruits to a more extreme party.

There was less possibility that the festival would politicize the non-Brahman communities, who were largely unaware of the burgeoning conflict between the British and the Brahmans. Tilak's *Kesari* articles might be construed as a long-term pious hope that the Marathas might eventually close ranks with the Brahmans. His immediate tactic was simply to involve the non-Brahmans in a quasi-political activity organized by Brahmans. If successful the demonstration could only strengthen the Brahman position but also indirectly involve the non-Brahmans in political protest and perhaps expose and educate them to the politics of dissent. The editorials underscored Tilak's philosophy that change must develop from within a society. The Brahmans could not hope to communicate their sense of alienation to their society from the comfortable precincts of the Congress; they had to work within the framework of traditional institutions.

The reorganized festival was extremely popular in Poona. Hindus, who had previously flocked to the *Muharram* festival, were conspicuously absent in 1894.[18] They turned instead to the Ganapati festival. For weeks before the procession, singing-parties marched and drilled throughout the city, chanting and reciting verses in honour of the god. Some of the *melas* were organized by Brahmans, but the majority were led by non-Brahmans, which seemed to substantiate Tilak's hope that the festival would be a broad-based affair.[19] The procession itself was a colourful occasion. It included a hundred *sarvajanik* ganapatis, conveyed in palanquins, carts, and horse-carriages, preceded by seventy-five bands of musicians, some seventy *melas*, twenty groups of *lejimvalas* (acrobats who dance to the music of the *lejim*), and a concourse of 25,000 people. They were in turn showered with sweets, parched rice, and *gulal*[20] by an estimated crowd of 50,000 which watched from the streets and balconies. The procession took three hours to proceed from Reay Market to Lakdi Bridge.[21]

The next year enhanced the reputation of the god. In Poona there

[18] *Mahratta*, July 8 and 15, 1894.
[19] *Balasaheb* Natu submitted a list of sixty-nine *mela* leaders of Poona in 1894: non-Brahman, 38; Brahman, 14; non-Maharashtrian, 4; unidentified, 13. BG, Judicial, 1894, Vol. 288, pp. 325–327.
[20] A red powder customarily used in religious ceremonies.
[21] *Kesari*, September 18, 1894; *Shri Shivaji*, September 14, 1894, *BRNP*, 1894, No. 38, pp. 13–14.

were an additional thirty *melas* and a similar increase in the number of *sarvajanik* ganapatis. Following the example of Poona, Bombay initiated its own *mela* movement and had thirty-five *melas* in 1895 and sixty-eight in 1896. The innovations were copied throughout the Deccan. Nasik had twelve *sarvajanik* ganapatis and thirteen *melas* in 1896; Ahmednagar had thirty-two *melas* in 1896 and forty-nine in 1898; Satara had thirteen *melas* by 1900 and Dhulia had fifteen in the same year.[22] "The Ganapati movement is spreading," noted a police officer in the Ahmednagar district in 1896, since "almost every town of any size in the district has its *melas* and Ganapatis now."[23] According to the official historian of the movement, the reorganized festival was celebrated in seventy-two towns outside of Poona by 1905.[24]

One of the reasons for the popularity of the revised festival was its decentralized character. The *mela* movement became a local and spontaneous effort of self-help. Citizens of a street, *peth,* or caste formed committees to collect subscriptions. They installed a public image and had a *mela* of their own. The leadership, activities, and constitution of the *mela* were determined by the local community.[25]

It was not until two years after the 1894 celebration that the Ganesh *Mandal* (society), a central co-ordinating body, was established. The desire for greater control of the festival came not from the Poona Brahmans but from government officials who increasingly demanded closer regulation of licenses for *melas,* censorship of songs, and stricter rules for processions. To meet official demands the Ganesh *Mandal* established four subcommittees in August, 1896. The managing committee was responsible for dealing with the authorities by arranging the hours and routes of processions and the granting of licenses. The duty of the second group, the working committee, was to move about the city and to supply the first committee with information relating to the number, constitution, and locality of the public ganapatis and *melas*. The third, the *mela* examining committee, was delegated the task of examining all songs and expurgating objectionable passages. The fourth, the rule-making committee, was to draw up rules for the guid-

[22]An appendix lists the number of *melas* in some important towns of the Deccan for selected years, 1894–1910.
[23]Bombay Police Abstracts, September 21, 1896, para. 1258.
[24]J. S. Karandikar, quoted in V. Barnouw, "The Changing Character of a Hindu Festival," *American Anthropologist,* LVI, No. 1 (February, 1954), p. 83.
[25]Oral evidence of Professor N. R. Phatak. Material supporting this argument is cited below.

ance of *melas*: their behaviour in the streets, in processions, and in the *mandaps* in front of the public ganapatis.[26]

In spite of the demands of the government for tighter regulation, the Ganesh *Mandal* was reluctant to supervise the activities of *melas* too closely. The Ganesh *Mandal* co-ordinated the final procession, negotiated with government officials, and arranged for public lectures, leaving the local organizations to their own devices. The *Mandal* consistently reaffirmed that it was not responsible for songs written by members of individual *melas*.[27] The leaders were clearly more interested in establishing and popularizing the movement than in regulating and controlling it. The festival was left to shape itself.

The manner in which the *mela* movement spread to mofussil towns further illustrates this. In the small town of Wai (Satara district) the *mela* movement was grafted to a local festival, the *Dvar* celebration, which amounted to a "beating of the city bounds." The Wai Ganapati celebration of 1894 was described by one Civilian:

> The melas composed of about 15–25 actual celebrants ... leave the city without playing music, march on each day to a village ... at each of the four cardinal points, worship a tree there and then on their return form one large procession at some point in or near to the city ... and then march on playing music and accompanied by flags and other sacred paraphernalia. There are usually about 6 or 7 melas but the number varies according as public negligence or private devotion subtracts or adds to their number. On arriving at some point in the town the large procession divides into two, the melas on the west side of the town go to the great temple on the river while those from the east go to the old temple of Ganapati. After this each mela then marches, still a compact unit, to its own quarters.[28]

It is apparent that the Wai festival did not have much in common with the Poona model and was shaped by local leaders. The influence exerted from Poona was indirect. The most important means of communication was the press, notably the *Kesari*, which was read throughout the Deccan and copied by smaller district newspapers. Visits to Poona by citizens of district towns was another means of spreading information about the festival. It was not until after 1900 that the Poona leaders made a concerted effort to champion the festival in the Deccan

---

[26]Bombay Police Abstracts, August 30, 1896, para. 1164.
[27]Oral evidence of Professor N. R. Phatak.
[28]B. C. Kennedy, Assistant Collector and Magistrate, to W. C. Rand, Collector and District Magistrate, Satara, October 2, 1894, BG, Judicial, 1895, Vol. 119, pp. 167–172.

through public addresses at district celebrations. By this time most towns of any size and note had initiated their own festival. The spread of the festival was a spontaneous occurrence, as was the spread of communal feeling throughout the Deccan after the Bombay riot of 1893.

A second reason for the popularity of the reorganized Ganapati festival was its revivalistic tone. Concerned with the amount of social and religious change, alarmed by the hostile attitude of the government toward Hindus, orthodox Brahmans and low-caste Hindus turned to Ganesh as a means of rectifying the balance in their favour. The Peshwas, the *Native Opinion* reminded its readers, were devotees of Ganesha and "extended their empire to the uttermost limits of Hindustan." It was fitting that the *mela* songs should honour the god who could "bring back prosperity to the land and the people."[29] Count Gubernatis was given a similar reply when he asked Ganapati devotees why they worshipped the god. Their reply was that "he brings us prosperity and abundance."[30] Many of the protest songs written for the 1894 festival contained revivalistic strains:

May this *Bhadrapad* holiday prove a source of happiness to the Arya people,
May the rains descend and the crops and trees bring forth fruit,
Parrots on seeing the sprouts will fly about with delight,
We shall see peacocks spread their plumage with exultation
The husbandmen carrying the grain will become elated
May the priestly class become satiated with deliverous food
What want of food and clothing will there be then for the poor?
Entreat all the diligent in protecting [our] religion.
Give up the *Dolas* [*tabuts*] and throw away the *Panjas* and *Nals* [*emblems*]
Chintamani is our titular deity who grants the fulfilment of vows
Celebrate this festival every year with pride
What will not be achieved by united action? Make this known to the wicked.[31]

Another verse proffered the following advice:

Dauntless were the Maratha sepoys and horsemen, O, Maratha brethren,
They carried their victorious arms beyond the Indus,
But you have become so passive now
Why don't you understand the vital point that religion is our duty?
You, who are skilful at work and who are brave, demonstrate your courage.

---

[29]*Native Opinion*, September 5, 1895.
[30]*Bombay Gazette*, November 6, 1886.
[31]BG, Judicial, 1894, Vol. 287, pp. 55–56.

Why have you abandoned Ganapati and followed the *tabuts* in procession?
Don't you feel ashamed?
The cow, our mother, is being slaughtered.
The fool follows the easy path.
Give up this evil habit and establish right thinking
Let us sing the virtues of the Aryans and follow our obligations.[32]

A number of sceptics questioned whether the worship of the god, within the loose structure and seeming disorder of a Hindu festival, could materially contribute to the Congress cause or achieve a political effect. The Bombay journal, *Indian Spectator,* advised the government not to take the *melas* too seriously, for the "days are yet to dawn when small disjointed parties of singing and dancing boys ... can have much political significance."[33] When the Bombay Police Commissioner visited the *melas* is 1895, he was greeted by a spirit of cordiality. He found the *melas* to be composed of "well-trained young men and boys of respectability" who sang verses which could not "possibly annoy or hurt the feelings of the most susceptible Muhammadan."[34] The Bombay procession proved orderly and inoffensive.

Some officials were inclined to detect a more sinister design in the innovations of the festival. In the opinion of one member of the government, the "small but noisy clique" which had organized the festival had no real interest in religion; "the object of all the recent agitation" was political.[35] The festival verses were directed, argued another official, not against the Muslims but against the rulers.[36] William Lee-Warner, an influential official, was anxious to prosecute the versifiers and restrict the innovations which went beyond the "proper and permissible object of celebrating a religious ceremony." The only question in his mind was whether the verses were "actionable."[37]

Lord Harris took a broader view. Admitting that some of the 1894 verses were "very insidious," he did not consider them "unreasonable from a religious point of view." Harris argued that the Hindu song-writers could not be blamed for encouraging in Hindu boys "a respect and preference for their own religion," and concluded that "if the

---

[32]*Ibid.,* pp. 251–252.

[33]*Indian Spectator,* September 13, 1896.

[34]Bombay Police Abstracts, September 9, 1895, para. 1216.

[35]H. M. Birdwood, Notes of September 2 and October 10, 1894, BG, Judicial, 1894, Vol. 287, p. 471, and Vol. 288, p. 136.

[36]Acting Commissioner, Central Division, to BG, October 2, 1894, BG, Judicial, 1894, Vol. 288, pp. 103–104.

[37]W. Lee-Warner, Notes of August 24 and 31, 1894, BG, Judicial, 1894, Vol. 287, pp. 425, 466–468.

Hindus like to have a public procession in honour of Ganapati, I don't see why they shouldn't."[38] The Harris view prevailed in 1894, and the public procession was allowed to go on despite a communal riot which had occurred the night before. Although this riot led to a closer control of the festival, Harris and subsequent governors did not view the festival as a threat, direct or covert, to the continuance of British rule until the festival became more openly political after 1905.

There is evidence to support the contention that the festival was an imperfect agent for disseminating the idea of nationalism and was a limited vehicle for conveying the message of the Congress to the non-Brahman masses. Because the Brahmans lived in certain wards of Poona and non-Brahmans in others, the *melas* were formed on a caste or community basis. Thus in some areas the *melas* tended to be exclusively Brahman, whereas in other areas they were non-Brahman.[39] The self-help character of the festival strengthened this tendency. Each local community organized its own *mela*. Given the character of Indian society, it was natural that the caste system should extend to the Ganapati observance. Of the forty-four *melas* in the Bombay procession in 1899, twenty-two were Brahman, four were Kamathi (labourers), two were Gujarati Bania and Marwadi, one was Khatri (weaver), and fifteen were Hindus of other castes.[40] The pattern was repeated in 1906. Fifteen *melas* were Brahman, ten were Maratha, two were Telugu, and fifteen were miscellaneous *melas*.[41] The seven *melas* reported in the town of Yeola (Nasik district) in 1896 were composed, respectively, of (1) Brahmans and Gujaratis, (2) Marathas, (3) Salis (weavers) and Khatris, (4) Vanis (traders) and Khatris, (5) Sonars (goldsmiths) and Darjis (tailors), (6) Pardeshis (foreigners), (7) Rangaris (dyers) and Sonars.[42] There are other references to *melas* based on economic groups, such as the Bombay mill-hands, and to groups based on families, such as the Patwardhans of Ratnagiri. Caste was also a factor in the composition of the Ganesh *mandals*. The Poona and Bombay branches were staffed by Brahmans, mainly Chitpavans, but the branch formed in the non-Brahman suburb of Mahim in 1901 was composed of Marathas.[43] Even the *Kesari* seemed to

[38]Lord Harris, Notes of August 14 and September 2, 1894, BG, Judicial, 1894, Vol. 284, p. 468, and Vol. 287, p. 470.
[39]*Poona Gazetteer*, III, 273-84.
[40]Bombay Police Abstracts, September 13, 1899, para. 1373.
[41]*Ibid.*, September 3, 1906, para. 690f.
[42]*Ibid.*, August 21, 1906.
[43]J. S. Karandikar, p. 157; *Kesari*, September 3, 1901.

admit the division of the *melas* on a caste basis when it commented in 1901 that while the non-Brahman *melas* of Poona were better organized that the Brahman units, the latter were superior in discipline and drilling.⁴⁴

If the procession brought together Brahman and non-Brahman *melas*, it did not necessarily educate or politicize the non-Brahmans. For, although the Brahman *melas* sang verses encouraging the Hindus to boycott the *Muharram* and in favour of temperance, swadeshi, and the program of the extremist party, the non-Brahman *melas* were almost exclusively religious in orientation.⁴⁵ Prizes for the best *melas* and the best, and most political, songs consistently went to the Brahman groups. Of all the *melas*, the songsters of the Brahman *Sanmitra Samaj Mela* (Good Friends' Society group) were the most popular. Its activities were described in a police report of 1905:

Of the 40 odd *melas* that of the *San Mitra Samaj* was as usual well to the fore. This year a third publication of songs has issued, the text is mostly political, and there is reason to believe that the printed version is not always adhered to, but verses couched in stronger terms, specially improvised for the delectation of select audiences, are used. Such songs were much appreciated by all who heard them, and they appeared to be to the taste of numbers of Government servants ... who formed a considerable portion of such audiences, strictures on Lord Curzon's *regime* and Government in general being vociferously applauded. Next in importance in the eyes of the public comes Bhor vakil's *mela*; its instruction in 'drill' by a Havildar in Military employ has, however been discontinued this year.⁴⁶

The *Indu of Bombay* stated in 1910 that the working classes had established many *melas* in "imitation of the Brahmin *melas*," but that they were free from the "political spirit and leaven" of the Brahman groups.⁴⁷ The official history of the festival seems to confirm this interpretation by its extensive coverage of the activities and songs of *melas* which were clearly Brahman, and by its limited reference to groups which were non-Brahman, such as the *Shur Maratha Mela* (Brave Maratha Group), the *Sahakhari Shetaki Mela* (Agricultural Co-operative Group), the *Chatrapati Sambhaji Mela* (Group associated with

---

⁴⁴*Kesari*, September 11, 1900.
⁴⁵This opinion was suggested by Professor N. R. Phatak, a resident of Poona during the most militant phase of the Ganapati festival, 1905–10. The evidence cited below seems to substantiate his view.
⁴⁶Bombay Police Abstracts, September 30, 1905, para. 942c.
⁴⁷*Indu of Bombay*, September 11, 1910, *BRNP*, 1910, No. 38, p. 27.

the Maharaja of Kolhapur), and the *Namdev Shimpi Mela* (Tailor Group connected with Namdev).[48]

The limited political involvement of non-Brahmans was probably due to Tilak's inability to discover political issues which would appeal to all sections of society. The communal issue provided a cause which was popular among a broad cross-section of society, but by 1896 the communal fires which had troubled the Deccan for two years were all but out. The pleas to Ganesha to restore material prosperity and correct the balance in favour of Hindus appeared to bring not replenishment but a serious famine and plague, and the harsh plague administration imposed on Poona in 1897. By 1900 there was a substantial decline in the numbers and the enthusiasm with which the festival was earlier celebrated. The reform paper *Sudharak* argued that the festival was on the decline.[49] Although this was denied by one of the leaders of the 1900 observance, only twenty-five *melas* were held in Poona at this time, substantially fewer than in the years 1894–96.[50]

It was not until after 1900 that the Ganapati festival recaptured the buoyant spirit of earlier years. This was due mainly to the increasingly political character of the festival. No longer did the Brahman versifiers attempt subtly to blend politics with religion, but openly exhorted the true patriot to wear swadeshi garb, to abstain from liquor, to support the *paisa* (penny) fund to regenerate Indian industry, and to oppose the policies of Lord Curzon, the moderates, and all the enemies of the extremists. The Bombay journal *Bhala* did not want the Ganapati festival if it was to remain strictly religious in character. It believed that it was necessary to breathe "some political fervour" into such festivals.[51] The following dialogue between the government and a *rayat* critical of the Bombay Land Revenue Amendment Bill of 1901 was a sample of the new types of Ganapati verses:

Government: You are poor and have no food and clothing, therefore we have introduced this Bill, but we are much concerned as to its operation.
Rayat: Oh Government! This is poison you are giving us, and we are altogether ruined now. This Bill is the beginning of future misery. The kindness of yours is a farce.

---

[48]The history of the *Sanmitra Samaj Mela* is narrated in considerable detail (Karandikar, pp. 378–436), but there is only passing reference to the non-Brahman *melas*.
[49]*Sudharak*, September 3, 1900, *BRNP*, 1900, No. 36, p. 30.
[50]*Native Opinion*, September 19, 1900; *Kesari*, September 11, 1900.
[51]*Bhala*, September 1, 1908, *BRNP*, 1908, No. 36, p. 32.

Government: The Demon Sawkar has troubled you much and thrust you into the deep sea of debt. He has attached your property and spoiled your reputation.

Rayat: The sawkar was our protector. You show us philanthropy only outwardly but actually cause dissension between us.[52]

Reviewing the altered character of the festival, the Bombay Police Commissioner wrote in 1910:

The movement which began as an opposition show to the local Musalman festival began to assume the character of an annual anti-Government eruption. Exhortations to use home-made clothes, the purity of Hinduism, social reform, the plague, Government measures generally and Lord Curzon in particular, the Congress, the Moderates, Lal, Bal and Pal and other persons of the official Demonology—these subjects under the tuition of the Extremist agents gradually formed the themes of the songs sung in the festival.[53]

The increasingly militant tone of the Ganapati festival resulted in its virtual suppression by 1910. By that time, officials had no compunctions about curbing the *mela* movement, since the festival had become what they considered to be "an engine for the dissemination and nourishment of vicious extremist propaganda."[54] By increasing censorship, by drawing up rigid rules for the conduct of the festival, by licensing each *mela*, and by insisting upon a complete register of the names and addresses of every *mela* singer, the government virtually stifled the *mela* movement.[55] Censorship of the Poona festival was further extended in 1916 when the government decreed that no pictures of humans could be carried and no names other than gods could be invoked in procession, and that the approval of the District Magistrate was necessary for any public speech.[56] By 1913 most of the *melas* had disappeared from Poona and the *Subodha Patrika*, organ of the *Prarthana Samaj*, could refer to the "practical disappearance of the Ganpati *melas*."[57]

The task of suppression in 1910 was made easier by the defamatory attack on the moderate leader, Gopal Krishna Gokhale, by Nilkanth Waman Bhide, a song-writer of the *Sanmitra Samaj Mela*. Incensed by the imprisonment and transportation of Tilak in 1908, Bhide, a

[52] Bombay Police Abstracts, September 29, 1901, para. 950.
[53] S. M. Edwardes, Bombay Police Commissioner, to BG, July 22, 1910, BG, Judicial, 1910, Vol. 139, p. 167.
[54] *Ibid.*
[55] *Kesari*, September 20, 1910; *Mahratta*, September 13, 1908, and September 25, 1910.
[56] *Kesari*, August 29, 1916.
[57] *Subodha Patrika*, September 7, 1913, *BRNP*, 1913, No. 37, p. 21.

Chitpavan lawyer, accused Gokhale of having conspired with the British to secure this severe sentence. Gokhale was castigated as the assassin whose hands were red with the blood of his brother. Adapting a scene from *Hamlet*, Bhide transposed the characters in a manner which would not be lost on the audiences who listened to the *mela*.

Mother [the British administration] look at my Bal [Tilak] and look at your Gopal [Gokhale] (refrain). Old hag your head has become bald ... Forsaking Bal, you have married a second time to Gopal. Bal has large, spirited and awe-inspiring eyes. Why are you sweet on this ill-starred paramour of yours? Look at Bal's bearing and royal lustre; do not turn away; look at your silly lover and kick him out. Bal is a Maratha hero. You deemed him arrogant. But this fellow hangs on your words only till his business is done. You thought Bal hardy. But he has received wounds on the battlefield. This creature has remained a Moderate because he is a eunuch in a harem ... This creature is the dirt of the gutter.[58]

At a meeting held in Poona to protest against the verses, a resolution moved by the Marathi novelist, Hari Narayan Apte, denounced the verses sung by the *Sanmitra Samaj Mela* as "containing vile criticism and false, unfounded and filthy charges against our respected fellow-townsman, the Honourable Mr. Gokhale."[59] Gokhale himself took action against Bhide and his publisher. The case was closed when Bhide agreed to make a public apology and to contribute 500 rupees to the Widows' Home run by Professor Dhondo Keshav Karve.[60]

In a recent autobiography, an educator recalls observing Tilak on the platform of the Gaekwad *Wada* listening to *mela* songs, such as those sung by the *Sanmitra Samaj Mela,* which were insulting to Gokhale and the moderates. While Tilak did not laugh and clap, in the manner of the assembled crowd, he did at least tolerate the performance. N. C. Kelkar, one of Tilak's chief lieutenants, was disturbed by the proceedings and protested to Tilak and the assembled leaders. Because no one took any notice of his objection, Kelkar left the platform as a protest.[61] The incident is confirmed in Kelkar's autobiography.[62]

[58]*Dnyan Prakash*, October 8, 1909, *BRNP*, 1909, No. 41, pp. 19–20. The text of the song has been reprinted in N. R. Phatak, *Adarsh Bharatasevak: Gopal Krishna Gokhale Yance Caritra (An Ideal Servant of India: Life of Gopal Krishna Gokhale)* (Bombay, 1967), pp. 391–394. It is translated in Appendix III.

[59]*Indu Prakash*, October 11, 1909, *BRNP*, 1909, No. 41. p. 20.

[60]A full account of the case appeared in the *Kesari*, November 9 and 23, 1909.

[61]Viththalrav Ghate, *Divasa Ase Hote...(So Were the Days...)* (Bombay, 1961), pp. 123–126.

[62]N. C. Kelkar, *Gatagosti Arthat Majhi Jivan-yatra (Past Events or the Story of My Life)* (Poona, 1939), p. 302.

Kelkar was equally disturbed by the tamasha tactics of some of the extremist newspapers. He was often at odds with the editors of the Marathi-language *Kesari* and *Kal* because they lavished abuse and invective on moderate opponents.[63] He was distressed by the campaign of the illustrated *Hindu Punch* to lampoon moderates, such as Gokhale, who were depicted in feminine form. As the leading moderate of Poona and as a Chitpavan Brahman, Gokhale bore the brunt of the criticism. The message of the *Hindu Punch* was clear: Gokhale, the mendicant politician, had forsaken his heritage, the masculine traditions of the Kshatriya Brahmans of Maharashtra.[64]

Whether Tilak approved of the attacks on Gokhale or whether he tolerated the excesses of some of his followers, tamasha tactics did produce problems for the leadership of the festival. The excessive zeal of Bhide gave the government a suitable excuse to suppress the *mela* movement. Tilak did not have the inclination to constrict Bhide's movements, even assuming that he had the means and personnel to do so. His forte was to light the fires of opposition and to stir up unrest against the rulers.

The political use of a Hindu festival helped to alienate other religious communities as well as the secular-oriented moderate party. The Parsi-edited *Indian Spectator*, reflecting the reaction of the moderate press, claimed that the mixture of religion and politics was a retrograde step. Progress, argued this newspaper, consisted in "moving more and more towards rationalism even in religion, and not towards the superstitions of bygone ages."[65] The Poona paper *Sudharak* questioned the national character of the Ganapati festival and suggested that the *Muharram* could be more appropriately labelled national, because Hindus and Muslims freely mingled in this festival.[66] Despite the claims of its organizers, the Ganesh festival was largely a regional affair. Since Ganapati was most revered by Maharashtrians and enjoyed greater popularity in Maharashtra than elsewhere, the new public honour accorded to the god was noticeably more enthusiastic in Maharashtra and the Marathi-speaking population of towns outside the region. In Bombay City the festival failed to evoke a responsive chord from the sizeable Gujarati Hindu population (20 per cent of the city total). There were very few Gujarati *melas*, and the festival was

---

[63] *Ibid.*, p. 306; Vidwans, pp. 256–261.
[64] Kelkar, p. 306; Ghate, p. 123.
[65] *Indian Spectator*, September 8, 1895.
[66] *Sudharak*, August 8, 1898, *BRNP*, 1898, No. 33, p. 20.

confined mostly to the Maharashtrian quarters of Girgaum and Thakurdwar.[67] The Bombay Ganesh *Mandal* was predominantly Maharashtrian. Significant figures were the Chitpavans, Dr. Moreshwar Ganesh Deshmukh, president of the *Paisa* Fund Committee, and the high court pleaders, Mahadev Rajaram Bodas and Daji Abaji Khare. Khare was a close friend of Tilak and one of the few moderates to support the festival actively.

There were, however, some advantages to be gained from the loose structure of the festival. It enabled individuals to develop their own projects within the larger festival framework. Antaji Damodar Kale, moved by the extent of the famine of the late 1890's, devoted his life to the *paisa* fund movement and established a *Paisa* Fund *Mela* to promote this cause. Shankar Ganesh Lawate, self-appointed tribune of temperance, likewise viewed the festival as a means of forwarding his mission and formed his own *mela*.

During this period the festival became a powerful vehicle for disseminating the ideas of the extremist party. Repeated in the marketplace and on the street-corner, the songs were an important means of spreading the revolutionary fervour which swept through Maharashtra after 1905. Damodar Hari Chapekar relates in his autobiography how he and his brother recited revolutionary *shloks* (verses) in the Ganapati festival, with appropriate gestures "to properly impress the drift of our *shloks* upon the minds of the assembled people."[68] In 1896, one year before the brothers struck down two British officers, Damodar published a book of Ganapati songs containing a "somewhat objectionable dialogue between a Hindu and a Muslim" which, if sung in public, the police considered, would give rise to bitter feelings.[69] Two other revolutionaries, Ganesh and Vinayak Savarkar, formed the Nasik *Mitra Mela* (Friends' Group of Nasik) in 1906, which later became the *Abhinav Bharat* (Young India Society). Sworn to secrecy, the members of the cadre read verses extolling Mazzini, Ramdas, and Shivaji, sang "exciting songs" in the Ganapati festival, and practised the martial arts. In the tradition of the earlier *mela*, the group printed its own books of songs. The *mela* thus formed an ideal model for the revolutionary cadre.[70]

[67] *Times of India*, September 14, 1895.
[68] *Source Material BHFM*, II, 993.
[69] Bombay Police Abstracts, August 24, 1896, para. 1120.
[70] *Source Material BHFM*, II, 395–416. The formation of this and several other revolutionary cadres led to a rash of extremist and terrorist activities in Maharashtra in the years 1908–11. By 1912 the government was able to expose the revolutionaries

From its inception the *mela* movement was potentially violent. It was an impossible task for the police of Poona, let alone the Ganesh *Mandal*, to effectively supervise the activities of the *melas* which marched more or less at will through the streets of Poona for weeks before the procession. Communal clashes were inevitable when some of the *melas* chose to march through the Muslim quarters of the city chanting verses which the residents regarded as objectionable.[71]

The tension of 1894 culminated in a communal riot the night before the scheduled Ganapati procession. One Muslim was killed. The *mela* of *Tatyasaheb* Natu, comprised of some fifty to seventy singers, had safely passed the mosque close to Daruwalla's bridge at eleven o'clock, but on returning an hour and a half later was instructed by the police to cease playing music in the vicinity of the mosque. In the words of the District Superintendent of Police:

They obeyed momentarily but struck up again against the remonstrances and efforts of the police, and on nearing the mosque the whole *mela* sent up a shout of defiance. It happened to be a Mahomedan festival and some 35 Mahomedans were in the mosque at the time. They dashed out and a riot commenced, the Hindus being driven back at first, but other Hindu *melas* were evidently in readiness close by, and in a few minutes some thousands of Hindus had collected around with sticks and stones, and the Mahomedans were put to flight; those taking refuge in the Musjid being severely beaten, one dying on the following morning.[72]

Local Officials considered that *Tatyasaheb* and his group had deliberately provoked a communal riot.

This contention was not upheld when *Tatyasaheb* and thirteen Hindus appeared in the Poona District Court. The prosecution failed to establish that the Muslims were assembled for religious purposes, to explain why they were at prayer at such a late hour. Since the police had no reason to anticipate the outbreak of disorder, they had no right to order the *mela* to forego its common-law right of playing music while in procession. The usually anti-Brahman *Times of India* summed up the trial by claiming that had the "Muslims kept their tempers and quietly continued" within the mosque there would have been no need for the prosecution.[73]

---

and to break up their groups. The revolutionary movement in Maharashtra was effectively stifled until 1927, when it surfaced again.

[71]District Superintendent of Police to District Magistrate, Poona, September 21, 1894, BG, Judicial, 1894, Vol. 288, p. 64.

[72]*Ibid.*, p. 68.

[73]*Times of India,* November 9, 1894.

To admit this, maintained the *Times of India,* was far from establishing the peaceful intent of *Tatyasaheb* on the night of the riot.[74] If he was willing to stop the music on the first occasion, why did he allow it to continue on the return journey? The most plausible explanation is that, rather than anticipating a riot, which would assume prior knowledge of the Muslim reaction, *Tatya* was intent on challenging the authority of the police order.

The 1894 Ganapati festival further embittered relations between the Hindu and Muslim communities of Poona City. Even before the riot of September, 1894, influential Muslims of the city had complained of the "inflammatory" Ganapati pamphlets in which the *Muharram* was "ridiculed" and the *tabuts* were described in "such offensive and disparaging language" which could only "incite the more inflammable sections of the two communities to breaches of the peace and bloodshed." The petitioners appealed for government censorship of the Ganapati songs and the forbiddance of "all mimicry, by the Hindus of Poona, of the rites, usages and observances connected with the Moharram."[75] Communal tensions were still evident in 1895 when the Muslims boycotted the elections to the Poona Municipal Corporation.[76]

With the return to relative political stability in Maharashtra, the government decided in 1919 to drop most of the festival restrictions, measures which had been conceived during the peak years of extremist and terrorist activity, 1905–10.[77] Although Ganesha was permitted to resume a political career, his political stock was never to reach the heights of the earlier period. Ganapati remains a political figure, but his festival is peripheral to the main propaganda thrust of political groups.[78] In the present-day celebration politics plays a rather minor role. Some *melas* dramatize local and international issues and the versatile Ganapati may preside over tableaus depicting support for or opposition to leaders such as Lyndon Baines Johnson and Nikita Khrushchev, but most *melas* are religious in orientation, preferring the deeds of Rama to the achievements of modern mortals.[79]

[74]*Ibid.*
[75]Substance of a petition from Abdulla Khan Ali Khan Mokasi, *inamdar,* and 370 others of Poona, to BG, July 31, 1894, and petition from Skaik Oomer, *sardar,* bahadur, and pensioner, and Kazi Syed Shumsuddin, and about 400 others of Poona to BG, August, 1894, BG, Judicial, 1894, Vol. 187, pp. 317–326, 419–420.
[76]*Times of India,* March 8, 1895.
[77]*Ibid.,* August 26, 1919.
[78]J. S. Karandikar, pp. 22–32.
[79]My observations of the 1966 Ganapati festival in Bombay and Poona.

Despite the decline in Ganapati's political reputation after 1910, Tilak's experiment of combining religion and politics was sufficiently instructive to be copied by other groups. Shortly after Tilak's death the *mela* movement was utilized by the *Satyashodak Samaj* non-Brahmans of Poona to challenge the political hegemony of Brahmans. The members of the *Chatrapati Mela*, organized in 1922 by Keshavrao Jedhe, chose to carry pictures of Gandhi, Shivaji, and the Maharaja of Kolhapur rather than of Tilak, and criticized the Poona Municipal Corporation, in their songs, for spending 15,000 rupees to build a statue of Tilak. Riots inevitably followed when the *Chatrapati mela* entered Gaikwad *Wada*, headquarters of the Tilak party. The Poona celebrations of 1922-27, the years during which Jedhe organized the *mela*, were dogged by similar outbreaks and by ensuing lawsuits.[80]

But in another sense Tilak's experiment of combining religion and politics was a telling success. Because he popularized a religious festival, Tilak won additional respect and support from those traditional leaders who had joined him in the opposition to the Age of Consent Bill. In organizing the festival, Tilak worked closely with the Natus and their party, who came to regard Tilak as a rising star in the Poona political firmament.[81]

In addition, Tilak was able to attract to the Ganesh *Mandal* some of the conservative and orthodox figureheads of Poona. Shrimant Wasudeo Harihar Pandit, better known as Baba Maharaj, a high-ranking *sardar* belonging to the priestly family of Kolhapur, helped in the organization of the festival. Although he was considered to be a "man of no capacity," he was an important traditional symbol because of the sanctity of his position.[82] Another orthodox supporter was the saintly *Annasaheb* Dr. Vinayak Ramchandra Patwardhan (1847-1917), whose long flowing hair was worn in the style of a *sadhu*. The son of a wealthy lawyer, *Annasaheb* studied arts, law, and medicine at Poona and Bombay, but was also familiar with palmistry and the occult

---

[80]Gail Omvedt, "The Non-Brahman Challenge in Poona, 1922-26" (unpublished paper, Maharashtra Study Group, May, 1971), pp. 15, 17-18.

[81]The principal figures of the Ganesh *Mandal* of 1896 were: Baba Maharaj, Tilak, *Balasaheb* Natu, *Annasaheb* Patwardhan, Ganesh Narayan Ghotwadekar, Bhau Rangari, Dr. Shankar Amrit Chobe, Dattopant Behere, Ramrao Patel Zambre, Balkrishna Ramchandra Paranjpe, Apparao Vaidya, Narayan Bapuji Kanitkar, and *Tatyasaheb* Dhamdera. The chief organizers of the 1896 festival were: *Annasaheb* Patwardhan, S. M. Paranjpe, Nana Narayan Bhore, Ganesh Narayan Ghotwadekar, and Kashinath Nilkanth Khasgiwale. Bombay Police Abstracts, August 30, 1896, para. 1164, and September 6, 1898, para. 1234.

[82]*Mahratta*, August 8, 1897; GI, Home, Public, B111-16, October, 1897.

sciences. During the 1870's he edited a newspaper and was an associate of Ranade's. After the failure of a revolutionary plot in 1880, Patwardhan retired penniless to an ashram in Madras were he remained for five years. When he returned to Poona, he reluctantly re-entered politics, though his main interests were the occult sciences and societies to protect orthodox religion and the cow. Like Baba Maharaj he was a useful symbol for the Tilak group.[83] Another recruit was the wordy, encyclopedic Professor Ganesh Shridhar Jinsiwale (1852–1903), who could monopolize a public platform for several hours. He was dismissed from Wilson College, Bombay, in 1890 for his very outspoken and ultra-conservative views on female education and the status of women. One of the leaders of the orthodox faction, Jinsiwale always carried a stick for protection.[84]

Tilak also obtained support from a second group, the college graduates, who became important assets for his fledgeling party. The most important were the Chitpavans, Narsinh Chintaman Kelkar (1872–1947), Shivram Mahadev Paranjpe (1864–1929), and Krishnaji Prabhakar Khadilkar (1872–1948), who were to become three of Tilak's closest associates. Kelkar, a fluent writer in English and Marathi, a littérateur and historian, became editor of the English-language *Mahratta* and later of the Marathi-language *Kesari* as well.[85] Inclined toward social reform, more liberal in religion than the defenders of tradition, a gentleman politician who did not believe that it was the duty of the extremists to oppose the government at every point, Kelkar was to have serious differences with most of the other

---

[83] *Kesari*, February 3, 1917; Chitrav, *Arvacin Caritrakosh* (Modern Biographical Encyclopedia) (Poona, 1964), p. 409; Aprabuddha, *Brahmarsi Shri Annasaheb Patvardhan, Sanketarekha Navabharatasya (Great Sage Shri Annasaheb Patwardhan, Pathfinder of Modern India)* (Poona, 1926); D. N. Shikhare, "Shri V. R. alias Annasaheb Patwardhan, A Spiritual Revolutionary," Note prepared by MHFM. Stanley Wolpert has argued that *Annasaheb* played an important role in the innovations of the 1894 festival. According to Wolpert, *Annasaheb*, the *moksha guru* (spiritual teacher) of Tilak, provided the inspiration for the changes. It is the view of Professor N. R. Phatak, however, that Tilak was too independent to rely upon any preceptor. There is no mention of the *moksha guru* relationship in Tilak's *Gita Rahasya*, where such an acknowledgment should be made. Nor is there any reference to this fact in *Annasaheb's* obituary article in the *Kesari* in 1917, written while Tilak was still alive. Professor Phatak, present in Poona from 1905, recalls that *Annasaheb* was not a very important politician. He was a useful figurehead who chaired an occasional public meeting.

[84] *Mahratta*, June 15, 1890; Ghate, p. 11.

[85] Kelkar came to Poona in March, 1896, and quickly became an important figure in Tilak's party. He wrote many of the editorials in the *Mahratta* and acted as an instructor in Tilak's law class.

members of the Tilak party. On more than one occasion he threatened to resign from the journals.[86] Kelkar was a "moderate" at heart; he disliked the ribald humour, the tamasha tactics, the tolerance of *gunda* (criminal)-style politics, and the more extreme position of the Paranjpe-Khadilkar faction. For the most part, he preferred to work within the defined frameworks of journalistic and constitutional agitation. As a leader he was an indecisive man who lacked the forcefulness to inspire others.

Paranjpe, one of the first graduates of the New English School and a master of arts from Deccan College, founded the Marathi-language *Kal* in 1898. As a student, Paranjpe was "stern, meditative, reticent ... proud and dignified, with a caustic tongue whenever he used it." He dressed in the "conservative Poona Sardar style, with ample personal decorations, and carried about himself a fascinating perfume."[87] Although phlegmatic and aloof, he was respected as a fiery opponent of British rule who could make effective use of sarcasm and invective. He became a Marathi essayist of some note.[88] Both he and Khadilkar,[89] the assistant editor of the *Kesari* and later editor, disliked Kelkar's relatively cool and detached prose in the *Mahratta* and consistently urged a harder and more militant line.

The graduates participated in the Ganesh *Mandal* because it provided the means of doing something outside the Congress and of answering the critics from the administration. Although the festival failed to politicize the non-Brahmans, it was nonetheless a novel attempt to woo the masses to the Congress cause. At a time when the methods of mass political protest had yet to be developed, this appeared to be a bold experiment with the rudiments of political power.

[86] Vidwans, pp. 256–261; Kelkar, *Gatagosti*, pp. 249–252, 295–299, 306–307, 323–324. The differences between Kelkar and the Paranjpe-Khadilkar faction became evident in 1897. Paranjpe criticized the *Mahratta* for being too sympathetic to the government and the moderates. It was Paranjpe's contention that the extremist party should not co-operate with the government even in times of severe plague. The differences reached a climax in 1907 when Kelkar wanted to resign from the *Mahratta* in order to disassociate himself from the tactics of the Marathi journalists. Tilak managed to avert this crisis. Because he was an effective journalist, Kelkar was a valuable asset to the Tilak party.

[87] M. R. Jayakar, *The Story of My Life*, 2 vols., Vol. I, 1873–1922 (Bombay, 1958), p. 100.

[88] Bombay Police Abstracts, "History Sheet of Shivram Mahadev Paranjpe, 1865–1927," File No. 3025/H, MHFM. V. K. Paranjpe, *Shivrampant Paranjpe: Vyakti Vakravata, Vadmaya (Shivrampant Paranjpe: His Life, Speeches and Writings)* (Poona, 1954).

[89] "Contribution to the Freedom Struggle of Shri Krishnaji Prabhakar Khadilkar of Poona, 1872–1948," Note prepared by MHFM.

Because no one had effectively tapped the resources of mass political power, appearances of power were an important element in politics in the 1890's. Tilak recognized the importance of myths. The most heartening aspect of the 1894 celebration, claimed the *Kesari,* was the manner in which Brahmans and Marathas had united in a common celebration.[90] Two years later the *Mahratta* maintained that the festival had proved to be a "powerful engine for imparting instruction to the masses."[91] Prior to this the *Mahratta* had published an improbable version of the beginnings of the revised 1894 celebrations. The movement to install public ganapatis was initiated by the non-Brahmans. It was only after the movement was well under way that the Brahmans joined in for fear that the "ignorance of the lower classes" might involve them in hardships at the hands of "already infuriated officials."[92]

Measured against the expressed hopes of its publicists, the reorganized Ganapati festival was a mixed success. Although it proved a means of politicizing Brahmans, it is questionable whether it added many non-Brahmans to the Congress ranks. It alienated some sections of Indian society, and at times it hindered rather than helped Tilak's cause.

But measured by the standards of the time it enhanced Tilak's stature and reputation as a leader. He acquired the support of the orthodox faction together with some of the young college graduates of Poona. He became a force not only in Poona but in the Congress as well. Tilak was aware that appearances were as important as the realities of power. It was difficult for any of his moderate critics to counter the myths propagated in Tilak's journals and to prove that Tilak was not doing what he claimed.

It was Tilak, rather than Ganapati, who benefited most from the reorganized festival. Ganapati's political stock was highest in 1894–96, and again in 1905–10, but by then he was a limited political force. The man Tilak used the god Ganesh as a stepping-stone to a bright political career. In the final analysis God Ganapati proved a diminutive recruit to the Congress cause. Despite the fervent prayers of devotees and the songs of the *mela*-singers, he failed to move the British or the non-Brahmans to recognize the rightness of the elite cause.

---

[90] *Kesari,* September 14, 1894.
[91] *Mahratta,* September 20, 1896.
[92] *Ibid.,* October 21, 1894.

Chapter V

THE DEVELOPMENT OF THE SHIVAJI TRADITION

> No one now cares for Seevajee. Over all those wide domains, which once owned him lord and master ... not one man now contributes a rupee to keep or repair the tomb of the founder of the Mahratta Empire.[1]

> Pride and admiration for our national heroes is a principal element in the sentiment of nationality and no nation can hope to rise that neglects its past heroes.[2]

The organization of a second festival to honour Shivaji, the founder of the Maratha empire, was probably due to the mixed success of the Ganapati festival. To graft politics onto the cumbersome form of a Hindu religious ceremony proved a difficult task. When all the singing and pageantry of the 1894 Ganapati festival died down, neither the Congress nor Tilak's fledgeling party had the substance of a mass following or the makings of a ward or grass-roots organization which might be used to disseminate the ideas of the Congress.

Whereas Ganapati was a quasi-political figure, Shivaji was a direct symbol of political action, the epitome of the Kshatriya tradition of Maharashtra. To recapture the martial spirit of the Maratha hero was a means of stimulating a resurgent Maratha nationalism. By honouring the person of the non-Brahman Shivaji, Tilak was selecting a popular symbol which directly appealed to communities outside the Congress sphere, for Shivaji was the one cause on "whom all the different castes of Maharashtra could focus their loyalty."[3]

A symbol was an important asset for the aspiring nationalist leader. It was an eloquent means of defining the program of the party, more effective than a dozen editorials in a newspaper. It was a way of establishing the legitimacy of the party by claiming the authority of a

[1]James Douglas, *A Book of Bombay* (Bombay, 1883), p. 433.
[2]*Mahratta,* April 12, 1896.
[3]*Kesari,* April 28, 1896.

heroic figure of the region. It was a method of appealing for the support of the non-Brahman majority of the region. More specifically, Tilak wished to appeal to men of wealth and standing, the princes and *sardars*, many of whom owed their position and landed estates to Shivaji. Because these leaders were respected by non-Brahmans, to appeal to them was one means of securing the support of the non-Brahman communities.

More than half the princely states of India were located in the Bombay Presidency. Although the majority of these states were in the northern regions of Gujarat, Sind, Kathiawar, and the Cutch, there was a sizeable number of princely domains in the Deccan and southern regions.[4] By far the most important southern state was Kolhapur, with a 1901 population of close to three-quarters of a million people and a Maratha ruler who traced his ancestry to the younger son of Shivaji. He was the acknowledged head of the Maratha princes. Throughout the Deccan and the southern divisions of the presidency were many smaller states and *jagirs* (land grants which entailed responsibilities to the state) ruled by Brahman or Maratha families who had been rewarded for their services to the Maratha Raj.[5] They varied in size from the state of the Chief of Sangli, who ruled over a territory of 1,112 square miles with a 1901 population of 226,128 people, to the pocket-sized principality of the junior division of Kurundwad, with only 114 square miles and 34,003 subjects in 1901. Outside the jurisdiction of the Bombay Government were the three large Maratha-ruled states of Baroda, Gwalior, and Indore. Baroda was the most important because of the independent spirit of its ruler, Sayaji Rao (1875–1925).[6]

The chiefs made up the first rank among the *sardars*. Below them were several ranks of titled gentry whose jurisdiction was limited to a handful of villages or who had the mere honour of a title. There were

---

[4] One-quarter, 6,908,648, of the 1901 presidency population of 25,424,235 lived in the princely states. Two-thirds of these people, 4,550,979, lived in the princely states in the northern regions of the province; the remainder, 2,357,669, resided in the states of the southern regions (Konkan, Karnatak, and Deccan).

[5] The majority of small feudatory states were ruled by Brahmans. Of the nine *jagirs* attached to Kolhapur, seven were ruled by Brahmans and two by Marathas.

[6] Figures derived from the 1901 *Census*.

	Area (square miles)	Population (1901)
Gwalior	25,133	2,933,001
Baroda	8,182	1,952,692
Indore	9,506	850,690

192 *sardars* in 1892, most of them in the Deccan.[7] They were the living representatives of the old Maratha state and, with their territorial interests, were the natural leaders of political movements. They were patrons of most of the political and educational institutions of the Deccan. It was a frequent claim of the elite press, however, that the *sardars* were politically apathetic, lacked an independent spirit, and were generally at the beck and call of the English Agent of the *sardars* and other officials. The *sardars*, complained the *Indian Spectator*, were the "step-sons of the British Government."[8] This claim was not unrealistic. When the *sardars* were enfranchised under the 1892 electoral scheme, they chose a government official to represent their interests in the legislative council—much to the dismay of the educated class.[9]

Some of the more influential chiefs took an interest in elite political and educational movements in the Deccan. The Chief of Aundh was president of the Poona *Sarvajanik Sabha*, and there were a good number of his fellow-chiefs among the vice-presidents. Although the chiefs did not actively participate in the business of the *Sabha*, which was carried out by a managing committee drawn from the educated classes, they did lend their patronage and gave financial support.[10] Their backing of the Deccan Education Society illustrates the importance of this role. From 1884 to 1910 the princes and chiefs contributed more than 200,000 rupees, which was more than half of the total subscribed to this project. Of this sum, seven Brahman princes contributed 122,140 rupees, seven Maratha princes added 43,500 rupees, and three Rajput rulers gave 32,000 rupees.[11]

---

[7]121 of the 192 *sardars* of 1892 resided in the Central Division, which roughly corresponded to the Deccan.

[8]*Indian Spectator*, May 21, 1893.

[9]*Mahratta*, April 30 and June 4, 1893.

[10]Some of the princely contributors to the *PSS* included:

	Rupees
Chief of Sangli	6,000
Chief of Gondal	5,000
Gaekwar of Baroda	4,000
Maharaja of Indore (Holkar)	4,000
Chief of Darbhanga	2,000
Maharaja of Travancore	1,000
Maharaja of Kolhapur	500

Among the subscribers to the *QJPSS* were the princes of Bavada, Bhavnagar, Bhor, Cutch, Dewas, Jaipur, Jamkhandi, Jamnagar, Jawar, Kurundwad, Limbdi, and Mysore.

[11]P. M. Limaye, *History of the Deccan Education Society* (Poona, 1935), Appendices, pp. 66–78. See the table on copy p. 143.

Prior to the 1880's both the *sardars* and the princes had neglected the memory of the founder of the Maratha Raj. The *samadhi* of Shivaji at the historic hill-fort of Raigad, which was also the place of his coronation, was in a state of disrepair. An Englishman who visited the fort found the modest memorial to be a mass of weeds and the adjacent temple to be "foul and dishonoured," with "its god cast down to the ground" and trees growing through the pavement of the *dharmashala* (pilgrims' rest house). No one, he concluded, cared enough for Shivaji to contribute a mite to repair and maintain the *samadhi*.[12] No one, he could have added, contributed to erect a *chatri* (awning) over the octagonal plinth, or provided for an annual pilgrimage to the shrine, honours usually accorded to important historical personages. While Shivaji's son, Rajaram, and Ramdas, were honoured in this manner, Shivaji was forgotten.[13] This suggests that the Marathas had lost in the nineteenth century some of the memory of Shivaji's achievements. The memory had to be recaptured in the 1880's and the 1890's.

The first attempt to erase the neglect of several centuries was made by Ranade. He convened a representative gathering of the *sardars* and citizens of Poona in May, 1885, to petition the local government to allocate funds to restore the *samadhi*. The government of Lord Reay, in response, set aside the annual sum of four rupees so that the historic plinth could be cleared of weeds and a railing be erected to prevent cattle from invading the hallowed ground. But for the untimely death of the Regent of Kolhapur, the movement might have assumed more significant proportions. Following the Poona meeting, the Regent sent an overseer to the fort to estimate the cost of erecting a *chatri*, but this project collapsed with his death.[14]

Ranade contributed more to the Shivaji revival by his writings on Maratha history in which he attempted to rehabilitate the name of Shivaji and to reassess the character of the Maratha empire. Ranade argued that the foundation of the Maratha Raj in the late seventeenth century was something more than the successful enterprise of an individual adventurer or the accidental kindling of a forest fire in the parched grass of the Sahyadri mountains—the view of the English historian Grant Duff. It was an "upheaval of the whole population," which had a strong sense of nationality, fostered by the bhakti poet-saints. By integrating the various castes and classes in his administration,

[12]Douglas, pp. 432–433.
[13]*Mahratta,* June 2, 1895.
[14]*Ibid.*; "The Shivaji Festival," Note prepared by MHFM.

Princely Donations to the Deccan Education Society, 1884–1910

	Rupees	Year Donated	
BRAHMAN DONATIONS			
Chief of Jamkhandi	1,000	1884	
Chief of Sangli	6,000	1884	
Chief of Miraj Junior	5,000	1891	
Chief of Ichalkaranji	18,500	1891	
Chief of Miraj Senior	11,000	1891	
Chief of Jamkhandi	33,500	1904	
Chief of Ichalkaranji	44,640	1908	as an endowment
Chief of Bhor	1,000	1909	
Chief of Aundh	1,500	1910	
TOTAL	122,140		
MARATHA DONATIONS			
Chief of Kagal	5,500	1886	
Gaekwar of Baroda	12,000	1889	
Maharaja of Kolhapur	10,000	1891	
Chief of Akalkot	1,000	1892	
Maharaja of Indore (Holkar)	1,000	1892	
Raja of Jawhar	4,000	1892	
Raja of Mudhol	10,000	1894	
TOTAL	43,500		
RAJPUT DONATIONS			
Maharaja of Bhavnagar	8,000	1891	
Ibid.	2,500	1902	
Maharaja of Gondal	20,000	1884	
Maharaja of Cutch	1,500	1902	
TOTAL	32,000		
OTHER DONATIONS			
Nawab of Junagadh	3,000	1886	
Raja of Benares	1,000	1901	
Limbdi Darbar	1,500	1909	
TOTAL	5,500		
TOTAL PRINCELY DONATIONS	203,140		
TOTAL DONATIONS	356,236		

Shivaji had acted, Ranade maintained, in accord with the national spirit propagated by the poet-saints.[15]

A second thesis developed by Ranade was that this spirit of nationalism was an expression of a deeper unity, which he likened to the Protestant Reformation, rather than a reaction against Muslim intolerance. For a number of reasons, particularly the small size of the Muslim population, Muslim rule was less influential in the Deccan than in other regions. Muslim power in western India was gradually "subverted by, and subordinated to, Hindu influence."[16] During the course of several centuries the Muslim population lost much of its exclusiveness and freely joined in Hindu religious movements. In return, the Hindus of the Deccan made common cause with the Muslims in their festivals and revered some of their fakirs. The spirit of "tolerance and moderation" was, Ranade considered, one of the "most stable elements of the national [Maratha] character."[17]

To Ranade, Shivaji was a catholic and moderate leader, a syncretistic figure who wished to unite the Maratha nation and to establish impartial rule. The legacy of Shivaji was not an exclusive Hindu or Brahman preserve but an ideal of national unity above religion and caste. Ranade also emphasized the non-violent character of Shivaji's government. Although there was a good deal of "wild-oats sowing" in the earlier exploits of Shivaji, the mature leader attempted to avoid violence and to capture forts without bloodshed.[18] In the administration set up by Shivaji the military was made subordinate to the civilian element.[19] Ranade's Shivaji was a pietistic general whose mind was moulded more by the forces of devotional religion than by Kshatriya values. From his youth he was fond of hearing the religious epics, and in his maturity he was inspired by the values of bhakti, religious enthusiasm, and self-discipline.[20]

In his interpretation Ranade attempted to expose the Muslim and British historians who depicted Shivaji as a robber extorting exorbitant taxes from his victims. Ranade, on the contrary, portrayed the Maratha general as a wise and humane leader whose constitutional ideas were in advance of his times. Ranade also criticized the folk historians who regarded Shivaji as an incarnation of the Lord Shiva. In the popular

[15] M. G. Ranade, *Rise of the Maratha Power*...pp. 5–6.
[16] *Ibid.*, p. 15.
[17] *Ibid.*, p. 13.
[18] *Ibid.*, pp. 26, 49.
[19] *Ibid.*, p. 72
[20] *Ibid.*, pp. 26, 75.

tradition the miraculous was a telling factor in the success of Shivaji's campaigns. He fought with no ordinary sword but with a divine weapon presented to him by the goddess Bhavani,[21] who could unleash supernatural forces to thwart the opposition. In 1659 the Muslim general, Afzal Khan, made the mistake of attempting to destroy the Hindu temple at Jejuri. The goddess Bhavani arranged for a swarm of bumble-bees to protect the sacred precincts. The Khan and his forces were stung into inaction, and wisely decided to leave the temple intact.[22]

Ranade was one of the first to turn to history to enhance the position of the Poona elite. To the critics from the administration, the Shivaji tradition was a means of demonstrating the unity of Maratha society. To those who sponsored the non-Brahman movement and railed against the Brahman establishment, history was useful for suggesting the essential compatibility of the interests of the various castes and classes. The Shivaji tradition helped to establish the legitimacy of the educated Brahmans of the *Sarvajanik Sabha* to lead their society and to be recognized by the British as the spokesmen of Maratha society. As Shivaji had achieved the political unification of the Maratha state, so the educated Brahmans, the heirs of Shivaji, would once again lead their society to a new level of political awareness and cohesion. Because of the failure of the princes and *sardars* to assume the mantle of leadership, and because of the new forms of political power, the educated Brahmans considered themselves to be the conscience of their society. It was their task to interpret modern ideas to the masses and to forge a new unity among Maharashtrians.

The elite Brahmans, in a number of ways, attempted to link themselves with the person of Shivaji. By successfully prevailing upon the *sardars* to act as patrons and figureheads for political associations, the Brahmans identified themselves with the living symbols of former rule. This concern for legitimacy reflected the ambiguous and uncertain position of the Brahman elite in the late nineteenth century. Cut off from the masses by virtue of education and participation in a western-style idiom of politics, the Shivaji tradition was an important means for the Brahmans to assure themselves of the essential similarity of their interests and those of Maratha society.

[21]The picture of Shivaji receiving the sword from Bhavani adorns many Maharashtrian homes. It ranks, with that of the equestrian Shivaji, as one of the more popular pictures of this leader.
[22]See *Jedhe Shakavali (Jedhe Chronology)*.

Tilak took up the work of Ranade in 1895. He convened a public meeting in Poona to raise a fund to repair the *samadhi* of Shivaji, to erect a suitable *chatri* and to arrange a permanent endowment which would provide the necessary funds for an annual festival at Raigad. "Pride and admiration for heroes," editorialized the *Mahratta*, was a "principal element in the sentiment of nationality."[23] Shivaji was a symbol around which the various groups of Maratha society could unite. The Shivaji tradition provided a further means by which the message of the Congress could enter the humblest cottages of the villages. Instead of writing history, Tilak organized a festival to commemorate the name of Shivaji. Since a festival was an important element of the folk tradition, it provided the means by which the miraculous could be harnessed to the cause of nationalism.

The meeting convened by Tilak in May, 1895, to launch the Shivaji appeal was a representative gathering. Five chiefs, a swami, and an array of lesser gentry were on the platform. One of the resolutions was seconded by a Muslim *sardar*. Telegrams of support for the venture were received from the Maharaja of Kolhapur and from Ranade, who had convened the 1885 meeting. The young Chief of Ichalkaranji promised an annual endowment of one hundred rupees. A broad-based committee was set up, including three chiefs (Ichalkaranji, and the senior and junior rulers of Kurundwad), a number of *sardars*, members of the Tilak party (*Balasaheb* Natu, Khasgiwale, and Baba Maharaj), supporters of Ranade (Gokhale and Jathar), and the Maratha champion of non-Brahman education, Gangaram Bhau Mhaske.[24] The Shivaji memorial committee was clearly a more influential and representative body than the group which had organized the Ganapati festival in 1894.

Tilak took great care to identify his endeavour with the moderate and catholic Shivaji tradition outlined by Ranade. To a question posed at the meeting as to whether the Shivaji committee was to be representative of all castes and religions, Tilak replied that the composition of the committee was not racial : anyone who admired Shivaji and subscribed to the fund could be a member of the committee. He pointed out that several Muslim *inamdars* (holders of an *inam*, a land grant) owed their *inams* to Shivaji, and thus were equally bound with the Hindu *sardars* to respect the memory of Shivaji. The festival was

[23] *Mahratta*, April 12, 1896.
[24] *Kesari*, June 4, 1895. The committee of fifty included three secretaries, Tilak, the Chief of Ichalkaranji, and *Sardar* Senapati Dabhade, and a treasurer, *Balasaheb* Natu.

not initiated "to alienate or even to irritate the Mahommedans," for, since "times have changed," Muslims and Hindus now found themselves "in the same boat."[25] Tilak assured the government that in the proposed celebrations there was "no disloyalty of any kind whatever."[26] The very moderate and catholic character of Tilak's Shivaji movement led reform papers such as *Sudharak*, which had criticized the reorganized Ganapati festival, to support the Shivaji festival.[27]

By adopting the moderate Shivaji tradition of Ranade, Tilak was attempting to establish the credentials of his party. In effect, he was claiming that the new party, with its interests in the activities of the common people and its attempts to involve them in Congress activities, was a more legitimate heir to Shivaji than the party of Ranade, which operated in the halls of the councils and the annual gatherings of the Congress. In view of the struggle between the Ranade and Tilak factions, it is likely that Tilak was attempting to capture some of the influence of the older leader by appropriating this important symbol of Maratha nationalism. By this action Tilak hoped to establish the legitimacy of his faction and thus to secure the support of the princes and the *sardars* who had previously aided Ranade in the *Sarvajanik Sabha*.

For this reason, Tilak was careful to establish the legitimacy of his movement. A delegation which included three chiefs (Ichalkaranji, Kagal, and Kurundwad senior), a number of *sardars*, Tilak, and Namjoshi requested the Maharaja of Kolhapur to act as president of the Shivaji Fund Committee, which post the Maharaja duly accepted.[28] Since the estimated cost of repairs to the *samadhi* and the provision of an endowment for the annual Raigad celebration amounted to 40,000 rupees, it was necessary, the *Kesari* stated, for the maharajas and *jagirdars* to assume responsibility for raising a substantial part of this sum.[29]

Although Tilak looked to the princes to provide the larger donations, he did not neglect the smaller contributors. The *Kesari* ran a singularly successful campaign to enlist the support of lesser figures by stating that no donation was too small and by promising that every *pai* (one-

[25] *Mahratta*, June 2, 1895; D. V. Tahmankar, *Lokamanya Tilak* (London, 1956), p. 65.
[26] *Kesari*, April 21, 1896.
[27] *Sudharak*, June 3, 1895, *BRNP*, 1895, No. 23, p. 19.
[28] *Mahratta*, September 1, 1895.
[29] *Kesari*, July 2, 1895.

third of a penny) would be acknowledged in the columns of the *Kesari*.[30] For months after this appeal the columns of his journal attested to the enthusiastic response. By August, 1895, three months after the launching of the fund, 6,000 rupees had been subscribed by over 15,000 people, five-sixths of the donations being in *pais* and annas. By December, 1895, the total had reached 15,000 rupees and the contributors numbered nearly 60,000.[31] The amount was sufficient for the committee to plan the first annual celebration at Raigad in May, 1896. Even the usually critical *Times of India* was impressed by the spontaneity of the movement and the many public meetings held throughout the Deccan to raise subscriptions.[32] What made the success remarkable, added the *Mahratta,* was that it was achieved without "organized efforts, central meetings or agents deputed to collect subscriptions."[33] This was probably the first journalistic campaign to evoke so enthusiastic and popular a response, and it might be considered the first successful mass campaign initiated by Tilak. It was a testimony to his bright journalistic career and his capacity to arouse enthusiasm for a particular cause through the medium of the press. The democratic character of the Shivaji fund, with its 60,000 subscribers by the end of 1895, contrasted noticeably with the two hundred princes and business magnates of Bombay who contributed 40,000 rupees in 1895 to raise a memorial to Lord Harris. The Shivaji fund was an impressive attempt to demonstrate the popular character of Tilak's party. Tilak was not slow to make journalistic capital out of the response. The enthusiastic manner in which Maharashtrians responded to the fund was a welcome sign of "national awakening". While some degree of national spirit had been present in the hearts of the people of western India, it had not before, claimed the *Mahratta*, assumed such an overt form.[34]

During the campaign of 1895 and 1896 to popularize the memorial fund, there were discordant notes in the Shivaji tradition, which was Hindu, violent, and xenophobic. The real mission of Shivaji was, in the opinion of certain journals, to protect the cow, the Brahmans, and the Hindu religion.[35] The Hindu character of the tradition was expressed

[30] *Ibid.,* June 4, 1895. Three *pais* = one *paisa*; four *paisas* = one anna; sixteen annas one rupee.
[31] *Mahratta,* August 11 and December 31, 1895.
[32] *Times of India,* June 11, 1895.
[33] *Mahratta,* August 11 and December 31, 1895.
[34] *Ibid.,* April 12, 1896.
[35] *Native Opinion,* June 2, 1895.

in a more negative form by the *Jagadhitecchu*, an orthodox Poona journal edited by one of the followers of *Balasaheb* Natu. A poem praised the manner in which Shivaji had trampled the Muslims under foot, had delivered his countrymen from their yoke, and had protected his country's religion.[36]

Such interpretations even found their way into the columns of the *Kesari*. In a letter to the editor, one writer railed against the fanaticism of the Muslims and suggested that had Shivaji been alive he would have burned with indignation at seeing Hindu temples demolished by Muslims and thousands of cattle slaughtered to feed the Europeans.[37] Another poem outlined what it considered would be Shivaji's advice to his descendants. It provided a curious mixture of the moderate and the violent Shivaji traditions. The poem began on a defiant note with Shivaji lamenting the impotent state of Hindus and their loss of independence. For this situation he suggested that they "have proper reverence for the good old Hindu religion ... be united and drive away all traitors."[38] The remainder of the poem was in a moderate and pro-British vein. If the Russians or other enemies of the rulers threatened India, the Hindus should combine with the British to drive out the invaders. The poet offered a strange formula for the advancement of the Hindus: "try and gain the favour of Englishmen by valourous deeds on the field of battle, ... preserve your heritage and revive the various industries, be grateful and obedient to the Queen."[39] The very naiveté of this appeal suggests that the violent reinterpretation of Ranade's Shivaji tradition was not the work of the editor of the *Kesari* but of some of his more orthodox and extreme followers. While Tilak was careful to observe a catholic stance in 1895 and 1896, he did not exclude from the *Kesari* columns the suggestions of variant, militant, and Hindu chauvinist traditions. On this occasion, as on many others, Tilak adopted an ambiguous stance. It is difficult to decide whether he did so in order to secure broader support for his cause and to confuse the British, or to make concessions to the opinions of his more orthodox followers.

The first celebration to honour Shivaji at the hill-fort of Raigad began on the morning of April 15, 1896, in the presence of several thousand *rayats* from the neighbouring talukas and a small but

---

[36] *Jagadhitecchu*, July 29, 1895, *BRNP*, 1895, No. 31, p. 22.
[37] *Kesari*, May 28, 1895.
[38] *Ibid.*, August 20, 1895.
[39] *Ibid.*

dedicated band of three hundred Brahmans from Poona, Ratnagiri, and Mahad, who had made the difficult journey to Raigad and had climbed the steep inclines of the hill-fort.[40] After a *kirtan* (devotional song) in honour of Shivaji, a portrait of the leader was unveiled to the cries of "Victory to Shivaji Maharaj!" In the address which followed, Tilak suggested that the object of the festival was to bring Maharashtrians together and to foster a feeling of confidence "which would be conducive to the maintenance of their religion and institutions." The meeting was not convened by Brahmans for the purpose of subverting the existing government, as supposed by some; the aim was simply to assist the administration by educating the masses and by engendering in them a sense of "unity, loyalty to their leaders, and a feeling of love and reverence for their national institutions." At a torch-light procession the portraits of Shivaji and Ramdas were carried to the accompaniment of music. The festival lasted for three days, and followed the usual form of a Hindu celebration with dances, gymnastic events, readings from the Hindu scriptures, ballads extolling the life and achievements of Shivaji, and the distribution of sweets and betel nuts.[41]

The character of the 1896 celebration together with the campaign waged in the *Kesari* suggests that Tilak was more concerned, in the Shivaji festival, with symbols which would enunciate the ideology of his party and establish its legitimacy than with direct politicization of the non-Brahmans. The inaccessibility of the hill-fort ensured that the political involvement of non-Brahmans at the Raigad celebration would be minimal. Whereas there was some direct attempt in the Ganapati festival to involve the non-Brahmans in a Brahman-sponsored movement, the main purpose of the Shivaji festival was to enunciate a symbol.

Despite his close adherence to the moderate Shivaji tradition, Tilak failed to achieve the substantial backing of the princes and the *sardars* on whom he had counted. The Shivaji fund, which had begun with an initial surge of enthusiasm producing 15,000 rupees in the seven months to December, 1895, languished in the following months because of the unwillingness of the Deccan aristocrats to make their expected contributions. By the time famine reached Maharashtra,

---

[40]Tilak and Professor S. M. Paranjpe were the only Poona leaders of significance to attend the 1896 Raigad celebration. Although the fort is only 80 miles from Poona, the journey is long and difficult because of the inhospitable terrain.

[41]Bombay Police Abstracts, April 27, 1896, para. 532.

late in 1896, the fund had come to a standstill with no addition to the December, 1895, figure.[42] The only princely donation came from the Gaekwar of Baroda, who gave 1,000 rupees in the early days of the fund. The amount, complained the *Mahratta,* was not nearly enough from the Gaekwar; it hoped that he would donate sufficient funds to create a permanent endowment. There was some logic to the point made by the *Mahratta,* for the prince had given 12,000 rupees to the Deccan Education Society in 1889 and 33,000 rupees from 1885 to 1889 to the Deccan Association to encourage education of Marathas at the secondary and tertiary levels.[43] The Gaekwar apparently considered investment in the Deccan Association a more profitable means of attaining the uplift of his fellow-castemen than the Shivaji movement.

Some officials felt that the Gaekwar was an extremist at heart, a not too secret admirer of the Tilak party. Lord Curzon complained in 1903 that he was the "sole important Prince" who was "not loyal to the British Government."[44] Several years later some officials prepared a "charge-sheet" against the ruler which accused him of harbouring revolutionaries in the Baroda service, notably Aurobindo Ghose and Keshav Ganesh Deshpande, of refusing to prosecute extremist newspapers, and of fostering poor relations between Baroda and the central government.[45]

More accurate assessments of the Gaekwar were made by Lord Hamilton, Secretary of State, and Sir George Clarke, Governor of Bombay (1907–13), who considered the prince to be a moderate rather than an extreme nationalist.[46] Although the Gaekwar was an independent spirit who resented British interference in his state, who came out in support of the Congress at an early date and was in favour of the programs of swadeshi and national education, he believed in the beneficence of the British presence.[47] The Gaekwar was at heart a social reformer: he identified caste and religious differences as the

[42]From December, 1895, to July 1, 1899, the fund increased from 15,000 to almost 20,000 rupees—due mostly to the interest on the original capital.

[43]*Mahratta,* July 7, 1895, and May 27, 1900.

[44]Curzon to Hamilton, March 12, 1903, Curzon Papers, MSS Eur. F 111/162.

[45]"British Government's Charge-Sheet against Sayajirao Gaikwad," compiled by MHFM.

[46]Hamilton to Curzon, September 11, 1902, and April 13, 1903, Hamilton Correspondence, MSS Eur. C 126/4 and 5; Clarke to Morley, November 2, 1909, Morley Papers, MSS Eur. D 573/42F.

[47]Stanley Rice, *Life of Sayaji Rao III: Maharaja of Baroda,* 2 vols (London, 1931), II, 139.

greatest impediments to the realization of Indian nationality.[48] He was one of the pioneers of the movement to improve the status of Untouchables and presided over a conference for the removal of untouchability in 1918.[49]

The Maharaja of Kolhapur gave no financial assistance to the Shivaji fund. This was disappointing to the Poona leaders, for the prince had given 5,000 rupees to the movement to memorialize the unpopular governor Lord Harris, 10,000 rupees to the Deccan Education Society in 1891, and 5,000 rupees to the Deccan Association from 1894 to 1899. An editorial of the *Mahratta* in December, 1895, stated, with a tinge of bitterness, that while the fund had become universally popular, support had yet to come from the pockets of the princes, "who as a rule are at the beck and call of influential Government officers whenever they chose to erect memorials to man like Lord Harris."[50] Five months later the *Indian Spectator* queried why the "miserable" sum of 15,000 rupees was all that had been subscribed to the fund: "The problem is inexplicable, even though we give its full weight the fact that the Sirdars and Jaghirdars hold back on account of the unmerited aspersions cast on the movement of being nothing more than an effort of the Brahmin Congress-*wallahs* to gain their own petty ends and make a selfish bid for the sympathy of the masses."[51]

Even with the return of a measure of prosperity in the years following 1900, the fund continued to languish. The main addition to the fund from 1896 to 1906 came from the six per cent interest accumulated in the Deccan Bank.[52] By 1900 the *Mahratta* was able to refer nostalgically to the time when princes took an active part in the Shivaji memorial movement. It was now necessary to rely on the "more patriotic and less timid" middle and lower classes.[53] The failure of the aristocrats to support the Shivaji movement was further underlined by the generous princely support of the fund set up to memorialize

[48] *Ibid.*
[49] *Ibid.*, II, 207; Philip W. Sergeant, *The Ruler of Baroda: An Account of the Life and Work of the Maharaja Gaekwar* (London, 1928), pp. 214–219.
[50] *Mahratta*, December 22, 1895. The princes of the presidency contributed the bulk of the 40,000 rupees to raise the memorial to Lord Harris.
[51] *Indian Spectator*, May 17, 1896.
[52] Progressive totals of the fund were listed in the *Kesari*:

December, 1895   15,000 (rupees)—0—0
July 1, 1899   19,854—7—$5\frac{1}{2}$
April 20, 1906   26,227—14—6

[53] *Mahratta*, May 6, 1900.

Ranade in 1901. The princely donations increased that fund to a total of 90,000 rupees by 1905.[54]

Because of the limited support for the Shivaji movement, only three of the proposed annual festivals at Raigad were held in the first eleven years (in 1896, 1900 and 1906). It was ironic that the leaders of the Shivaji movement, who despised those who advocated mendicant tactics, had themselves to appeal to the Bombay Government in 1906 for financial assistance to complete the task of restoration and commemoration. The Bombay Government looked favourably on the 1906 petition and donated 5,000 rupees toward the cost of erecting a *chatri* and repairing the tank at the hill-fort. The restoration of the plinth, the repair of the adjacent temple, and the maintenance of the fort road were to be left to private subscription.[55] The assistance of the government did not end the problems of the memorial committee. The commemorative objective of the movement was not completed until 1925, some five years after Tilak's death and thirty years after the commencement of the effort.[56] The memorial fund demonstrated the ability of Tilak to initiate a novel and popular program but also his inability to bring it to fruition.

The violent reinterpretation of the Shivaji tradition may have been one reason why the princely donations to this movement failed to materialize. It occurred at a time when the Deccan was engulfed by a severe famine, the worst since the 1870's, and the spectre of death in the form of bubonic plague. Initially the Bombay Government adopted moderate measures to root out the disease, but when these failed and the plague spread from Bombay City into the Deccan, the government resorted to harsh measures. In order to carry out a house-to-house

---

[54]*Ibid.*, September 17, 1905. Some of the princely donations to the Ranade memorial fund included :

	Rupees
Chief of Miraj	3,000
Maharaja of Kolhapur	2,000
Maharaja of Bhavnagar	2,000
Chief of Jamkhandi	2,000
Chief of Ichalkaranji	1,500
Gaekwar of Baroda	1,000
Chief of Ramdurg	1,000
Chief of Akalkot	1,000
Chief of Vishalgad	1,000
Chief of Kagal Junior	300
Chief of Bavada	200

[55]*Ibid.*, April 29, 1906, and May 12, 1907.
[56]"The Shivaji Festival."

search to ensure that plague cases be discovered and isolated and to apply the necessary sanitary measures, the governor called out the European troops and established a plague administration headed by a military officer, W. C. Rand, who had a reputation for severity. In view of the breakdown of municipal government in Poona, the unwillingness of many of the local leaders to help the plague administration, and the harsh policies implemented by Rand, it was inevitable that misunderstanding, resentment, and obstruction should develop in the relatively orthodox centre of Poona.[57]

In the light of the frustration and bitterness engendered by a harsh plague administration that violated orthodox Hindu sentiment, Tilak reinterpreted the Shivaji tradition in a more violent form. At the annual gathering held in Poona in June, 1897, to honour Shivaji's birth, a lecturer, Professor Bhanu of Fergusson College, touched on one of the perennial issues of Maratha history, Shivaji's killing of the Muslim general Afzal Khan. By prior arrangement the two leaders had met on the battlefield to resolve a military stalemate between the powerful Bijapur army and the Maratha guerrilla force. Secretly armed, Shivaji was able to outwit his opponent. The controversy revolved around whether Shivaji had struck the first blow, had dishonoured the agreement with the Muslim general, and had committed murder, or whether Shivaji had anticipated an attack from Afzal Khan and had acted in self-defence. Shivaji's action, according to Professor Bhanu, was above reproach, for the cause of Maratha freedom placed him above the usual canons of morality. This argument was developed by Tilak in the *Kesari* when he commented on Bhanu's speech:

Let us even assume that Shivaji first planned and then executed the murder of Afzal Khan. Was this act of the Maharaja good or bad? This question which has to be considered should not be viewed from the standpoint of the Penal Code or even of the *Smritis* of Manu or Yajnavalkya or from the principles of morality prescribed in Western or Eastern ethical systems ... Great men are above the common principles of morality. These principles do

[57] It has been customary to blame Rand for all the violence which emerged in Poona City and to underestimate the problems he faced. Moderate measures to confine the bubonic plague to Bombay City had failed. The Poona municipal administration had proved ineffective in handling the crisis. Many of the leading citizens had left the city and others, such as S. M. Paranjpe and *Balasaheb* Natu, refused to co-operate with the Rand administration. Rand had intended to include Indians in the search parties, but few volunteers were forthcoming. The house-to-house inspections were conducted by European troops. While Rand contributed to the ensuing political crisis by his tactless manner and harsh policies, he was hampered by the extent of the panic and the poor relations between the British and Brahmans.

not reach the place on which great men stand. Did Shivaji commit a sin in killing Afzal Khan? The answer to this question can be found in Mahabharata itself. Shrimat Krishna preached in the *Gita* that we have a right even to kill our own *guru* and our kinsmen. No blame attaches to any person if he is doing his deeds without being actuated by a desire to reap the fruit of his deeds.[58]

The meaning of Shivaji's action was made clear: the cause of Maratha freedom justified violent means. If the comments were not a "direct incitement to violence against Rand himself," notes Tilak's biographer, Stanley Wolpert, "they provided moral sanction for such an action."[59] By emphasizing Shivaji's defeat of the Muslim general, Tilak was drawing attention to the foundation of the Maratha Raj, carved out of the Muslim empire. While Tilak was careful to avoid the language of community interest, his followers were not. The spectacle of Afzal Khan's defeat was, according to Professor Bhanu, one in which "every Hindu, every Mahratta must rejoice.[60]

Within a week Rand was dead. He and Lieutenant Ayerst were struck down by the Chapekar brothers, who sought to emulate the "desperate enterprises" of Shivaji as a means of attaining independence. In his autobiography, Damodar Chapekar relates how exasperated he was by all the discussion at the Shivaji festival and complained of the childish behaviour of the participants who failed to learn a lesson from Shivaji's life. To the Chapekars the lesson was clear. It was expressed in a *shlok* which they sang at the festival in honour of Shivaji: "Listen. We shall risk our lives on the battlefield in a national war. Do not look upon our utterances in the presence of many people as a mere farce. We shall assuredly shed upon the earth the life-blood of the enemies who destroy (our) religion. We shall die after killing only."[61]

A Shivaji Club formed in Kolhapur took the same violent inspiration from its preceptor. Founded in 1893 on the prototype of Poona societies, by 1898 it had a membership of three hundred men, who formed Ganapati choirs and were taught the skills of riding and gymnastics and the use of arms in preparation for a small-scale rebellion. The club was raided by the Maharaja of Kolhapur in 1897 and declared illegal by him two years later.[62]

[58]*Kesari,* June 15, 1897, quoted in Wolpert, pp. 86–87.
[59]Stanley A. Wolpert, *Tilak and Gokhale...* (Berkeley, 1962), pp. 87–88.
[60]*Kesari,* June 15, 1897.
[61]*Source Material BHFM,* II, 992–993.
[62]G. P. Pradhan, "Lokamanya Tilak and the Revolutionaries," *Mahratta Annual,*

While the violent interpretation of the Shivaji tradition inspired revolutionary activity, it impeded the potential support of the Deccan aristocrats for the Shivaji movement. Many princes were reluctant to support openly the program of a militant party which had lost the favour of the British administration. With the rise of extremism, the princes withdrew their patronage from the Shivaji movement and the Poona *Sarvajanik Sabha,* which had been captured by the Tilak forces in 1895.[63]

The Brahman chiefs of Ichalkaranji and Vishalgad, who were under the jurisdiction of Kolhapur, were two exceptions to this pattern of princely loyalty. The Maharaja of Kolhapur suspected that they were encouraging sedition, attending meetings of the Tilak forces, and indirectly contributing to the coffers of the extremist faction. Pressure was brought to bear on the feudatories when their "powers of residuary jurisdiction" were withdrawn by Kolhapur in 1910. The powers were not restored until 1917.[64]

The conflict which developed between the Poona promoters of the Shivaji festival and the Maharaja of Kolhapur, Shahu (1894–1922), the living symbol of Shivaji's empire, was a second reason for the failure of the Shivaji memorial fund. Differences between the two parties dated from the accession of the prince to the Kolhapur throne in 1894. Prior to this, a succession of minors and the insanity of the Maharaja's immediate predecessor had enabled the Chitpavan prime minister of Kolhapur to become a powerful figure in the state. He proceeded to appoint his fellow-castemen to important posts in the administration. The new Maharaja reversed this trend. To reform the administration, he appointed a prime minister from the Kayastha Prabhu (writer) caste.[65]

The young ruler subsequently took a keen interest in the education of Marathas. In order to recruit promising non-Brahman graduates,

---

1967 (Poona, 1967), pp. 7–8, 87; "Shivaji Club Kolhapur: A Centre of Revolutionary Activities, 1895–1909," Note prepared by MHFM; "Contribution of Krishanji Prabhakar Khadilkar."

[63]The stalemate in the Shivaji fund suggests that it was unlikely that the princes were secret contributors to the Shivaji movement. The *QJPSS* was suspended for twenty years, 1897–1917; when it was resumed no princes were found on its rolls as officers or contributors.

[64]A. B. Latthe, *Memoirs of H. H. Shri Shahu Chhatrapati—Maharaja of Kolhapur,* 2 vols (Bombay, 1924), I, 339–340; II, 358.

[65]Valentine Chirol, *Indian Unrest* (London, 1910), p. 65.

he consulted with Gangaram Bhau Mhaske of the Deccan Association.[66] As a patron and later as president of the Deccan Association, and as a champion of Maratha education, the Maharaja incurred the wrath of the Poona Brahman press. When the Maharaja gave a large sum of money to establish hostels for Maratha students at Kolhapur, he was roundly criticized by the *Mahratta*: "A ruler of a state should be practically above caste or sectarian prejudices. Such was Shivaji; and the value of his example lies in the fact that he encouraged merit wherever it was found and by his wonderful tact organized the different sects into a nation."[67] The journal later argued that, while it did not object to Maratha rulers spending thousands of rupees to ensure that their castemen were educated, it did object to the effort "to make a hot-house growth of one caste."[68]

The Maharaja took his views to their logical conclusion when he issued the resolution of July 26, 1902, reserving 50 per cent of future vacancies in the Kolhapur state service for members of the "backward classes."[69] By introducing this measure the Maharaja hoped to quicken the pace of non-Brahman education. In his opinion the limited progress of non-Brahman education was due to the insufficient rewards of higher education for the lower castes. The result, complained the *Mahratta*, was to make admission to the state service a racial question; it amounted to placing caste considerations over merit.[70]

The issues of non-Brahman education and the composition of the Kolhapur service were complicated by two other controversies, the Vedokta question and the Tai Maharaj case. The Vedokta question, which emerged in 1901, concerned the claim of the Maharaja of Kolhapur to Kshatriya status both for himself and for the Maratha community as a whole. Although the Kolhapur Brahmans admitted the right of their ruler to claim full Vedic ritual, which was an admission of twice-born status, they insisted that the Maharaja should undergo penance for allowing the practice of Vedic ritual to lapse in his family. The Maharaja's refusal to accept this condition was the crux of the con-

---

[66]Latthe, I, 95.

[67]*Mahratta*, October 6, 1901. The Maharaja gave 4,000 rupees to the permanent fund of the Victoria Maratha Students Institute at Kolhapur, promised an annual contribution of 500 rupees, and gave property valued at 800 rupees for extensions to the Institute.

[68]*Ibid.*, October 16, 1902.

[69]The backward castes were considered to be those groups other than the advanced communities, namely, the Brahmans, Prabhus, Shenvis, and Parsis.

[70]*Mahratta*, August 2 and 17, 1902.

troversy. When the Brahmans were equally adamant, the ruler confiscated the property of the high-priestly family and a number of other Brahman families of Kolhapur. The Brahman press both in Kolhapur and in Poona was critical of the manner in which the Maharaja was coercing his Brahman subjects to admit the entitlement of the Marathas to Vedic ritual. While it was not wrong for a community to elevate itself in the caste system, argued the *Mahratta,* there should be a bona-fide belief in the claim to higher status; it should not be based on vindictiveness or an attempt to offend the religious susceptibilities of Brahmans. The Poona Brahmans believed that the Maharaja's campaign was inspired by "personal vindictiveness and rancourous hatred of Brahmans."[71]

The Tai Maharaj case centered around the adoption of a son for the widow of Tai Maharaj after the death of her husband, Baba Maharaj, in 1897. Tilak and three of the trustees of the estate favoured the adoption of a boy from the Nizam state. The fifth trustee, Nagpurkar, wished the selection to be made from Kolhapur. Initially, Tai Maharaj accepted the majority decision and adopted a boy from Aurangabad in June, 1901. One month later Tai Maharaj changed her mind and declared the Aurangabad adoption to be invalid. She proceeded to adopt a second son from Kolhapur in August, 1901. The adoption of the second boy took place with the approval of the Kolhapur Darbar and in the presence of the Maharaja. Tilak wired a protest to the Darbar.[72] The subsequent litigation proved long and costly for Tilak. It was not until July 21, 1920, shortly before his death, that the Bombay High Court removed all the obstacles to the adoption of the Aurangabad choice. Throughout the long and arduous case, Tilak and Kolhapur were ranged on opposite sides. In the opinion of one Bombay governor, Sir Stafford Northcote (1900–03),[73] the Vedokta controversy was Tilak's means of obtaining revenge for the Maharaj case.[74]

Whether the root cause of the Kolhapur-Poona conflict was personal animosity created by the Tai Maharaj case, the issue of Maratha education, or the status of the Marathas, the British took advantage of

[71]*Ibid.,* October 20, 1901.
[72]For a summary of the initial phase of the Tai Maharaj case see D. P. Karmarkar, *Bal Gangadhar Tilak* (Bombay, 1956), pp. 119–130.
[73]Henry Stafford Northcote (1846–1911), Baronet of Exeter, educated at Eton, Merton College, Oxford, Conservative member for Exeter, 1890–99, Surveyor-general of Ordnance, 1886–87.
[74]Northcote to Hamilton, May 1, 1902, Hamilton Correspondence, MSS Eur. F 123/36.

these differences and encouraged the Maharaja to continue his anti-Brahman stand. While the British were not much impressed with the Kolhapur ruler (Northcote referred to him as an "arrant coward" and Hamilton spoke of him as a "weak vessel"),[75] they did consider him to be a useful ally. Because he was a "thoroughly loyal" prince and a counter-elite symbol, he was an asset who could be used to weaken the dominant position of the Poona Brahmans and to question their claims to be the true heirs of Shivaji. At the height of the Vedokta controversy, Northcote wrote to Hamilton that the Maharaja was on the point of giving in to the Brahmans when "he luckily came to Mahableshwar," and "we quietly instilled a little pluck into him." The interview was effective, for, on returning to Kolhapur, the ruler "struck the Brahmins a counter blow by suspending certain payments to them."[76] Several months later the governor was optimistic about the prince. With the proper advice from the Political Agent, Colonel Ferris, and with a "little determination on his part," Northcote considered that Kolhapur ought to "master the Brahmans."[77] It was his hope that the Bombay Government would help Kolhapur as much as they could. He considered that the British ought to make common cause with the Maharaja, for "we are subject to a common danger from the preponderance of Brahmins in the public services both of the British government and of the Native Princes, and I only wish we had a more resolute ally than this timid prince."[78] When the Kolhapur ruler visited the Secretary of State in 1902, Hamilton told him that he "ought to stand up to the Brahmins," to which the prince acquiesced.[79]

The British encouraged the emergence of a counter-elite movement at Kolhapur. It proved to be an effective means of countering the ideas publicized at the time of the Ganapati and Shivaji festivals that the interests of Brahmans and Marathas were similar and that the Brahmans were the recognized leaders of their society. In a sense the British were challenging a myth by attempting to demonstrate the validity of a counter-myth. The British were as concerned with myth-making as were the elite Brahmans. The rulers recognized the symbolic

[75]*Ibid.*, Hamilton to Curzon, August 20, 1902, Hamilton Correspondence MSS Eur. C 126/4.
[76]Northcote to Hamilton, May 1, 1902.
[77]Northcote to Curzon, October 4, 1902, Curzon Papers, MSS Eur. F 111/206.
[78]Hamilton to Northcote, October 16, 1902, Hamilton Correspondence, MSS Eur. F 123/37.
[79]*Ibid.*, September 4, 1902.

importance of the Maharaja of Kolhapur.

Although Tilak's movement was hampered by the opposition of Kolhapur and was limited by a shortage of funds, the effort to revive the memory of Shivaji was a striking success within Maharashtra. Since the time of Tilak, Shivaji has been the guiding inspiration for political parties of all perspectives within Maharashtra. As the symbol of the ruling state Congress party, portraits of the soldier-statesman occupy pride of place in government offices next to the non-violent father of the Indian nation. The Congress Shivaji is a syncretistic figure who stands for impartial democratic rule in the interests of all classes and communities, together with an active pursuit of Maharashtrian and national interests.

The name of Shivaji is so powerful in Maharashtra that no politician can ignore it. Each political party of the region must define its program in terms of Shivaji. During the movement for *Samyukta* Maharashtra, which was led by a coalition of opposition parties, the name of Shivaji was invoked as a supporter of the unilingual state of Maharashtra, which was set up in 1960. For intellectuals the new state provided an opportunity to realize the social and political ideals established by Shivaji. Politicians and parties vied with each other in their attempts to gain Shivaji's endorsement for their particular programs. It is ironic that even the "anti-imperial" Communists can take pride in the empire of Shivaji. According to one Communist writer, Shivaji was a leader of the oppressed peasants against the powerful landlord class. It was a historical accident that the exploiters tended to come from one communal group and the exploited from another.[80] In a similar manner Hindu communal politicians have attempted to appropriate the Shivaji tradition. According to Veer Savarkar, a revolutionary nationalist who became a leader of the Hindu Mahasabha, Shivaji stood for a powerful Hindu state, one in which cows would be protected, Brahmans supported, and the laws and customs of Hindus preserved. Shivaji also demonstrated the need for a forceful policy abroad based on well-equipped military forces and strong leadership at home. The rule of a "benevolent great leader like Shivaji" was preferable, according to Savarkar, to the present "weak-kneed democracy": India needed Shivaji rather than Buddha.[81] Another member of the

---

[80]Lalji Pendse, *Dharma Ki Kranti? (Religion or Revolution?)* (Bhadgaon, 1941); Aloo J. Dastur, "The Pattern of Maharashtra Politics," in Iqbal Narain (ed.), *State Politics in India* (Meerut, 1967), p. 190.

[81]Dhananjay Keer, *Veer Savarkar* (2d ed., Bombay, 1966), pp. 450, 497.

Hindu Mahasabha warned the Congress leaders of independent India that the modern-day followers of Shivaji would not tolerate a weak policy toward Pakistan. He warned the national government that Shivaji might yet ride again:

The Sindhu belongs to us ... It is well known that in his last days Shivaji Maharaj was thinking of capturing Banaras, the holy city of the Hindoos. His descendants took their horses from the banks of the Bhima, to drink water on the banks of the Sindhu. Sadashivrao Bhau Peshwa literally hammered the Moghul throne and broke it into pieces. It is regrettable that now a days, anti-national elements have got an upper hand. I declare here that even if the whole of India sleeps, Maharashtra will rise again and recapture Sindhu. Oh sacred Sindhu, how can we forget you.[82]

The most recent appropriation of the Shivaji tradition has been by the sub-national society, Shiv Sena, formed in Bombay in 1966. The group was established to protect the interests of the sons and daughters of Maharashtra from the competition of immigrants from other regions, chiefly South Indians. Bal Thackeray, the leader of the society, declared that the Shiv Sena "derives its name and draws its inspiration from the national hero of Maharashtra, Shivaji the great."[83] The main platform of the Sena is expressed in the rallying slogan, "Maharashtra for the Maharashtrians." Thus the more national tradition propounded by Ranade and Tilak has been cast aside by the Sena.

The Shiv Sena represents a modern variant of the militant tradition of Maharashtra. The name of the society, literally, "the army of Shiva," underlines its purport. Like the Poona prototypes of the late nineteenth century, the cadre of the Shiva Sena is based on respect for the charismatic leader, who attains his power by martial words or deeds. In all these societies the leader establishes his authority by virtue of his own personality and ingenuity rather than by the power of tradition or of the bureaucracy. Bal Thackeray rose from obscurity and did not have the backing of the Congress party or any other group. Thackeray set up a closely knit organization in which the chief is the benevolent leader, who could be a dictator. Thackeray, who is known as the *pramukh* (chief), exercises absolute control over the *shakha pramukhs* (branch chiefs), who are handpicked and dismissed by him. The leader of the Shiv Sena does not mind being called a dictator since he believes that a dictatorship might be preferable to the present democratic government. He is reported to have once said that the

---

[82]N. B. Khare, *My Political Memoirs or Autobiography* (Nagpur, 1959), p. 443.

[83]R. S. Morkhandikar, "Shiv Sena—An Eruption of Sub-Nationalism," *Economic and Political Weekly*, II, No. 42 (October 21, 1967), p. 1906.

"country needs a 'Hitler.'" Members of the Shiv Sena take a pledge which binds them to such objectives as employing only Maharashtrians, purchasing articles sold by Maharashtrians, and not selling land to "outsiders."[84]

During Tilak's lifetime there were attempts to popularize the Shivaji tradition in other regions of India. Shivaji was a "Swadeshi hero," Tilak suggested to a Bengali audience in 1907, one who "took a bold stand against the tyranny of his time." Shivaji was also a national figure who fought against the Mughals, not because they were Muslims but because they were "oppressive, tyrannical and despotic rulers."[85] Behind this Maharashtrian enthusiasm there was an occasional note of insecurity, which was indicative of a "tongue-in-cheek" approach to this campaign to nationalize the Maratha hero. When some of the leading Congress delegates of 1895, from regions other than Maharashtra, supported the Shivaji movement, the *Mahratta* could not suppress a note of surprise: "It proved that under the Pax Britannica the Bengali in spite of the Mahratta ditch, the Madrasi in spite of Shivaji's unkind treatment of his ancestors, the Guzerati in spite of being 'royally looted' were prepared to forget the past and honour the greatest Indian hero of modern times."[86]

In spite of the efforts of Ranade and Tilak, Shivaji did not become a national hero. With the declining national importance of Maharashtrian leadership after the death of Tilak, Congress leaders from other regions of India were less inclined to eulogize the Maratha soldier-statesman. Gandhi categorized him as a "misguided patriot."[87] According to one Maharashtrian politician, Gandhi's position was a product of Gujarati chauvinism. On one occasion Gandhi warned of the dangers of a Maratha resurgence: he is reported to have said that "if these Marathas are brought together they will sack our Surat again."[88] There is, however, a more obvious and plausible reason for Gandhi's limited interest in the Shivaji tradition. As a propagandist of non-violent political action, Gandhi drew greater inspiration from the quietist traditions of the Jains than from the martial exploits of Shivaji. Gandhi's attitudes toward India's generals of the past was well

[84]*Ibid.*, pp. 1903–06.
[85]Tahmankar, pp. 64–65.
[86]*Mahratta*, January 5, 1896.
[87]*The Collected Works of Mahatma Gandhi*, XXVI, Jan.–April, 1925 (Delhi, 1967), p. 491.
[88]Khare, p. 407.

indicated in a debate with a revolutionary which appeared in *Young India* in 1925. The revolutionary contended that the people of India were the descendants of Shivaji, Ranjit, Pratap, and Govind Singh. Gandhi maintained, however, that the true descendants of such leaders were the military classes—merely one segment of Indian society. Gandhi thus maintained that non-violence was the dominant tradition in India. Because Shivaji resorted to violent tactics to achieve his purpose, he was a heroic but misguided patriot.[89]

With even less regard for Maharashtrian susceptibilities, the young Nehru once dismissed Shivaji as a "predatory adventurer."[90] However, once he became prime minister, Nehru was forced to bow to Maharashtrian enthusiasm and as "an act of rectification" unveil a statue of the equestrian Shivaji on the very spot where he had killed Afzal Khan.[91]

The organization of the Shivaji festival illustrates the important role which symbols played in the struggles of nationalist parties. Given the insuperable problems of organizing an effective mass movement in the 1890's, a myth provided an alternative avenue toward politicization. By linking his party to the heroic name of Shivaji, Tilak also provided a means of establishing the legitimacy of his program and of directly appealing to the princes and descendants of Shivaji for support. In some immediate purposes the festival was a limited success. Because some Deccan aristocrats had personal or caste reasons for restraining their generosity toward Tilak and because others were too timid or disliked an extremist party, completion of the memorial fund was delayed for three decades. But in a larger sense the Shivaji tradition was successfully redefined so that it stimulated political activity among a significant segment of regional society. The symbol continues to inspire the Maratha people.

[89] *Collected Works of Gandhi*, XXVI, 488–491.
[90] Khare, p. 407; Dastur, p. 190.
[91] Dastur, pp. 189–190; S. V. Kogekar, "A Profile of Maharashtra," *Economic Weekly*, XII, No. 1 (June, 1960), p. 847.

Chapter VI

THE FAMINE CAMPAIGN AND THE DECCAN PEASANTRY

> The Irish methods and the organisation of the Land League have been closely studied by certain Irreconcilables in Poona, and their proceedings were not very dissimilar from those practised by the Parnellites.[1]

> Our leaders have yet to reach the *rayat* to agitate in a constitutional manner.[2]

With the failure of the 1896 monsoonal rains, the Deccan was confronted with the gloomy prospect of a famine which threatened to be worse than the last serious dearth of 1876–77.[3] Grain riots during October and November, 1896, heralded the coming scarcity. Mobs looted the shops of grain merchants in a number of towns.[4] Despite the extensive failure of the autumn crops and the winter sowings, the Government of India appeared reluctant to recognize the existence of famine and to institute programs of relief.[5] The provincial government, also, seemed reluctant to grant the suspensions and remissions of the land revenue which had been specified in the Famine Relief Code drawn up after the famine of the 1870's. The code stipulated the manner in which the government should relax the land revenue collection and organize relief at such times.[6] The result was a general holding back of

[1] Hamilton to Northcote, February 21, 1901, Hamilton Correspondence, MSS Eur. F 123/32.
[2] *Kesari*, December 15, 1896.
[3] Hon. J. Woodburn (Member of the Viceroy's Council) to Elgin, November 19, 1896, Elgin Papers, MSS Eur. F 84/69.
[4] Yawal (Khandesh district), Hubli (Dharwar district), Karad (Satara district), Kelve-Mahim (Thana district), Kolhapur, and other places in the Bombay Presidency.
[5] A recent commentator, defending the famine policy of Elgin and the Government of India, argued that Elgin was well aware of the situation, but, to avoid undue alarm, refrained from publicly referring to the famine and quietly organized relief programs. Piarea Lal Malhotra, "The Internal Administration of Lord Elgin in India, 1894–1898" (unpublished Ph.D. dissertation, University of London, 1966), pp. 204–209.
[6] *Ibid.*, pp. 197–199.

the land revenue which in some cases amounted to a spontaneous combination of landholders to resist paying the full amount of revenue.[7]

The social dislocation and distress provided Tilak with the opportunity of launching a third mass movement to demonstrate the interest of his party in the welfare of the Deccan *rayat*. Revenue payment and famine relief were issues of substance through which Tilak could stake his claim to be a mass peasant leader. Whereas the princes and the *sardars* were reluctant to support the Shivaji memorial fund, the landowners were vitally concerned with revenue and relief.

The elite Brahmans had long been concerned with the condition of the peasantry and the land revenue policies of the government. Shortly after its formation the *Sarvajanik Sabha* petitioned the administration, arguing that the revised assessments of the early 1870's were too high and contributed to the impoverishment of the peasantry. To dramatize their hostility toward the new assessments, the *Sabha* sent agents to the villages in 1873 "to whip up the *kunbis*' [cultivators] opposition to rates imposed under the new survey and to explain the reasons for their poverty."[8] From the accounts of the campaign it is not clear whether the agents attempted to organize directly no-tax combinations or whether the combinations were spontaneous by-products of the preaching of the agents. In the several districts visited by the agents of the *Sabha,* there were combinations to withhold payment of the rent, which officials suspected to be the work of the *Sarvajanik Sabha*.[9]

Several years later the Poona *Sabha* again sent agents throughout the Deccan to collect information on the nature and extent of the 1876–77 famine. On the basis of these reports Ranade drew up a series of "Famine Narratives" which were critical of the limited attempts of the government to counter the famine and provide relief.[10] Ranade made a life-long study of the land revenue policies of the Bombay Government. He was a supporter of the Deccan Agriculturalists' Relief Act of 1879, which attempted to lessen the alienation of land and to alleviate peasant indebtedness to the *sawkar*.

By taking up the agrarian program of Ranade, Tilak was again attempting to establish the credentials of his party. Because of its

---

[7]Combinations to withhold payment of land revenue were not infrequent in time of famine. See below for a discussion of earlier no-rent campaigns.

[8]Ravinder Kumar, "The Deccan Riots of 1875," *JAS*, XXIV, No. 4 (August, 1965), p. 630.

[9]*Ibid.*, pp. 630–631; James C. Masselos, "Literal Consciousness..." (Unpublished Ph.D. dissertation, University of Bombay, 1964), pp. 395–397.

[10]Masselos, pp. 488–493.

practical efforts to explain land legislation to the *rayat*, his party was taking on the mantle of the *Sarvajanik Sabha*. This was another attempt to make the ideology of the Congress relevant to the illiterate masses and to enable national politics to enter the humblest cottages of the villages.

To dramatize his interest in the oncoming dearth, Tilak first tackled the problem of the rising cost of grain in Poona City. With the prospect of famine, Bania and Marwadi dealers bought up and hoarded the stocks of grain in the city in order to capitalize on the anticipated shortage. The existence of widespread speculation led to a sharp increase in prices which alarmed the populace. A riot threatened to erupt in the city. To counter the "unholy and unjustifiable speculations" of the grain merchants,[11] Tilak and his supporters raised the sum of 5,000 rupees to establish fair-price grain shops in Poona. The endeavour was successful and resulted in "breaking down the ring which had been formed by the grain dealers, much to the relief of the suffering poor."[12]

This action was an example of Tilak's pragmatism, his willingness to deviate from his usual principles of action. Normally, he opposed interference with or regulation of the free pattern of society. Unlike Ranade, Tilak opposed the extension of the remedial Deccan Agriculturalists' Relief Act in the 1890's.[13] At the same time he disapproved of factory legislation.[14] In part this was because Tilak was a conservative, but it was also because his main aim was to select issues which dramatized the conflict between the British and the Indian people. It was Tilak's contention that the ills and tensions within Indian society were due to alien rule, or at least that such problems could be shelved and better solved when Indians ruled themselves. The curbing of the grain dealers indicates that Tilak was not doctrinaire and was capable of a pragmatic and humanitarian approach. One of Tilak's strengths was his flexibility: he was willing to experiment with different ideas and techniques of organization.

Tilak's more important work in 1896 was the criticism of the Bombay Government's unwillingness to suspend or at least remit part of the land revenue assessment in view of the extensive failure of the crops. From mid-October a series of *Kesari* articles criticized the unwillingness of the government to apply the Famine Relief Code. "It was provided by law," stated the *Kesari*, "that in the event of the failure of

---

[11] *Mahratta*, October 18, 1896.
[12] "Life of Bal Gangadhar Tilak," p. 18.
[13] *Mahratta*, January 31, 1892.
[14] Tilak's attitude toward factory legislation is discussed in Chap. VIII.

the crops to a particular extent, assessment should be remitted or its recovery postponed." It was the duty of the government officers to grant remissions and for the people to "firmly and perseveringly but peaceably to ask for it." Such concessions, the *Kesari* was careful to point out, were "our just and legal rights." The watchword of the famine campaign was that "law and not force should reign supreme": if it is necessary to fight "we must do so constitutionally," as it is only when we act in this way that grievances will be redressed.[15]

To collect information on the extent of the famine and to explain the famine code to the people, Tilak deputed agents from the *Sarvajanik Sabha*[16] to visit various districts of the Deccan and the Konkan in October, 1896. He urged Poona students, who finished their examinations in November, to carry the famine gospel to their villages.[17] It was only when the peasants learned to demand their rights that government officers would "cease to be insolent" and go beyond their legal authority. The code, Tilak pointed out, clearly set forth that no one should pay the assessment who was not able to do so.[18]

To carry out the famine campaign, Tilak relied on men who were active in elite circles of Poona. The principal agents were young and inexperienced graduates, the newer recruits attracted to the Tilak party by its activist and extremist character. Among them was the twenty-two-year-old Achyut Sitaram Sathe, a Chitpavan and a recent master of arts from Allahabad who was studying law in Poona. Sathe, one of the secretaries of the Famine Committee of the *Sarvajanik Sabha*, was to be one of the principal agents, since he was familiar with the colloquial idiom of the villagers as well as being fluent in English.[19] The other Famine Committee secretary was the Shivram Mahadev Paranjpe. N. C. Kelkar was another young graduate to carry the famine message of the *Sabha*. Although Kelkar wrote very good prose, both English and Marathi, he was not a very effective public speaker. A fourth student was Shankar Ganesh Lawate, later to become the champion of the Poona temperance movement. For the rest, Tilak relied on whomever he could secure: the Maratha historian, V. K. Rajwade, an astrologer, Mahadkar, an itinerant cow protection

---

[15]*Kesari*, December 15, 1896.
[16]The forces of Tilak and *Balasaheb* Natu captured the managing committee of the Poona *Sarvajanik Sabha* in July, 1895. The moderates responded by forming a new society, the Deccan *Sabha,* in November, 1896.
[17]"Life of Bal Gangadhar Tilak," p. 17.
[18]*Kesari*, December 15, 1896.
[19]N. C. Kelkar, *Gatagosti Arthat Majhi Jivan-yatra* (Poona, 1939), p. 213.

preacher, Narayan Shivram Barve, and a number of others.

From October, 1896, to April, 1897, the agents of the *Sabha* combed the districts of the Deccan and the Konkan. They visited every district with the exception of Kanara in the extreme south of the presidency.[20] They lectured both in the large mofussil towns and in the smaller hamlets. The hardest-working agent, though not necessarily the most effective, was the former Nagpur cow protection preacher, Barve, who stumped the inhospitable terrain of the Ratnagiri district and succeeded in arranging a meeting on most days. His itinerary was impressive. The week of February 23–28 was typical of Barve's crowded schedule. He spoke at the taluka town of Devrukh on the 23rd, 24th, and 28th of February to audiences of 200, 60, and 60, respectively. He addressed two meetings in the village of Bhadkumbe of 200 and 700, respectively, on the 25th of the same month. The next day he spoke to 700 in the village of Washi.[21] As a paid agent of the Nagpur Cow Protection Society and a Chitpavan Brahman, Barve was well equipped to carry out such a campaign.[22] During a much shorter period, December, 1896, to January, 1897, the speaking itinerary of Sathe was equally impressive and more taxing because of the larger audiences he attracted.[23]

To discover the extent of the famine and to determine the response of officials to it, the *Sarvajanik Sabha* armed its agents to make inquiries under seventeen headings concerning the state of the crops, the extent of the scarcity, the character of the relief, and the remissions and suspensions asked for and granted.[24] A second pamphlet issued by the *Sabha*

[20]The map, based on newspaper and police reports, indicates a few of the towns visited by the agents of the *Sabha*.
[21]Bombay Police Abstracts, March 12, 1897, para. 453.
[22]*Ibid.*, July 25, 1896, para. 977, and February 26, 1900, para. 449.
[23]*Kesari*, December 29, 1896. From December 15 to 25, 1896, Sathe addressed meetings in the following towns in the Thana and Kolaba districts.
The figures in parentheses represent the estimated attendance.

December	15	Panvel
	17	Pen
	18	Panvel (4,000)
	20	Pen (8,000)
	21	Roha (5–6,000)
	23	Goregaon
		Nagontha (3–4,000)
	25	Revdanda

[24]Bombay Police Abstracts, November 16, 1896, para. 1573. The pamphlet, dated November 1, 1896, was issued under the names of the two famine secretaries, Sathe and Paranjpe.

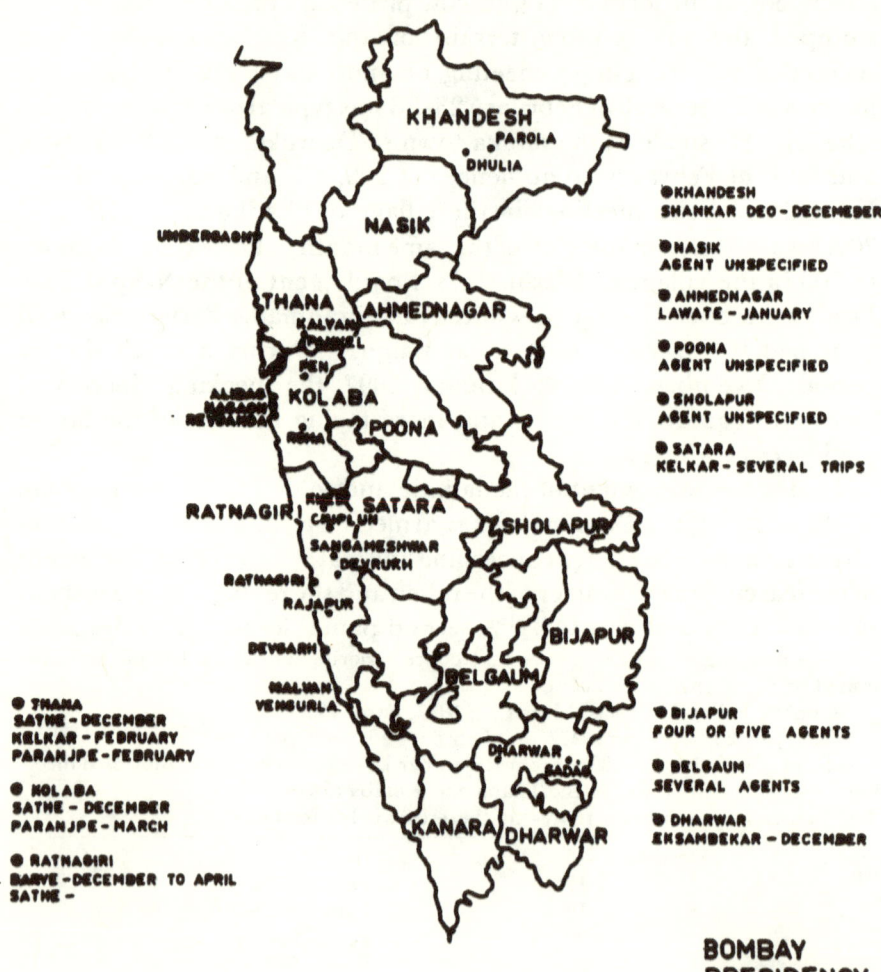

urged the people to take action: "There exists a rule in the Famine Code that assessment should be remitted by those persons whose crops amount to less than four annas in the rupee ... The people should be made to understand this; moreover the elders of each village should confer together and should send poor people to the Mamlatdar or Collector with a petition requesting that their case may receive attention." If the people could not prepare a petition themselves, the author of the pamphlet, Wasudeo Ganesh Joshi, manager of the Chitrashala Press, promised to draft a petition and to send it to the head of the village.[25] Petitions printed by the *Sabha* were widely circulated. The Collector of Thana discovered that by November, 1896, "hundreds, if not thousands of petitions for remission mostly printed or lithographed" had been sent to his office. He concluded that "undoubtedly some organisation had devised and distributed the forms; but it can only be assumed that it was the Sarvajanik Sabha."[26] Tilak arranged for 6,000 copies of the Famine Code to be printed in Marathi and distributed by the *Sabha* agents. They also prepared their own pamphlets, which repeated the arguments of the *Kesari* editorials, and hawked these throughout the Deccan.[27]

The Bombay Presidency Association and the Deccan *Sabha* took a keen interest in famine conditions and deputed agents to collect information on the extent of the scarcity. The one agent of the Bombay society travelled extensively throughout the troubled districts of the Deccan and wrote lengthy reports which adorned several columns of the *Times of India*. The Bombay association submitted a short representation to the government urging it to institute an extensive relief program. A committee of twelve was formed to raise a subscription to aid famine relief.[28] The Deccan *Sabha* appointed four agents who collected data which formed the basis of six memorials to the government urging it to lighten the load of the revenue collection.[29] Neither of these associations went as far as the Poona *Sarvajanik Sabha* in attempts to organize resistance to the collection of revenue.

Although Tilak's agents were careful to keep within the law, they

[25]*Ibid.*, January 13, 1897, para. 141.
[26]Collector of Thana to Commissioner, Northern Division, May 31, 1897, BG, Revenue (Famine), Vol. 122, pp. 125–126.
[27]"Resistance of the Famine-Stricken People in Maharashtra during the Period, 1876–1903," Note prepared by MHFM.
[28]"Minutes of the Council of the Bombay Presidency Association," II, 67.
[29]D. V. Ambekar (ed.), *The Deccan Sabha Poona: Golden Jubilee Celebration* (Poona, 1947), pp. 22–23; *Gujarati*, January 31, 1897.

alarmed the police and local officials, who could not understand why such "malcontents" were permitted to "prowl about the country and unsettle the minds of the people."[30] Most officials agreed with the District Magistrate of Kolaba in attributing the worst motives to the agents of the *Sabha*:

> The action of the Sarvajanik Sabha in this district is most mischievous, stirring up discord and strife where there was none, and fanning and inflaming what discontent existed. From beneath the mask of philanthropy and public spirit which they wear before Government and the press, there peeps out at these meetings the seditious political agitator. Professing the wish to render loyal assistance to the Government, they are in reality trying to hamper and annoy the authorities in every possible way by cutting off the revenue from land and from excise and working up the people to a state of mind likely to result in mob violence and open defiance of the law, which they will then describe as the despairing protest of an oppressed population against the cruel tyranny of their rulers.[31]

Such was the official mentality that when Sathe addressed some 2,000 cultivators and tribals at Khatalvad (Kolaba district) on December 13, 1896, he and his audience were cordoned off by some three hundred policemen who waited with loaded guns, together with the Assistant Collector and other officials, for Sathe to make a false step. The Assistant Collector's intention was to have the police ready "to pull him [Sathe] down at the first incitement to disorder."[32] Sathe did not provide the officials with this opportunity. During his three-hour address he went no further than to say that "if the crops had failed they should not pay anything to the government"—a perfectly legitimate statement.[33]

Within a week, officials arrested Sathe and another lecturer, Govind Vinayak Apte, after a meeting at Borle (Kolaba district) on December 18. Apte, who was not an official agent of the *Sabha,* had urged his listeners to take the law into their own hands and disobey the forest and abkhari (excise) rules. Because the government had not responded to the petitions of the people, Apte suggested that they should go to the forests to collect firewood and to tap toddy (palm juice which becomes fermented after tapping) trees without asking permission. Sathe had spoken in a similar vein, but had stopped short of urging the people to

---

[30]Bombay Police Abstracts, January 25, 1897, para. 264.
[31]*Ibid.*, December 19, 1896, para. 1746.
[32]Collector of Thana to Commissioner, Northern Division, May 31, 1897.
[33]*Kesari,* December 15, 1896.

take the law into their own hands.³⁴ In the trial which followed, Apte was sentenced to one year's imprisonment and a fine of 200 rupees. Sathe, the accredited agent of the *Sarvajanik Sabha*, escaped unscathed.³⁵

The government found its opportunity to discredit the *Sabha* when its Dharwar agent, Anantrao Joshi Eksambekar, went beyond lawful bounds in a pamphlet issued in January, 1897. Eksambekar incorrectly stated that the government had ordered the remission of land revenue where the crop return was six annas, and its postponement when the revenue was twelve annas, and argued that the revenue was being collected in defiance of the orders of the government.³⁶ The Bombay Government wrote to the *Sarvajanik Sabha* inquiring whether Eksambekar was an official agent of the *Sabha* and whether it accepted responsibility for the statements made in its name. After a lapse of five weeks the Poona *Sarvajanik Sabha* answered in ambiguous terms. It admitted that Eksambekar was a deputed agent, but did not categorically condemn or approve his statements. The *Sabha* argued that it could not be held responsible for pamphlets which it had not officially approved. It further contended that the statements of Eksambekar were a product of the many contradictory rumours which were current at the time. If Eksambekar had "perhaps inadvertently" relied upon one of these "more or less ill founded rumours," he was not entirely at fault because they were a result of the unusual delay in publishing official government orders.³⁷ The government was not mollified by the *Sabha*'s rationalization of its agent's "mistake." The Bombay Government, as a result, issued a resolution stating that the Poona *Sarvajanik Sabha*, as it was at present constituted, would cease to be recognized as a body which had any claim to address the administration on public policy. The issue was clear: "A statement which must be known to be false is not repudiated and there is offered explanation of its being made which is manifestly inadequate, while the letter furnished no indication of any desire to discountenance action which tends to cause unnecessary trouble to the administration, to induce landholders to bring on themselves coercive processes and to be injurious to the public interests."³⁸

³⁴Bombay Police Abstracts, January 3, 1897, para. 69.
³⁵*Mahratta*, February 21, 1897.
³⁶Collector of Dharwar to Commissioner, Southern Division, January 21, 1897, BG, Revenue (Famine), Vol. 122, pp. 8–10.
³⁷*PSS* to BG, March 9, 1897, BG, Revenue (Famine); Vol. 122, pp. 77–80.
³⁸Resolution dated March 17, 1897, BG, Revenue (Famine), Vol. 52, p. 230.

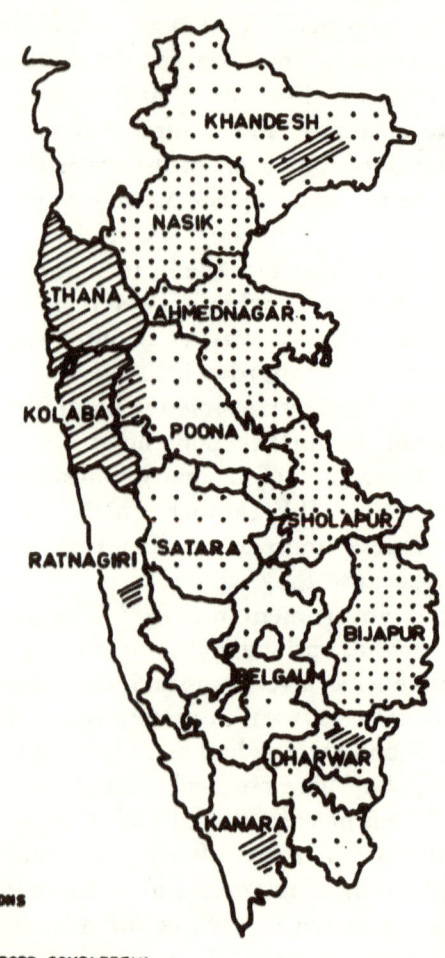

The dramatic success of the *Sabha*'s no-rent campaign was the cause of this hostile official reaction. In the Thana and Kolaba districts the seed of revenue dissent fell on fruitful ground. In other districts, Ratnagiri, Poona, Khandesh, and Dharwar, there was a worth-while yield. In the Kolaba district, people in the thousands collected to hear the famine gospel proclaimed by Sathe.[39] The listeners, who quietly absorbed the speeches, were not only rich Brahman landlords, but also cultivators, tribals, and fishermen, since most sections of rural society were affected by the dearth. The results were dramatic. Following the preachings of Apte and other emissaries from Poona, reported the Collector of Kolaba, "the expectations of the people grew stronger and stronger" and combinations to withhold the payment of revenue resulted. At several places the camp of the collector was mobbed by petitioners clamouring for relief.[40]

The report of the Collector of Thana clearly establishes the significant role played by the *Sabha* in provoking these combinations:

The machinations of the Society [the *Poona Sarvajanik Sabha*] whether private or public have had a great effect in causing the cultivators to withhold payment of the tax till the last possible moment. This is exemplified by the fact that the people of Mokhada, who, owing to the entire absence of roads, cannot be reached by agitators, paid both installments before the rich Pandhurpeshas of the rest of the district had paid the first, although the Mokhada cultivators are all of the semi-barbarous class that might be expected to feel the pinch of distress before any others.[41]

It was the opinion of the Collector that the postponements erred on the side of liberality, and the failure of the *rayats* to pay the revenue was due not to any real inability but rather to the doctrines preached by the *Sabha* and the "innumerable agents which it possessed in the Brahman landlords of the district."[42]

One reason for the success of the *Sabha*'s campaign was the existence of rural organizations of landowners throughout the mofussil which co-operated with the *Sarvajanik Sabha* agents by distributing pamphlets and by organizing and publicizing meetings. Some of these bodies were branch societies of the Poona *Sabha*, since it had been the policy of Ranade from the 1870's to establish networks of rural *sabhas*.[43] But

[39]*Kesari*, December 29, 1896.
[40]Collector of Kolaba to Commissioner, Central Division, July 15, 1897, BG, Revenue (Famine), Vol. 122, pp. 200–201.
[41]Collector of Thana to Commissioner, Northern Division, May 31, 1897.
[42]*Ibid.*
[43]Masselos, p. 365. By 1873 the *PSS* had established regional *sabhas* at Satara, Wai, Karad, Dharwar, Shiwandi, Ahmednagar, Nasik, and Sholapur.

the most vigorous taluka associations of 1896 had no direct affiliation with the Poona body and appear to have been locally organized groups of wealthy landowners of the taluka. In many instances the movement to withhold the payment of revenue was launched by these local bodies well before the Poona agents appeared on the scene. The District Magistrate of Kolaba commented on the combinations in his district, which were evident by November, 1896: "The landlords of this district are combining to refuse payment of the land revenue unless they are granted wholesale remission. R. L. Gharat and the Alibag Taluka Association are the leading spirits. The Sabha of Nagaon, a large village between Alibag and Revdanda, is taking an active part in the movement."[44]

The Alibag Taluka Association was a body of local landholders formed in the early 1880's to protest against the increase in the survey settlement in the taluka. From 1893 to 1895, when the papers pertaining to the settlement were being considered by the Bombay Government, the Alibag society waged a vigorous campaign in public meetings, articles in the press, and questions in the Bombay Legislative Council. The leading spirit behind the association, Ramchandra Lakshman Gharat, wrote numerous letters to the *Times of India* advertising the campaign and published a book in 1896, *Alibag Revision Settlement*, that catalogued the unsuccessful efforts of the association to secure redress of its grievances.[45] Gharat was not a Poona politician; he was from Bombay, and a member of the Council of the Bombay Presidency Association, a Khatri by caste, a schoolteacher by profession, and a landholder in the taluka.[46] He was one of a number of Bombay politicians who owned land in the districts bordering the city and helped to organize rural associations to champion the causes of rural landowners.

Another Bombay figure to take an active part in land agitation was the Parsi, Manekshah Jehangirshah Taleyarkhan (1847–1900). He chaired a meeting of the landholders of the Panvel Taluka (Thana district) in December, 1896, to petition the government to remit part of the assessment.[47] Taleyarkhan was a lawyer, a founding figure of

[44]Bombay Police Abstracts, November 9, 1896, para. 1567.

[45]Ramji Lakshman Gharat, *Alibag Revision Settlement: Being a Series of Letters Indicating a Departure in the Land Revenue Policy of the Bombay Government as Applied to the Konkan Districts* (Bombay, 1896). The book was published under the authority of the Bombay Presidency Association.

[46]Gharat was a member of the Council of the Bombay Presidency Association from 1895.

[47]*Times of India*, January 2, 1897.

the Bombay Presidency Association and an active member of its council, and a prominent person in university, municipal, and city politics. He was probably a landowner in the Panvel Taluka, since he was a persistent critic of the Bombay Government abkhari policies. He wrote two pamphlets in the 1880's complaining of the excessive taxation of toddy and the restrictions on the toddy industry imposed by the abkhari legislation of 1878.[48] Taleyarkhan was one of a number of Parsis, many of whom owned land in the toddy talukas of Alibag, Panvel, and Umbargaon, who formed a Parsi liquor lobby. They attempted to popularize the view that toddy was an innocuous beverage, the harmless drink of the masses, which did not need to be regulated as the government seemed to believe.[49] The two other champions of toddy were the indefatigable Pestonji Behramji Dantra, a landowner in the Dahanu Taluka, and the prolific Dinshaw Edulji Wacha (1844–1936), who wrote copiously on this issue as he did on every other public question.[50] It was ironic that the success of the Poona campaign in Kolaba was due in part to the activities of the moderately inclined Bombay politicians. It was equally ironic that support for the Poona politicians, later to champion total abstinence, came from the Parsi liquor lobby.

The advanced state of rural organization in the Kolaba and Thana districts was undoubtedly due to land speculation of Bombay capitalists. In these two districts land alienation had reached a more advanced stage than anywhere else in the presidency. In some talukas of Thana 70 per cent of the land had changed hands from the original owners, cultivators, tribals, and fishermen, to non-resident Parsi, Brahman, and Bania capitalists chiefly from Bombay City.[51] The proximity of the city combined with the limited sophistication of the Thana and Kolaba inhabitants meant that the districts were drawn within the vortex of Bombay City.

The Poona campaign capitalized on the rural distress and dislocation resulting from the famine. There was considerable dissatisfaction among tribals and cultivators at the government's policies of restricting

[48] Manekshah Jehangirshah Taleyarkhan, *Notes on the Taxation of Toddy in Bombay* (Bombay, 1885), and *Some of the Results of the Bombay Abkhari Act* (Bombay, 1887), IOL tracts. The 1897 legislation raised the tax on each toddy tree in the Alibag Taluka from one to twelve rupees.
[49] For the British view see Reay to Cross, July 22 and November 6, 1889, Cross Papers, MSS Eur. E 243.
[50] Dinshaw Edulji Wacha, *Indian Abkari Administration* (Bombay, 1888).
[51] GI, Revenue and Agriculture, Land Revenue, A1–2, January, 1901, pp. 7, 49, 62.

the consumption of toddy and of limiting access to the forests. Five thousand tribals met at Bassein (Thana district) early in November, 1896, to complain about the rigorous forest rules. The meeting was presided over by the Bombay politician, Daji Abaji Khare.[52] There was a riot in the town of Kelve-Mahim, in the same district, in which government records were burned to protest restrictions on the free use of toddy.[53] The police considered that the timing of the *Sarvajanik Sabha* campaign was unfortunate since it coincided with the agitation against the forest and toddy rules.[54] The Poona agents took advantage of this situation. They campaigned not only against reassessments but against the forest and toddy rules, and exhorted their audiences to wear country-made cloth, to abstain from liquor, and to protect cows.

The famine distress in the districts of Kolaba and Thana was limited. Its main impact was felt to the east of these districts, above the narrow coastal plain and across the plateau districts of the Deccan and the Southern Maratha Country.[55] While the *Sabha* agents traversed these chronically affected districts, they tended to concentrate on areas where there was an encouraging response to the famine message, which happened to be the areas least affected by the famine. There may be some truth in the assertion, frequently made by officials, that the withholding campaign was championed by wealthy landowners who were well able to pay the revenue due.[56]

Elsewhere in the Central Division the Poona agents had considerable influence in only two districts, Poona and Khandesh. There were few combinations in the districts of Nasik, Ahmednagar, Sholapur, and Satara, though these were the worst hit by famine. In three talukas of Khandesh (Dhulia, Erandol, and Amalner) the combinations were strong, and many were attributed to the *Sarvajanik Sabha*.[57] In the western and central divisions of Poona district, which escaped the brunt of the famine, there were a number of "determined pay-no-rent leagues" chiefly in the villages "within easiest reach of or with residents

[52]*Times of India*, November 9, 1896.
[53]*Gujarati*, December 6, 1896.
[54]Bombay Police Abstracts, December 22, 1896, para. 10.
[55]The map indicates the districts worst hit by famine. T. W. Holderness, *Narrative of the Famine in India in 1896–97*, Cd. 3812, 1898, p. 429; *Further Papers Regarding the Famine and Relief Operations in India During the Years 1896–97*, II, Cd. 8388, 1897, pp. 480–482.
[56]Collector of Thana to Commissioner, Northern Division, May 31, 1897.
[57]Commissioner, Central Division to BG, July 6, 1897, BG, Revenue (Famine), Vol. 122, p. 150.

FAMINE CAMPAIGN AND DECCAN PEASANTRY   137

most frequently in communication with Poona."[58] Very few combinations were organized in the eastern portion of the district, which was severely hit by famine.[59]

The greatest response to the *Sarvajanik Sabha* in the Southern Division occurred in the Dharwar district. The promises of Eksambekar fell on responsive ears in the divisions of Gadag, Ron, and Mundargi in this district and by January, 1897, there were "distinct signs of conspiracy" to refuse payment of land revenue, and a deluge of petitions for remissions were presented to officials on lithographed forms.[60] Although Barve conducted an extensive grass-roots campaign in Ratnagiri, the results were disappointing. Except for a few combinations in some of the southern talukas, there was little resistance. The Collector maintained that this was because the campaign did not suit the *khoti* farmers of the district. It was his opinion that the *khots* had no desire for a relaxation of the revenue, that their object all along had been to overestimate the revenue for the sake of their own rents.[61] Like the landowners of Kolaba and Thana, the *khots* of the Konkan were well organized. The Bombay lawyers, Daji Abaji Khare and Mahadev Rajaram Bodas, were active in the largest *khoti* association at Ratnagiri.[62]

The response elsewhere was not promising. Several emissaries visited Belgaum without achieving much.[63] The agents were warned off the premises of the Bijapur district by the Deshastha Brahman Collector, G. D. Panse. The Collector warned the *Sabha* agents that if they attempted to organize combinations in his district they would be arrested and prosecuted. The warning had salutary effects.[64] N. C. Kelkar, the agent to the Satara district, was more cordially received

---

[58]Assistant Collector, W. S. D. Poona to Collector, Poona, June 11, 1897, BG, Revenue (Famine), Vol. 122, pp. 143–145.

[59]Assistant Collector, E. S. D. Poona to Collector, Poona, June 8/9, 1897, BG, Revenue (Famine), Vol. 122, pp. 139–140.

[60]Bombay Police Abstracts, January 9, 1897, para. 185; Collector of Dharwar to Commissioner, Southern Division, June 25, 1897, BG, Revenue (Famine), Vol. 122, pp. 166–167.

[61]Collector of Ratnagiri to Commissioner, Central Division, June 26, 1897, BG, Revenue (Famine), Vol. 122, pp. 170–171.

[62]Bodas, an associate of Tilak, was the General Secretary of the Ratnagiri Khots' Association in 1899.

[63]Commissioner, Southern Division to BG, July 7, 1897, BG, Revenue (Famine), Vol. 122, p. 156.

[64]Collector of Bijapur to Commissioner, Southern Division, May 20, 1897, BG, Revenue (Famine), Vol. 122, pp. 161–163.

there. Because his brother was employed in the service of the Satara Collector, Kelkar met him on more friendly terms and was able to explain the purpose of the *Sabha*'s campaign.[65] Elsewhere, officials were less approachable, since they viewed the activities of the Poona agents with suspicion and antipathy. No agents visited the Kanara district, but combinations in two talukas, Sirsi and Sidapur, were organized by persons who had visited Poona and made use of printed notices issued by the *Sabha*.[66]

For his third mass movement Tilak had chosen a more popular issue and had achieved a measure of success which had eluded him previously. Nevertheless, the role of Tilak and the *Sarvajanik Sabha* in famine resistance should not be exaggerated. The chief duty of the *Sabha* was to work within the existing network of rural organizations and to co-ordinate the opposition to revenue and famine policies. The *Kesari* editorials provided a sharp focus for discontent. The *Sabha* distributed pamphlets and petitions and the agents addressed large gatherings; this was the extent of the *Sarvajanik Sabha* campaign of 1896–97.

The success of the movement was due in large measure to the reluctance of the Bombay Government to grant sufficient remissions and suspensions of land revenue in 1896 and to make its policy of intended remissions known at an early stage of the famine. The two famine commissions of 1898 (Sir A. L. Lyall) and 1901 (Sir A. P. Macdonnell) severely censured the provincial administration and made what Curzon referred to as a "rather formidable indictment" of the Bombay famine administration and the Bombay system of land revenue.[67] There were three main criticisms of the Bombay revenue system. The first was that the assessments in the presidency were too high and too rigidly applied. The commissions also criticized the manner in which remissions and suspensions were granted in times of famine. Whereas suspensions in other parts of India were granted in advance on the basis of an area (an entire district or a division), the Bombay system was based on the inquiry of the local official who decided the merits of each individual case. The third and most damning criticism was that the Bombay Civilian was less well acquainted

---

[65]Kelkar, *Gatagosti*, p. 213.

[66]Collector of Kanara to Commissioner, Southern Division, June 7, 1897, BG, Revenue (Famine), Vol. 122, pp. 167–169.

[67]Curzon to Hamilton, April 22 and June 5, 1901, Curzon Papers, MSS Eur. F 111/160.

with the *rayats* than officials in other regions. According to Macdonnell, because the duties of the Bombay Civilian were separated from the survey settlement, and because of the lack of registration in Bombay, the district officers were less familiar with the wants of the peasant than elsewhere.[68]

Macdonnell's views were reiterated by the Viceroy and the Secretary of State and, in fact, by everyone other than the partisans of the Bombay revenue system. Lord George Hamilton, the Secretary of State (1895–1903), did not agree with the claim of R. C. Dutt, the nationalist theoretician, that famines were caused by over-assessment, but considered that there might be some truth to Dutt's statement in the case of Bombay: "My impression is that, if there is any part of India where assessment is too high, it is there [in Bombay], for a good many of the settlements were made during a period of exceptionally high prices which Indian cotton obtained during the American war and that has formed to a large extent the basis of subsequent settlements."[69] Such comments were frequently made in the 1890's.[70] Hamilton suggested another reason for the rigidity of the Bombay settlements. Because land agitation was more developed and systematized in Bombay, a stiffer official attitude toward concessions prevailed in the presidency.[71] The Lyall Commission also subscribed to this view when it maintained that the Bombay Government "felt it necessary to be rather harder" in the matter of famine suspensions and remissions "than it would have otherwise been in consequence of an agitation originating in Poona."[72]

In times of famine the Bombay system of individual suspensions was, according to Curzon, perfect in theory but almost unworkable in practice. The system had been tried in Madras, the Punjab, and the North-West Frontier Provinces and found wanting. The "more business-like and generous system" was to make a general reduction

[68] *Report of the Indian Famine Commission*, 1898, Cd. 9178, 1899, p. 186; Curzon to Northcote, May 21, 1900, Curzon Papers, MSS Eur. F 111/201; Hamilton to Northcote, July 3 and September 24, 1902, Hamilton Correspondence, MSS Eur. F 123/34 and 37.

[69] Hamilton to Sandhurst, July 20, 1900, and Hamilton to Northcote, April 18, 1900, Hamilton Correspondence, MSS Eur. F 123/29; Hamilton to Curzon, April 18, 1900, Curzon Papers, MSS Eur. F 111/159.

[70] John R. McLane, "The Development of Nationalist Ideas and Tactics and the Politics of the Government of India, 1897–1905" (unpublished Ph.D. dissertation, University of London, 1961), pp. 31–32.

[71] Hamilton to Curzon, August 3, 1900, Curzon Papers, MSS Eur. F 111/159.
[72] *Report of the Indian Famine Commission*, 1898, p. 186.

for a district at the beginning of a famine and then to investigate the legitimacy of the suspensions afterward. In Bombay the opposite idea prevailed: every man should pay the revenue unless he could prove his inability to do so. A better system, in the opinion of Curzon, was that everyone should profit by a general reduction except those who could clearly pay the revenue due.[73] The Viceroy went on to maintain that he considered the Bombay remissions of 1896–97 a "little stiff."[74]

Although the third charge against Bombay was a polemical one which was impossible to prove, Hamilton adduced some plausible reasons in support of the contention that the Bombay official was less in touch with the peasantry than Civilians elsewhere. Lacking a class of landed gentry, such as the Bengal *zamindars,* who could provide a conservative and stabilizing influence, the Bombay Government had no aristocracy on which to rely. Many of the landowners were of the Maratha Brahman community who were considered to be an unreconciled community. It was therefore natural for Civilians to react against the Irish methods of the Poona "Irreconcilables" and adopt stiffer attitudes toward the remissions and suspensions of revenue.[75]

All three charges were vigorously denied by the Bombay Governor, Sir Stafford Northcote. He became quite disturbed by what he considered to be a campaign of Macdonnell and officials outside of Bombay to discredit the Bombay revenue system. Macdonnell, Northcote claimed, made no secret of the fact that he was out to "go for" the Bombay system. The worst fears of the Governor were confirmed by the manner in which the Commission went about its task. When the Commission was convened in Bombay, Macdonnell browbeat the witnesses and did not permit the Bombay administration to see the evidence taken. "We were condemned unheard by his Commission," complained Northcote to Curzon. To salvage the respect of the province, the Bombay Government demanded that it should at least be permitted to consider the report and to "have a chance of defending ourselves before it is signed."[76] This did not occur, for both Curzon and Hamilton agreed with Macdonnell's diagnosis of the flaws in the Bombay revenue system.

[73]Curzon to Northcote, May 21 and July 26, 1900, Curzon Papers, MSS Eur. F 111/201 and 202.
[74]*Ibid.,* April 5, 1900.
[75]Hamilton to Northcote, February 21, 1901, and July 3, 1902, Hamilton Correspondence, MSS Eur. F 123/32 and 34.
[76]Northcote to Curzon, February 3 and 14, 1901, Curzon Papers, MSS Eur. F 111/203; Northcote to Hamilton, February 15, 1901, and October 16, 1902, Hamilton Correspondence, MSS Eur. F 123/30 and 35.

Because of this barrage of criticism and further famine difficulties in the northern regions of the province, Northcote reluctantly came to admit some of the arguments of his critics. If the Bombay system was at fault, he wrote in 1902, it was not because of the character of Bombay officials but because "we attempted the impossible" by trying to discover how much each individual cultivator could pay. Whereas the Civilian in northern India could deal with the large landowners and did not have to deal directly with the people, the Bombay Civilian was at a disadvantage, for there was no similar class in the presidency. The task of the Bombay official, argued Northcote, was much harder than elsewhere because of the disloyal press, the activities of the "agitators," and the fact that Maharashtrians were "grievance mongerers." These were the very arguments which Hamilton had pressed on Northcote in 1901. Northcote also came to admit that the Bombay policy of granting suspensions at the time of famine on the basis of individual inquiry, while good in theory, was impossible to implement. Bombay did not have the *"trustworthy* machinery to effect it." As a result the Government agreed to a number of changes in the Bombay famine system: to abandon individual inquiry and substitute the practice of suspension and remission by area; to devise a "liberal automatic scale" which would regulate remissions and suspensions according to the value of the crops.[77]

While Northcote did not accept all the criticisms levelled by the famine commissions, he did admit the charge that the Bombay famine system, as it had operated in 1896–97, was too stringent. By implication he accepted the view that the remissions and suspensions of this time were not as prompt or as generous as they might have been under the systems prevailing elsewhere. In a sense Northcote accepted in 1902 some of the chief arguments of the *Kesari* of 1896. In championing famine relief, Tilak had discovered a cause which was to win grudging approval of the Viceroy, the Secretary of State, and, belatedly, the Governor of Bombay himself.

In 1896 the Bombay Government was not prepared to admit the faults of their revenue system. Officials were alarmed by the number and extent of the no-rent combinations which they attributed to the bad faith of the Poona agents. Under the famine code local officials had the power to cancel tenure when necessary. Coercive measures were effectively used to nip the Poona-sponsored movement in the bud.

---

[77]Northcote to Hamilton, October 16, 1902.

One of the most effective methods was to make an example of the richest landowners. This happened in Khandesh:

> Some of the richest defaulters—Marwadis, Banyas, Sowkars, and so forth—were immediately selected and on the 21st January orders summarily forfeiting their lands, transferring them to padit [government land], and directing the recovery of arrears by seizure of moveable property were sent to the villages. The recalcitrant Khatedars had of course been expecting the usual tedious procedure of notices, jaghirnamas etc., etc., and thinking that they were going to give Government the maximum of trouble with the minimum loss to themselves. The instantaneous forfeiture of their lands completely paralysed them.

This result of this action was spectacular:

> The rank and file seeing the collapse of the bigger men rushed at once to the chawris with their haftas, lest a like thing should befall them also. And thus the net result of the agitation and the strike was that the Government revenue came in more quickly and more plentifully than it would otherwise have done: and that I fear a good many people have paid who could ill-afford it and who have been deemed by us entitled to suspensions and possibly remissions had they been left alone to ask for them in the ordinary way. Since that 21st January nothing more has been heard of agitators.[78]

The net result of the *Sabha* agitation in Khandesh was an increase rather than a decrease in collection of revenue. This seems to confirm the very point made by the Lyall Famine Commission that the Bombay Government reacted negatively to the Poona-sponsored movement and exacted more revenue than the scarcity demanded. This also suggests that the *Sarvajanik Sabha* agents were not very successful in lightening the famine burden of the *rayat*. The people who flocked to hear the agents in December and January stayed away from the meetings in February when they discovered that the agitation had proved abortive.[79]

Coercive measures were effective in many other districts. Following a meeting at Kalyan (Thana district) eighteen of the chief defaulters were arrested; one of them, who was unable to pay the arrears, found himself in the cells of the *mamlatdar's* office.[80] Similar actions indicated the mind of the government and the futility of further combinations. The lesson was salutary and the movement collapsed by the end of January, 1897. The combinations were further weakened by the

[78]Commissioner, Central Division to BG, July 6, 1897.
[79]*Ibid.*
[80]Collector of Thana to Commissioner, Northern Division, May 31, 1897.

administration resolutions of January 9 and March 17, 1897, which indicated the extent to which the local government was prepared to grant remissions and suspensions.

While the Bombay Government put out the fires of rural unrest, it was sufficiently alarmed by the extent of the agitation to suggest legislation to prevent any future recurrence. The Advocate General of Bombay pointed out that the common law of England, which covered "conspiracies" of the no-rent variety, was not applicable to India on this point. He suggested that a section or sections of the common law of England and Ireland concerned with the law of conspiracy should be added to the Indian Penal Code. The Advocate General thought that it was desirable to go beyond the law of England and Ireland and to make it an offence for one person to incite the withholding of revenue, whether or not it was possible to prove that such person was acting in concert with others.[81] The Government of India, in reply, argued that the existing clauses of the Bombay Famine Code were stringent enough to make additional legislation redundant. It also referred to the successful action taken to quash a similar "conspiracy" in Oudh eighteen years before, when combinations were formed throughout the south and the east of the province to resist paying the revenue: "It was, we thought at the time, all the more formidable, because it was organized and propagated by those secret methods, which are natural to the people of the East. It was an exceedingly successful conspiracy. The revenue payments in many districts came to a stand still, the Native revenue officers were beaten and maltreated when we tried to sell the lands of defaulters, no one would bid for them, and we were nearly baffled." The law on recovery of the revenue of northern India included a provision by which tenure could be confiscated for fifteen years. The Bombay Government had similar coercive powers in its famine regulations, which obviated the need for further legislation.[82] The Secretary of State, who took a similarly grave view of the agitation, was later to reflect on its character in the following terms: "I wonder if, in the course of the next generation or two, a Parnell will arise who will combine the ryots in refusing to pay land revenue. It would be an awkward situation, and I sometimes used to think that Tilak and Co. had got the idea into their heads. The Irish methods and the organization of the Land League have been closely studied by certain irrecon-

[81] BG to GI, February 20, 1897, BG, Revenue (Famine), Vol. 122, pp. 33–52.
[82] J. Woodburn to Sandhurst, May 17, 1897, BG, Revenue (Famine), Vol. 122, pp. 107–118.

cilables in Poona; and their proceedings were not dissimilar from those practised by the Parnellites."[83]

In one sense Tilak's movement was a failure. It did not induce the provincial government to lighten the famine load of the peasant. It brought a harsher and less generous famine administration. In the face of this, the no-rent agitation collapsed. But in another sense Tilak's endeavour was a telling success. It was to have a profound influence on land legislation for more than a decade. The administration was sufficiently alarmed by the rural agitation of 1896–97 to postpone remedial legislation, which it came to believe was necessary to prevent the growing instances of land alienation. The government which had ignored the party of the Ganapati and Shivaji festivals could no longer afford to make light of the party which could hamper the collection of land revenue. For perhaps the first time, the Poona Brahman elite forced the administration to heed its position.

The need for remedial land legislation was first felt after the Deccan riots of 1875. The commission which investigated the 1875 unrest found that one-third of the *rayats* on government land were embarrassed by debt. In many instances landownership had been transferred to the money-lender.[84] To rectify this situation the Deccan Agriculturalists' Relief Act was passed in 1879. The extent of the legislation was limited because its framers did not believe that the prohibition of land transfer could be justified, since it would subvert the form of property.[85] A second commission, set up in 1891 to consider the working of the 1879 legislation, concluded that while the *rayat* had benefited from the legislation, it had failed to stop the transfer of land—it had merely retarded this trend. Although the 1891 commission admitted that the transfer of landownership from the peasant to "rack-renting aliens" was a serious matter, it did not consider the situation drastic enough to demand further legislation.[86] The Macdonnell famine committee of 1901 flatly disagreed with this conclusion. Macdonnell maintained that the 1879 legislation had completely failed to relieve indebtedness

---

[83]Hamilton to Northcote, February 21, 1901, and November 27, 1902, Hamilton Correspondence, MSS Eur. F 123/32 and 37.

[84]The commission investigated twelve villages in the Ahmednagar district. It found that one-eighth of the occupancies had been transferred to the money-lender.

[85]GI, Revenue and Agriculture, Land Revenue, A37–38, October, 1905; Viney Chander Bhutani, "The Administration of Lord Curzon: Socio-Economic Policies" (unpublished Ph.D. dissertation, University of New Delhi, 1966), pp. 168–184.

[86]Although Lord Harris was critical of the 1879 act, his council considered that the legislation had improved the position of the *rayat*.

and land alienation. He urged the Bombay Government to introduce more radical legislation along the lines of the legislation prepared for the Punjab, which became the Punjab Land Alienation Act of 1901.[87] The time for palliative measures, Macdonnell argued, had passed. The advanced state of land alienation, as much as 70 per cent in some talukas, demanded radical action.[88]

When approached by the Government of India concerning this matter, the Bombay Government of Lord Sandhurst concurred with this view. The Bombay administration was alive to the political dangers which could result from any deterioration in the land system. The Poona *Sarvajanik Sabha* had exhibited great facility in organizing all manner of agitation, and in the course of time the network and efficiency of the Poona machine could be expected to increase with the spread of education and the improvement in communication facilities:

The Governor in Council must record it as his deliberate opinion that if the rayats, as a body, are in the course of time deprived of their lands by the action of our laws to the extent that a further continuation of *laissez-faire* policy renders inevitable, machinery is already in existence prepared to take advantage of the discontent and serious consequences may follow. The time for action, in the opinion of the Government, has now certainly come.[89]

The governor, Lord Sandhurst, dissented from the majority opinion. He predicted that the enactment of radical land legislation would constitute a more immediate political threat than the long-term deterioration of rural relations:

I am unable to perceive that there is in the Deccan, as there seems to be in the Punjab, a strong public opinion in favour of the land-holder being regarded as a tenant for life. Again we have in the Deccan a class, possibly small, but certainly clever, active and unscrupulous, who are ever on the look out for some means of embarrassing Government, and who for some years past have been seeking a cry that would secure them the support of the rayats. To this end they have taken up cow-protection, the Shivaji and Ganpati movements, the no-rent agitation of 1897, forest grievances, plague measures and active criticism of famine relief, all in turn: and the proposed scheme for restricting the alienation of land will, it seems to me, give them just what they have been looking for.[90]

[87] GI, Revenue and Agriculture, Land Revenue, A37–38, October, 1905.
[88] The districts most affected by land alienation in 1900 were Thana (55 per cent of land alienated), Kolaba (45.04 per cent), Ratnagiri (38.3 per cent), and Ahmednagar (35.02 per cent).
[89] BG to GI, October 7, 1899, GI, Revenue and Agriculture, Land Revenue, A1–2, January, 1901.
[90] *Ibid.*

The dilemma which faced Sandhurst and succeeding governors was whether it was better to introduce radical land legislation and face political agitation, or to follow a *laissez-faire* policy, with the definite possibility that the condition of the cultivating classes might degenerate in the near future and become easier prey for the provincial "agitators."

The next provincial administration of Lord Northcote sidestepped the whole issue. It twice rejected the suggestion of the Government of India to consider introducing legislation on the Punjab lines to prevent land alienation. The Bombay Government denied the existence of the land ailments diagnosed by the Macdonnell commission. It maintained that peasant indebtedness was not the serious problem depicted by Macdonnell, since it was no worse than had existed in 1818. Because the Punjab legislation was a novel and radical experiment, it was maintained that Bombay should wait to ascertain the effectiveness of the measure before it followed suit. In such an important area caution was needed.[91]

The Northcote administration was far from moderate when it introduced what it considered to be an innocuous land bill in 1901. The purpose of the bill was twofold: to secure authority to occupy certain unassessed waste-lands, and to re-grant land which had been forfeited and become derelict because of the inability of the owners to pay revenue arrears in famine years. However, what began as a limited emergency measure, approved by Curzon and Hamilton, ended as an "absurd mess," since the legislation was loosely worded and was "introduced and steered with a minimum of discretion and skill."[92] Curzon was "staggered" to find out, after the bill had been introduced to the Bombay Legislative Council, that what he thought was a limited measure to apply to isolated tracts was applicable to 50 per cent of the land in some districts, and to 20 per cent of the total area of the presidency. This could have amounted to an estimated cost of 750,000 rupees. While Northcote privately assured the Viceroy that he did not intend to act on such "heroic lines," the Bombay Government never publicly denied the statement of its revenue member, made at the first reading of the bill, that the legislation could be applied to this very large area if the government were so inclined.[93] The member in charge of the bill thus gave the impression that "state-landlordism was the

---

[91]Bhutani, pp. 173–176.
[92]Curzon to Hamilton, September 11, 1901, Curzon Papers, MSS Eur. F 111/160.
[93]Curzon to Northcote, July 4, 1901, and Curzon to Hamilton, July, 1901, Curzon Papers.

aim of the Government."[94] In view of the extensiveness of the proposed legislation, the Bombay Government acted rashly in hurrying the bill through the Council. The contents of the bill were published on May 18, 1901, the first reading was on May 30, and it was passed on August 24 of the same year. The bill was drafted and introduced before the results of two important famine commissions had been published.[95] It was with "extreme reluctance" that Curzon finally approved the "perilous license" with which the provincial administration had acted. To reject the bill would have appeared a victory for the Congress politicians.[96]

The 1901 bill sparked a "fierce" and "hysterical clamour" the like of which had not been witnessed in the presidency before.[97] The bill was greeted with a barrage of petitions from the premier provincial associations and a host of taluka and district bodies. Meetings against the bill were held in every prominent town of the province.[98] The agitation was spontaneous and represented one of the rare occasions when rural and urban elites vied with each other to denounce the gargantuan creation of the Bombay administration. The climax of the campaign took place when five non-official members walked out of the Bombay Legislative Council during the third reading of the bill. Leading the popular forces was Gopal Krishna Gokhale, who, following the death of Ranade several months before, took up his preceptor's mantle and became the foremost Indian commentator on Bombay land revenue policy. He was supported by the "lion of Bombay," Pherozeshah Mehta, who dominated the Bombay congress scene. The third dissident was the Brahman doctor, Sir Balchandra Krishna Bhatwadekar, an active member of the Council of the Bombay Presidency Association. The fourth figure was the Chitpavan lawyer, Daji Abaji Khare, active in Bombay and Konkan politics. The support of a *sardar*, the Chief of Ichalkaranji, added weight to the popular cause.

It was argued by Hamilton and Northcote that the political fervour

[94]McLane, p. 201.
[95]The Macdonnell commission and the Machonochie inquiry. The latter investigated famine administration in Gujarat.
[96]Note by Curzon, September 24, 1901, GI, Legislative, A1–25, October, 1901.
[97]Note by Curzon, August 8, 1905, GI, Revenue and Agriculture, Land Revenue, A37–38, October, 1905.
[98]Petitions were received not only from leading presidency association but also from district associations, such as the Sholapur People's Association, and from meetings of cultivators in small towns and villages.

against the bill was manufactured by money-lenders and lawyers,[99] but the extent of the opposition belies this. Of the principal factions in the presidency, only the Tilakites had clear links with the money-lending class. Some of the leading figures of this group came from *sawkar* families. Tilak himself opposed the extension of the Deccan Agriculturalists' Relief Act in 1891, which was designed to prevent the *rayat* from falling into the clutches of the money-lender. But this does not prove that the Tilak party was a spokesman of *sawkar* interests. Tilak was a conservative who opposed any state regulation of land ownership.

The same accusation could not be levelled at Ranade and his disciple Gokhale, since they had favoured the remedial legislation of 1879 and its extension in 1891. They had also advocated measures, such as the establishment of agricultural banks, to relieve peasant indebtedness. They were not, however, prepared to support the 1901 bill, since it represented a step toward the introduction of radical legislation on the Punjab lines, which Ranade and Gokhale considered would be disastrous.[100] It has recently been argued that nationalist leaders such as Ranade, who opposed radical land legislation, were devoid of altruism because they sought to conserve their landed interests.[101] While it is true that Ranade underestimated the seriousness of rural dislocation and helped to prevent the implementation of effective corrective measures, it should be stressed that the land debate in Bombay was clouded by the limitations of the Bombay revenue system. There was, after all, some truth to the nationalist assertion that the ills of the Deccan were due to excessive assessments and the unfortunate famine policies of the local administration.

The opposition to the bill was equally vigorous in Bombay and was championed by the leaders of the Bombay Presidency Association. While some elite figures owned land outside the city, the majority were mill-owners, merchants, professional men, or landlords, who tapped urban sources of wealth. As the men of privilege within the city, they tended to oppose all government efforts to regulate the pattern of society. Their *laissez-faire* approach to land legislation was simply an extension of their ideas on factory acts, liquor control, and property

[99] Northcote to Hamilton, August 1, 1901, and Hamilton to Curzon, July 25, 1901, Hamilton Correspondence, MSS Eur. F 123/31 and C 126/3.

[100] GI, Legislative, A1–25, October 1901. Although Ranade died several months before the 1901 land revenue debate in the Bombay Legislative Council, his views were frequently quoted by critics of the legislation.

[101] McLane, p. 213.

regulation. Most of the Bombay newspapers opposed the extension of the Deccan Agriculturalists' Relief Act in 1891. It was the view of the Parsi editor of the *Kaiser-i-Hind* that the 1879 act had not worked, because it was opposed to all principles of political economy and had left the peasantry worse off than before.[102] Wacha expressed his opposition to the 1901 bill in the following terms: "You are right in saying I go further than you. I go to the first principle and say that the Government has no business to restrict the right on the plea that it is the state landlord. Mark my word, everywhere there is a tendency to drive the thin end of the wedge and assert the right of land ownership which from the days of Cornwallis has been persistently repudiated."[103]

The Bombay Government's traumatic experience of 1901 together with the two no-rent campaigns underlined the political danger of introducing radical land legislation in the province. When Curzon asked the Bombay Government of Lord Lamington (1903–07)[104] to reconsider the introduction of a bill to prohibit land transfer, he emphasized that the local administration would have to weigh the need for such legislation against the political consequences. In a sense Curzon summed up the official dilemma in regard to land revenue policy in Bombay and the role which the local "agitator" played in the situation:

In Bengal the agitator cannot in 19 cases out of 20 get hold of the cultivator, because the interests and point of view of the agitator are urban not rural, political and not economic, while the cultivator under a permanent settlement is in an entirely different position, so far as the Government is concerned, from his fellow-cultivator elsewhere.

In Bombay, on the other hand, the political agitators, as they attempted to do at the beginning of the famine of 1896–97, and again at the time of the Revenue Act of 1901, will exert the whole of their machinery to produce discontent, strikes, and possibly even risings among the peasants by spreading among them poisoned counsels and interested lies. . . . We have, as statesmen, to balance the disadvantages of agitation, even vehement and malignant and formidable agitation, now, against the disadvantages of allowing the Bombay cultivating classes to degenerate in the not remote future into

[102]*Kaiser-i-Hind*, October 18, 1891; *Indu Prakash*, September 21, 1891; *Indian Spectator*, February 21, 1892.
[103]Wacha to Gokhale, June 11, 1901, Gokhale Papers, 569/57.
[104]Charles Wallace Alexander Napier Ross Cochrane-Baillie (1860–1940), second Baron Lamington, educated at Eton, and Christ Church, Oxford, Conservative member for North St. Pancras, 1886–90, Governor of Queensland, 1895–1901.

rack-rented serfs upon their former lands—a far easier prey, and a much more fruitful soil, for the political agitator of the future.[105]

The decision of this and succeeding administrations not to proceed with a Punjab bill was a testimony to the successful manner in which the Poona leaders, Tilak and Ranade in particular, altered the course of land legislation in the province.

Tilak's famine campaign of 1896–97 did not improve the lot of the Deccan peasantry, but this was not his chief aim. His intention was to secure an issue which would dramatize the interest of his party in the *rayat*, and demonstrate that the urban intellectuals of Poona could organize an effective rural protest movement. As a political realist, Tilak was aware that the effective politicization of the agrarian masses was a long-term project, and he therefore settled for lesser aims. The rural unrest of 1896 provided the temporary straws which Tilak eagerly grasped to make political capital for his party. By 1903 the British had learned their lesson and adopted a more cautious land policy in Bombay. In so doing they removed many of the grievances which Tilak had so adeptly championed. As a result, Tilak turned next to Bombay City, to the mill-hands and merchants, for his next mass movement.

The 1896–97 no-rent campaign was Tilak's first successful endeavour to organize a mass protest. Unlike his previous efforts, Tilak this time found a pertinent issue which concerned landowners and cultivators. The resistance was brief, but it profoundly alarmed the government. The Bombay administration which made light of the party which had planned the Ganapati and Shivaji celebrations could ill afford to overlook the rural resistance of 1896–97.

[105] Note by Curzon, August 8, 1905, GI, Revenue and Agriculture, Land Revenue, A37–38, October, 1905.

Chapter VII
POONA AND BOMBAY

> Admittedly Bombay stands foremost in commercial pursuits, but this activity is gained somewhat at the expense of political energy, earnestness and enthusiasm.[1]

> Poona is, we freely admit, not a manufacturing or commercial centre. It is ... rich in political traditions.[2]

The famine campaign demonstrated Tilak's capacity to organize a rural protest of some magnitude, but it did not provide him with a peasant-based party or a continuing program of forward action. Having failed to woo the non-Brahmans effectively in the Ganapati festival or to enlist the princes in the cause of Shivaji, and enjoying only temporary success among the Deccan *rayats,* Tilak gradually turned to the greater prize of Bombay.

The city provided two possibilities of political gain for the Tilak party. One was to enlist the non-Brahman labour force and, if possible, business to their cause. The other goal was to undercut the position of the ailing Bombay Congress party, to demonstrate the limitations of its leadership, to contrast its lack of constituency with the broadening Poona base, and thus to discredit the Bombay party and its programs. Having effectively rebuffed the Ranade party in Poona and having experimented with the rudiments of political power, Tilak hoped to demonstrate his political strength in the premier city of the region. This would provide a means of capturing control of the nationalist movement in western India.

Although separated by only 120 miles, the cities of Bombay and Poona were and are markedly dissimilar. The 1901 population of Bombay (776,006) was seven times that of metropolitan Poona (111,381). The crowded islands of Bombay supported a dense population of 35,273 to the square mile compared to Poona's more comfortable ratio of 165 to the same area. Whereas Bombay's population was

---
[1]*Mahratta,* September 6, 1891.
[2]*Ibid.*

152   THE MYTH OF *Lokamanya*

steadily increasing, Poona's growth rate was modest.[3] As the historic seat of the Peshwas, a centre of the powerful Chitpavan community, and the intellectual and linguistic focus for Marathi-speakers, Poona was the recognized cultural capital of Maharashtra. Homogeneous in culture and language, dedicated to the refinement and perpetuation of the great traditions of Hinduism and the cultural heritage of the Marathas, Poona was a relatively traditional city. Bombay, by comparison, was modern, heterodox, and cosmopolitan, an entrepôt city which readily imported materials and ideas from other societies, tempering the old with a heady dose of the new. The promising commercial prospects of India's second maritime port attracted labourers and entrepreneurs from a variety of communities and regions.[4]

The character of the elite groups of the two cities reflected these differences. The elite of Poona was relatively traditional, Brahmanical, and exclusive. Its members were recruited primarily from one *jati*; there were never more than a handful of non-Brahmans and non-Hindus on the managing committees of the elite societies. In Bombay, by comparison, men of diverse religious and cultural backgrounds

[3] Figures derived from censuses from 1872–1911.

	Bombay City	Poona Municipality	Poona City, cantonment and suburbs
1872	644,405	106,188	118,886
1881	773,196	99,622	129,751
1891	821,764	118,790	161,390
1901	776,006	111,381	153,320
1911	979,445	117,256	158,856

[4] Figures derived from the 1901 *Census*. Religion (per cent)

	Bombay City	Poona	Bombay Presidency
Hindu	65.5	94.0	78.4
Muslim	20.1	4.7	17.9
Parsi	6.0	0.2	0.3
Christian	5.8	1.1	0.8
Jain	1.8	0.0	2.1
Others	0.8	0.0	0.5

Language (per cent)

	Bombay City	Poona	Bombay Presidency
Marathi	53.6	90.2	40.6
Gujarati	20.6	1.4	28.1
Hindi-Urdu	14.6	5.4	4.4
Sindhi	8.4	0.0	11.5
Kanarese	0.0	0.0	12.0
South Indian languages	1.1	1.3	3.0
Others	1.7	1.7	0.4

co-operated with each other and British capitalists in the interests of profit and mutual advance.

The affiliations of the active members of the Council of the Bombay Presidency Association, the Bombay branch of the Indian National Congress, indicate the diversity of the Bombay elites. From 1885 to 1909 there were forty-two members of the Council who attended twenty or more meetings.[5] They can be classified as follows:

		Per cent
Hindu	23	55
Parsi	14	33
Muslim	4	10
European	1	2
TOTAL	42	

The twenty-three Hindu members can be further identified in terms of region and caste:

Region		Per cent
Maharashtrian	13	57
Gujarati	9	39
South Indian	1	4

Caste		Per cent
Brahman	16	70
Non-Brahman	7	30

A third of the total active membership and more than half of the active Hindu members were Maharashtrian. However, these figures exaggerate the Maharashtrian proportion of the elite communities, since the Bombay Presidency Association was dominated by one element of the Bombay elites—the professionals. The occupations of the forty-two members have been clearly indicated on next page in Table I.

Very few Maharashtrians were found among the business groups. There was only one Maharashtrian mill-owner out of the forty-six who operated the eighty cotton mills in the city in 1908.[6] Non-Hindus operated fifty-three of the eighty mills as given in Table II.

[5] These forty-two members of the Council are listed in Appendix 4.
[6] *Indian Textile Journal*, August, 1908, p. 348.

I.

		Totals	Per cent
Professional		32	76
Lawyers	24		
Doctors	4		
Journalists	2		
Educator	1		
Engineer	1		
Business		7	17
Merchants	6		
Mill-owner	1		
Unidentified		3	7

II.

	Firms	Mills	Mill-hands
Hindu	20	27	27,500
Parsi	13	21	27,500
Muslim	6	10	11,000
European	4	14	16,200
Jewish	3	8	14,800
TOTAL	46	80	97,000

Most of the Hindu mills were owned and operated by Gujaratis, chiefly from the Bania communities.[7] Although well represented in the professions of the city, the Maratha Brahman exhibited a strong bias against commercial enterprise. There was no strong Vaishya (mercantile) community in Maharashtra to take advantage of the ample entrepreneurial opportunities in nineteenth century Bombay City.[8]

Unlike the Poona elite, which could look back to those advantageous

---

[7]The three Hindus who operated the largest mills in 1908 were from the Gujarati Bhatia community:

	Number of mills	Employees
Vithaldas Damodar Thackersey	3	3,623
Dwarkadas Dharamsi	3	3,362
Goverhandas and Mulraj Khatau	2	3,089

[8]Much of the trade of Maharashtra was in the hands of Gujaratis and Rajasthanis because of the more fertile soil, the better systems of transportation, and the superior sea-ports, to the north of Bombay, and greater capital formations.

pre-British days when Brahmans were the temporal and spiritual rulers of their society, the merchants and manufacturers of Bombay City tended to regard the British presence as beneficent, since many fortunes were built on the foundation of European protection and technical skill. The co-operation of European and Indian personnel and capital was one of the unique features of commercial enterprises of Bombay City. Although most of the mills were owned by Indians, they still depended on Europeans for skilled labour and technical advice. There were only three or four mills in 1889 which had no European element. Indians, wrote Dinshaw Wacha at this time, make "fair weather captains" as a rule, but "when there is a squall they are at their wit's end."[9] The table below indicates that the European element was considerable in 1896:[10]

	Europeans	Indians
Mill managers	27	28
Carding masters	20	31
Spinning masters	21	31
Mill engineers	23	38
TOTAL	91	128

The majority of Maharashtrians who migrated to Bombay City were non-Brahmans, chiefly from the overcrowded tracts of the Konkan south of Bombay. They came in search of employment in the expanding mill industry and the service organizations. Brought up in the shadow of the western *ghats*, and known as *ghatis*, they accounted for the bulk of the 97,000 mill-hands in 1908. They also provided the backbone of the Bombay army and comprised 70 per cent of the Bombay police force.[11] The *Times of India* estimated in 1896 that there were 300,000 *ghatis* in Bombay City.[12] Whereas the British looked on Brahmans as disloyal and definite security risks, they regarded the illiterate non-Brahman labourers as dependable material on which to build their rule in western India.

[9] Wacha to Naoroji, June 4, 1889, Naoroji Papers.
[10] S. M. Rutnagar, *Bombay Industries: The Cotton Mills* (Bombay, 1927), pp. 297–311.
[11] *Papers Relating to the Revision Settlement of* 152 *Villages in the Dapoli Taluka of the Ratnagiri Collectorate* (Bombay, 1903), p. 14; "Bombay Bill No. 30 of 1879 to amend the law relating to the settlement of villages held by Khots," GI, Revenue and Agriculture, Revenue, B3-4, May, 1880.
[12] *Times of India*, March 28, 1896.

The Bombay labouring classes were not well organized in the 1890's. As late as 1896 the *Times of India* could exult over the peacefulness and docility of the hands: "Thrice happy, Bombay! A large trade emporium with a labouring population full of gentleness and meekness, content to give a full day's labour for the barest necessities of life, and never to presume to question the justice or generosity of their employers."[13] But if labour was relatively quiescent in the 1890's, there were portents of future strife. The mill-hands figured prominently in the communal riots of 1893 which lasted four days and resulted in eighty deaths. The Hindu labourers participated in a manner which the Bombay Government of the day considered ominous: "The Hindu mill-hands ... not only retaliated upon the Muslim aggressors, but did so in large and apparently organized gangs; and it is difficult to avoid the conclusion that the heaviness of the Muhammedan death-toll in proportion to the comparative numbers of the Hindu and Muhammedan population is largely due to the capacity for co-operation which the Bombay mill-hands are beginning to display."[14]

In more ordinary times the working classes were comparatively docile. Narayan Meghaji Lokhande, the Mali (gardener) heir-apparent to Jotiba Phule, editor of the *Din Bandhu*[15] and secretary of the Deccan Phulmali community of Bombay, attempted to organize labour without noticeable success. He formed the Bombay Workers' Conference in 1884 to campaign for a stronger factory act.[16] The Conference was succeeded by the Mill-Hands' Association, established in 1890 with Lokhande as president, which agitated for shorter hours and improved working conditions. Since there was "no membership, no rules and regulations and no funds," the Association was more of a welfare organization than a trade union, and Lokhande was a self-appointed adviser to and tribune of the mill-hand.[17] The Association collapsed with the death of Lokhande in 1901.

In comparison with the moderate means of the Tilakites, the members of the Bombay Presidency Association were men of wealth and influence. Many of them enjoyed lucrative practices in the Bombay High Court. Pherozeshah Mehta was typical of the group. As the son

[13] *Ibid.*
[14] BG to the Secretary of State, October 26, 1893, BG, Judicial, 1893, Vol. 195, p. 233.
[15] The *Din Bandhu*, a weekly Anglo-Marathi journal with an average circulation of 1,500, was critical of Brahmans.
[16] Reisner and Goldberg, *Tilak and the Struggle for Indian Freedom* (New Delhi, 1966) pp. 533–534.
[17] V. S. Karnik, *Indian Trade Unions: A Survey* (Bombay, 1960), p. 4.

of a successful merchant, Mehta had been brought up in comfortable circumstances. Because of a profitable legal practice, he had few financial worries. Polished in manners, elegant in his attire, which included a fashionable velvet collar, Mehta enjoyed the life of a Bombay aristocrat, who could afford a good house in the city and an attractive retreat at the hill-station of Matheran. For his excursions to the mofussil Mehta engaged a sizeable retinue which even included a barber.[18] Dinshaw Wacha, who stated in 1888 that he was "as poor as a Church mouse," was an exception to the general affluence of the group.[19] The Council of the Bombay Presidency Association included some of the wealthiest men of the city. Tribhovandas Mangaldas Nathubhai, the president of the Gujarati Kapole Bania caste, was a successful merchant and one of the largest property-holders in the city.[20] Another active member of the Council was the Bhatia, Vithaldas Damodar Thackersey, who employed more labourers than any other Hindu mill-owner in 1908.[21] The Tyabji brothers, Badruddin, Amiruddin, and Camiruddin, came to be recognized as heads of the Muslim Suleiman Bohra community by virtue of the extensive business fortune acquired by their father, who established commercial houses in London, China, and Karachi. Badruddin was the president of the third Indian National Congress meeting. Amiruddin was a joint secretary of the Council of the Bombay Presidency Association for a number of years.[22]

By virtue of their wealth and education, the elite figures of the Association held dominant positions in their respective communities. They contributed handsomely to charitable institutions of their castes, they funded scholarships for promising students, and they formed *mitra mandalis* (friendly societies) to improve the educational status of their community and to promote social reform within it.[23] Their status enabled them to become spokesmen for their communities. Thus, among the ranks of the Bombay nationalist society were some of the most influential men of the city.

[18]Homi Mody, *Sir Pherozeshah Mehta: A Political Biography* (Bombay, 1963), pp. 1, 115–116.
[19]Wacha to Naoroji, August 7, 1888.
[20]Nathoobhai attended 45 meetings of the Council of the Bombay Presidency Association from 1885 to 1909.
[21]Thackersey, who employed more labourers than any other Hindu mill-owner, attended 12 meetings of the Council from 1903 to 1908.
[22]R. H. Jalbhoy, *Portrait Gallery of Western India* (Bombay, 1886).
[23]Goverhandas and Mulraj Khatau donated 100,000 rupees for Bhatia education

Although the professional elite tended to dominate the proceedings of the Bombay Presidency Association, they did have important links with the businessmen of the city. A significant number of manufacturers and merchants were prepared to underwrite the programs of the Association and to attend the occasional public meetings to demonstrate their support for the platform of the Bombay nationalist party. Jamshedji Nasserwanji Tata, the Parsi pioneer of the iron and steel industry, attended only four meetings of the Council in a decade, but usually could be persuaded to provide financial support when necessary. Prominent mill-owners connected with the Bombay Presidency Association included the two Bhatias, Thackersey and Dwarkadas Dharamsi; the Parsi Avestic scholar, Khurshedji Rustomji Kama; and the Jain mill agent, Veerchund Deepchund. Among the mercantile supporters were the Kapole Banias, Nathoobhai and Harkisondas Narotumdas; a banker who was the director of several stock companies; the Modli Bania, Vijbhookhundas Atmaran, who was the senior partner of a cotton, wheat, and seed business; Damodurdas Thackersey Moolji, a Bhatia merchant who also owned a mill and was president of the Native Piece-Goods Merchants' Association in 1893; and the Bhunsalay Kshatriya contractor, Vundrovandas Purshotumdas.[24] Many others took only a minor interest in the Council meetings, but could be persuaded to donate funds for the work of the Association.[25]

There was much overlapping in the interests of the professional and business elites of the city in the 1890's. Many of the leading citizens were involved in a variety of business and professional concerns. Wacha was both a mill agent and a journalist. Manekshah Taleyarkhan was a lawyer, a landowner, and a spokesman of the toddy interest. Ramchandra Lakshman Gharat was a schoolteacher and a spokesman of the landholders of the Alibag Taluka. K. R. Kama was a mill-owner, a religious reformer, and director of a newspaper. Nathoobhoy,

---

in 1896. In the same year Nathoobhoy gave 25,000 rupees to his community for similar purposes. *Indian Spectator,* March 1 and May 17, 1896.

[24] Purshotamdas attended 44 Council meetings, 1885–93; Atmaran, 51, 1885–1905; Narotumdas, 1, 1885; Deepchund, 7, 1896–1905; Moolji, 13, 1885–93.

[25] The Council entrusted the task of collecting 25,000 to 30,000 rupees, required for the 1889 Congress meeting, to a committee of Hindu businessmen, including Nathoobhai, Damodurdas Thackersey, Vijbhookhundas Atmaran, Vassonji Khimjee, Vundrovandas Purshotumdas, Hariprasad Suntokram, Jivandas Moolji, and several others. Wacha to Naoroji, July 9, November 1 and 15, 1889.

a successful merchant, invested his money in property within the city. Badruddin Tyabji and Pherozeshah Mehta, the sons of prosperous merchants, preferred the law. Amiruddin Tyabji remained a merchant. Lakhmidas Khimjee was both a piece-goods merchant and a mill-owner. Damodurdas Moolji was an office-holder in both the leading mercantile and manufacturing associations. It was logical for a business magnate to diversify his wealth in order to secure larger profits and to safeguard his interests should one sector become depressed. The Bombay elites were a series of connected interest groups sharing a common concern to preserve their dominant economic and political status in the city.[26]

The more articulate members argued that commercial and industrial advancement were practical means of regenerating the country. It behooved the government and other Indian communities to recognize this important role. Differences within the elites were largely issues of tactics regarding the best means of preserving their interests. Some argued that it was sufficient for the Bombay business leaders to present their views to the British through the existing channels of mercantile and manufacturing associations. Others maintained that greater pressure should be brought to bear on the rulers in order to pursue a more vigorous campaign for recognition. The Indian National Congress provided a means by which the Bombay leaders could combine with other regional groups and strengthen their case.

Bombay politicians thus had greater potential sources of wealth to tap than their Poona counterparts. Wealth in Bombay was of the expanding variety, concentrated in the hands of individuals who did not have the responsibility of ruling a principality. There was also a tradition of philanthropy among business magnates, notably of the Parsi community. They provided endowments for charitable institutions and embraced laudable political and educational endeavours. The support which Bombay businessmen gave to the Poona-sponsored Deccan Education Society, which primarily benefited Maharashtrian students, was indicative of the potential of Bombay philanthropy. From

[26]According to Masselos, pp. 587–597, and Dobbin [Christine Dobbin, "Competing Elites in Bombay City Politics in the Mid-Nineteenth Century (1852–83)," in *Elites in South Asia*, Edmund Leach and S. N. Mukherjee (eds.), (Cambridge, 1970), pp. 74–94], conflict between the western-educated professional group and the *shetias* (merchants) was a key factor in Bombay City politics in the pre-Congress years. While this division persists after 1885, it seems less significant. With the spread of education and the rising threat of extremists in the 1890's, distinctions between merchants, manufacturers, and professionals become blurred.

1884 to 1910 the Deccan Education Society received greater support from Bombay City than from Poona. The major donations came from the following sources:[27]

	Rupees
Princes	203,140
Poona City	41,475
Bombay City	51,646
Other	59,975
TOTAL	356,236

More than half the Bombay City donations came from non-Maharashtrian sources:

Donations		Rupees
Maharashtrian		22,646
Non-Maharashtrian		29,000
Gujarati	18,000	
Parsi	10,000	
Bene Israel	1,000	
	TOTAL	51,646

Such connections helped the Bombay Presidency Association to establish itself as the most powerful branch organization of the Congress. Bombay also had a quality and depth of leadership which few other cities could match. Lawyers who could write and speak good English and who practised in the Bombay High Court were presidential timber for the annual Congress meetings. Bombay Presidency provided nine of the twenty-three Congress presidents from 1885 to 1907, eight of whom were from Bombay City.[28] During the same time the Congress met six times in Bombay Presidency, more than in any other region.[29]

[27]P. M. Limaye, History of the Deccan Education Society, 1880–1935 (Poona, 1935), Appendices, pp. 66–76.

[28]The Congress presidents from 1885 to 1907 came from the following regions: Bombay, 9; Bengal, 8; Madras, 2. There were also four English presidents. The Bombay presidents of the Congress were: 1886, Dadabhai Naoroji; 1887, Badruddin Tyabji; 1890, Pherozeshah Mehta; 1893, Dadabhai Naoroji; 1896, Rahimtoola Sayani; 1900, Narayan Chandavarkar; 1901, Dinshaw Wacha; 1905, Gopal Krishna Gokhale; 1906, Dadabhai Naoroji.

[29]The Congress met the following number of times from 1885 to 1907: Bombay, 6;

The pre-eminent position of the Bombay politician was also reflected in his dominance of the Bombay Provincial Conference, the regional branch of the Congress. From the year 1892, when the Bombay Provincial Conference became a region-wide organization, until the last united conference of 1906, nine of the ten presidents came from Bombay City. The tenth president came from Karachi.[30] Although the Tilak forces preferred the hustings of the street-corner and the market-place to the dry constitutional proceedings of a provincial conference, they did recognize the importance of the regional association. It was both a symbolic representation of presidency power and a means of exerting provincial pressure on the national body. For this reason Tilak tried to capture control from the Bombay president, Goculdas Parekh, of the provincial conference held at Satara in 1900. The attempt failed.[31]

But all was not well with the Bombay Presidency Association. The most active year of the society was that of its founding in 1885, when the Council met seventeen times and organized three public meetings. No succeeding year provided a similar surge of activity and enthusiasm. The number of council meetings provides a barometer of the fluctuating interest, the "fits and starts,"[32] of political activity in Bombay:

United Provinces, 4; Bengal, 5; Central Provinces, 2; Madras, 4; Panjab, 2. The Congress met at four different places in the Bombay Presidency: 1885, Bombay; 1889, Bombay; 1895, Poona; 1902, Ahmedabad; 1904, Bombay; 1907, Surat. All five Bengal meetings were held at Calcutta.

[30]The Bombay Provincial Conferences were as follows:

Year	Venue	President	Affiliation
1888	Poona	Vishnu M. Bhide	PSS
1889	Poona	Gopal Hari Deshmukh	PSS
1890	Poona	Kazi Shahabudin	PSS
1891	Poona	Govind Dhondo Limaye	Satara
1892	Poona	Pherozeshah Mehta	BPA
1893	Ahmedabad	Rahimtoola M. Sayani	BPA
1894	Bombay	Javerilal Yajnik	BPA
1895	Belgaum	Dinshaw Wacha	BPA
1896	Karachi	Narayan Chandavarkar	BPA
1900	Satara	Goculdas Parekh	BPA
1901	Bombay	Tahilchand Khemchand	Karachi
1902	Sholapur	Chimanlal Setalvad	BPA
1903	Dharwar	Daji Abaji Khare	BPA
1906	Surat	Balchandra Bhatwadekar	BPA

[31]*Kesari*, May 15, 1900.
[32]Wacha to Naoroji, January 2, 1888.

COUNCIL MEETINGS OF THE BOMBAY PRESIDENCY
ASSOCIATION

Year	Number held	Average attendance (out of 50)
1885	17	14.6
1886	11	14.9
1887	11	11.1
1888	6	7.8
1889	6	10.0
1890	4	7.8
1891	4	8.8
1892	6	11.7
1893	6	14.2
1894	9	11.1
1895	7	14.8
1896	11	12.4
1897	11	14.8
1898	9	11.1
1899	7	14.2
1900	6	11.2
1901	7	13.6
1902	6	10.8
1903	6	11.8
1904	3	12.0
1905	11	15.8
1906	10	11.5
1907	7	14.2
1908	10	14.9
1909	10	15.2

Three years after the founding of the association, Wacha bemoaned the lethargic spirit of Bombay politics when he wrote that "the spirit of political activity which was so visible and strong three years ago is nowhere."[33] The same point had been elaborated by another member of the Council, Narayan Chandavarkar:

Except when some big question is on the *tapis*, Bombay takes things easily ... Like the British lion, she is roused only when some exciting imperial topic gets to the front. And when she is roused at all, she puts forth all her strength, and then it is you see her at her best. But once the humdrum of ordinary

---

[33] *Ibid.*, October 5, 1888.

life is again on her, she retires into obscurity and you can hardly get her to take more than a passive interest in what passes around.[34]

From its inception the Bombay Presidency Association was plagued by the passivity of the majority of its members and the defections of some of its leading spirits. The majority of the Council failed to attend meetings or appeared infrequently. The real work of directing the Association fell on the hands of a few. The table indicates the attendance record of Council members who were sufficiently interested to attend at least one meeting:[35]

Number of meetings attended (1885–1909)	Number of individuals
150–205	1
100–149	1
80–99	2
60–79	5
40–59	11
20–39	21
10–19	18
1–9	42
TOTAL	101

Increasingly, the Bombay Presidency Association came to represent a small informal cabinet, which Wacha referred to as "our inner circle."[36] It met regularly, sometimes daily, at Pherozeshah Mehta's office. The most important members were Mehta, Wacha, N. V. Gokhle, Chimanlal Setalvad, and Daji Khare.

A more serious handicap to the work of the Association was the defection of some of the more influential figures. Sir Jamsetjee Jeejeebhoy, head of the Parsi community and the first president of the Association, resigned within the year of assuming office. The prominent Parsi historian, Dosabhoy Framjee Karaka, left the same year. They were joined five years later by the second president, Sir Dinshaw Petit, who increasingly grew "funky about political bodies."[37] Behramji

[34] *Indu Prakash,* January 2, 1888.
[35] To avoid distortion, the table does not include those who joined the Council after 1900. It also leaves out a sizeable number who failed to attend one meeting after their nomination. "Minutes of the Council of the Bombay Presidency Association," Vols. I–III.
[36] Wacha to Naoroji, October 7, 1899, and September 5, 1903.
[37] *Ibid.,* June 25, 1898.

Merwanji Malabari, the radical social reformer and Parsi editor of the *Indian Spectator*, resigned in 1895.[38] Malabari's resignation was prompted by the fear that it was dangerous for the Bombay society to be allied to a National Congress which was veering toward an extremist organization. It was impolitic for Bombay politicians, who had benefited from the British presence, to work with leaders such as Tilak, who was not only an outspoken critic of British rule but also an organizer of mass agitation outside the Congress meetings.

There were other reasons for the declining number of active members. Narayan Ganesh Chandavarkar, one of the joint secretaries for more than ten years, progressively came to view social reform and the theistic program of the *Prarthana Samaj* to be more pertinent to his interests than the purely political program of the Association. Others came to believe that political and social progress could best be achieved through alternative avenues of action. Some chose to work in caste associations and attempted to improve the social and educational status of their fellow-members. Others worked for industrial and commercial progress, considering that advance in these sectors would achieve more than the purely political program of the Bombay Presidency Association.

The shrinking elite support for the Association can best be illustrated by reference to the city press. Initially, the society could count on the support of the leading Indian newspapers of the city: Malabari's English-language *Indian Spectator*, the two Gujarati dailies, *Jame Jamshed* and *Bombay Samachar*, the weekly Anglo-Gujarati, *Kaiser-i-Hind*, and the Gujarati weekly, *Gujarati*, and the three most important Anglo-Marathi journals, *Indu Prakash*, *Native Opinion*, and *Subodha Patrika*. The only important Indian newspaper opposed to the Congress was the Anglo-Gujarati weekly, *Rast Goftar*, edited by the irascible Parsi, K. N. Kabraji.[39]

But in 1885 there began an erosion of this broad support. The *Jame Jamshed* and the *Indian Spectator* joined cause with the *Rast Goftar* in the 1890's, arguing that it was politically dangerous for Parsis and respectable businessmen to align themselves with the Congress. *Native Opinion* became a convert to the "left" by making common cause with the extremists. When Wacha, the editor of the English columns of the *Kaiser-i-Hind*, had a serious political disagreement with its owner, he

---

[38]Malabari attended thirteen meetings of the Council from 1885 to 1887.
[39]Wacha to Naoroji, June 4, 1889.

complained to Naoroji that save for the *Gujarati* no other Anglo-vernacular weekly "advocates our cause" and serves as a "counterblast to the *Rast*."[40] However, with the spread of militant nationalism in 1905, even the *Gujarati* was to waver. While the editor of the *Gujarati* columns, Iccharam Desai, supported the extremist program of swadeshi and boycott, the editor of the English columns, N.V. Gokhle, advocated more orthodox Bombay views.[41]

The declining elite support for the Bombay Presidency Association can further be indicated by the growing alienation of elite communities from the Bombay Congress cause. This trend was particularly evident in the politically aware Parsi community which accounted for one-third of the active members of the Council of the Association, although the community represented only one-twentieth of the city population. As one of the best-educated and advanced communities, the Parsis had long exercised a significant role in city politics well above their numerical strength.[42] The defection of some of the leading Parsi figureheads caused Wacha to complain in 1889 that he was "really ashamed" of his community, particularly its "so called leaders," which he characterized as "invertebrates."[43] The anti-Congress cause found a standard in the *Rast* and an influential figurehead in Sir Muncherjee Merwanji Bhownuggree, the second Parsi to be elected to the House of Commons, as a Conservative in 1895.[44] The supporters of Bhownuggree included the mill-owner, N. N. Wadia, the ex-Council member, Shapurji Bharucha, later to be a chairman of the Bombay Native Share and Stockbrokers' Association, and Hormusji Chichgur.[45] The majority of Parsis sought to avoid the Scylla of the trenchant critics of the Congress and the Charybdis of the protagonists of the Bombay Presidency Association by defining their position in apolitical terms. This was the gist of a 1904 letter in which Wacha

---

[40] Wacha to Naoroji, July 16, 1898, and May 7, 1904.

[41] "Annual Report of the Native Press of the Bombay Presidency for the Year 1906," GI, Home, Public, B1–2, August, 1907.

[42] The Parsis were one of the best-organized communities in the city. Despite their numbers they consistently returned more than one-quarter of the elected representatives to the Bombay Municipal Corporation. The percentage of the community who voted in municipal elections was higher than that of any other community.

[43] Wacha to Naoroji, November 15, 1889.

[44] Bhownuggree represented Bethnal Green from 1895 to 1900. The Association leaders were disheartened by Bhownuggree's election in 1895 because it coincided with the defeat of Dadabhai Naoroji, the first Indian to be elected to the House of Commons. Naoroji had been elected as a Liberal in 1893.

[45] Wacha to Naoroji, July 5, 1895, and November 7, 1896.

complained to Naoroji that the Parsis were becoming "intensely materialistic" and eschewing all forms of politics. "If Mehta and I were to retire," complained Wacha, there would not be a single Parsi "who could be pointed out to fill our vacancy."[46]

While Tilak was expanding the base of his party and appealing to an ever-broadening circle, the Bombay leaders were experiencing the very opposite. There were almost 300 members of the Bombay Presidency Association in 1885, and in 1886 an additional 95 were recruited, but ten years later there were only 500 members—350 resident and 150 mofussil. It was a frequent complaint of Wacha that many members were not sufficiently interested to pay their annual dues, ten rupees for townspeople and six for non-residents. Some members accumulated arrears of five years despite "all sorts of dunning." In 1898 dues amounting to 3,675 rupees had still to be realized from the three preceding years. Wacha anticipated that at least half this amount would have to be written off as a dead loss.[47] The unwillingness of members to pay arrears was a good index of Bombay political lethargy, for the number of elite figures who could not afford this amount must have been few.

There were several reasons for this erosion of elite support and for the declining vitality in the body politic, the Bombay Presidency Association. The basic cause was the natural timidity of the Bombay politician to participate in an organization which might be viewed with disfavour by the government. Because his pre-eminent position had been achieved under British aegis and to some extent with British support, the Bombay leader considered that any criticism of the Raj should be circumspect and moderate. He disliked the growing demands of the Congress politician; he disdained the militant tactics of the extremists. He questioned whether it was in the interests of the Bombay elites to antagonize the rulers and to work within the framework of a movement which had incurred official disfavour.

Another serious handicap to the work of the Association was the full-time business and professional interests of its members. Involved in entrepreneurial pursuits, active in joint stock companies, engaged in successful High Court practices, the typical elite had little time to devote to a political society. The Bombay Presidency Association was one of many political organizations in the city. The Bombay leader

---

[46]*Ibid.*, September 7, 1904.
[47]*Ibid.*, October 22, 1897, and October 8, 1898; *Indu Prakash*, April 12, 1886.

took part in other spheres of activity such as caste, municipal, and university politics. A nationalist society was simply one means of securing social, political, and economic advancement. By the 1890's it was widely doubted whether such an association provided the best means of protecting the essential interests of the Bombay elites.

One of the objects of Tilak, when he turned to Bombay City, was to contrast the shrinking influence of the Bombay Presidency Association with the burgeoning Deccan party. Tilak considered that the Bombay Congress party had two basic weaknesses: it represented a clique which did not have the active support of the elites within the city; and it lacked a constituency. Despite their wealth and influence, the Bombay leaders did not have the capacity and interest to develop a broader political base. Because they had no concern for mass political organization, they had no means of forcing the British to heed their demands.

It was ironic that, while the Bombay Presidency Association could count on the support of some of the leading citizens of the city, it could not count on the support of their communities. As the recognized presidential family of the Borah community, the authority of the Tyabji brothers to act as spokesmen for the community interests was unquestioned, but their authority did not necessarily extend to issues outside the immediate interests of the Borahs. The Tyabji brothers found it difficult to rally their co-religionists to the Congress cause. In an important letter to A. O. Hume in 1888, Badruddin suggested that, in view of the growing Muslim hostility, the Congress should be prorogued for five years, which would "give us an opportunity of reconsidering the whole position and if necessary retiring with dignity." While many educated Muslims were in favour of the Congress, Badruddin considered that the majority of the community were against it.[48] The situation was to worsen after 1893 rather than improve. The communal riots of 1893 and the rise of a militant Hindu party in the Deccan were not inclined to allay Muslim suspicions of the Congress party.

The members of the Bombay Presidency Association had a wide audience when they spoke as community leaders, but as secular nationalists, advocating the program of the Congress, their audience was small. Dedicated to a pan-regional and secular idea of nationalism,

---

[48]Badruddin Tyabji to A. O. Hume, October 27, 1888, Tyabji Papers, quoted in *Source Material BHFM,* II, 80–82.

holding to a loyalty which was above caste and community, and expressing themselves in decorous English, they formed a caste and community of their own. These nationalists represented no community and had no effective constituency.

The failure of the Association to establish a journal of its own was proof of this very fact. The need for an English-language journal to disseminate the views of the Bombay nationalist leaders was felt as early as 1883, when the *Voice of India* was launched to fill the void. But the *Voice* was never a practical or paying proposition. Within a year it was quietly absorbed by the *Indian Spectator*.[49] A second English-language journal, the *Champion*, was published in 1896 by an English member of the Council, W. A. Chambers, a Fabian socialist and a theosophist. The endeavour lasted only five years and collapsed in 1901. Thus the society had to rely on journals whose primary commitment was to communities, to regional or interest groups who were not always secular or pan-regional in their views. The *Kaiser-i-Hind*, for instance, catered chiefly to the Parsi community, whereas the *Gujarati* was more interested in the activities of the Gujarati Hindu population. Poona was more fortunately placed. For three decades the *Sarvajanik Sabha* had its own English-language journal. In the 1890's Tilak edited an English-language and a Marathi-language journal. By identifying themselves with a religion, a region, and to some extent with a community (the Brahmans), the Poona extremist leaders could count on the potential support of a much broader constituency.

Tilak's interest in Bombay was an attempt to demonstrate the superiority of a Poona-led movement to a Bombay-led one. The leaders of the two centers had long been rivals. It was sometimes suggested in Poona that Bombay leaders, because they were tainted by business interests and dependent on the British by virtue of their wealth, were not the fittest leaders of the Congress movement. The Poona Brahmans considered themselves more capable of directing the national movement because of their closer ties with society and tradition.

The Bombay leader had similar prejudices. He considered that he was better equipped to shape the New India by virtue of his pragmatic approach to politics and his constructive efforts to lay a firm foundation for industrial advancement. The Bombay nationalist prided himself on his vision of a secular India which was above caste, creed, or region.

---

[49] *East and West*, August, 1904, pp. 845–854.

He tended to regard his Poona counterpart as provincial and parochial in outlook.

This rivalry manifested itself in a number of spheres. The annual Industrial Conference, which was initiated by Poona leaders in 1891, was one such area. Several Bombay journals criticized the idea of convening an Industrial Conference in Poona. The *Gujarati* commented: "We think it is a mistake to hold the Industrial Conference every year at Poona instead of the centre of industrial and commercial activity, like Bombay; and if it is to grow and expand, like our Provincial Conferences and National Congresses, it must be removed from its orthodox home into more bracing and healthy climes, to imbibe new ideas and receive fresh vitality."[50]

The *Mahratta* defended the right of Poona to hold the conferences:

Poona is, we freely admit, not a manufacturing or commercial centre. It is ... rich in its political traditions. But it would be a mistake to infer from this that the city is incapable of leading a movement like the present one. Before capitalists can be induced to take part in any commercial or industrial movement, they and the public must be educated as regards the industrial and commercial requirements of the province; and there can be little doubt that Poona can do this work—and as a matter of fact has done it—with greater enthusiasm and ability than any other town in the presidency. Bombay, we speak of native Bombay, is richer than Poona, but the attention, as well as the time of our Bombay commercial men, is entirely taken up by their pursuits; and in consequence the work of formulating a scheme of commercial revival must be done by other hands.[51]

But the Bombay journals were not convinced by such reasoning or by Tilak's suggestion, at the second conference, that the caste system could be adapted to industrial needs.[52] Most of the Bombay press agreed with the *Kaiser-i-Hind*, which expressed its doubt that a system of "fossilised conservatism" could benefit industry.[53]

The Bombay Provincial Conference was another arena of conflict. The first conference, in 1888, was organized by Poona politicians who failed to consult Bombay. Wacha expressed his chagrin at this slight: "Provincial Conferences have been held in Bengal and Madras. Poona holds one today. Bombay has held herself aloof, as Poona has not deigned to consult her prior to calling the Assembly. I regret this

---

[50] *Gujarati*, September 22, 1895.
[51] *Mahratta*, September 6, 1891, and September 22, 1895.
[52] *Indian Spectator*, September 11, 1892; *Indu Prakash*, September 12, 1892.
[53] *Kaiser-i-Hind*, September 11, 1892.

incident. We should work in unity. However, I dare say next year that there will be more harmony."[54]

Prior to the 1890's such incidents were the exception rather than the rule. Ranade, the dominant figure of Poona in the 1870's and the 1880's, worked harmoniously with the Bombay leaders. His moderate creed was essentially similar to the Bombay viewpoint. At this time it was believed that the roles of the cities were complementary rather than antithetical. A Bombay newspaper defended the right of the Poona Brahmans to hold an industrial conference: "If Poona Brahmans are not men of action, that does not prevent them from being men of thought."[55] Narayan Chandavarkar went further to praise the contribution of Poona politicians whom he considered to be more reliable and steady in their political work than the Bombay politician who could be roused to significant effort only when the "political wind is blowing high." Chandavarkar's preference was for the "plodding and active politician of Poona," who was always at his post, working "unhasting and unresting."[56]

But with the rise of Tilak, city relations worsened. Wacha refused to accept the chairmanship of the 1891 provincial conference because he feared the activities of Tilak's party. Despite the urgings of Mehta, Telang, and Chandavarkar, Wacha declared that he was reluctant to accept the post: "There is a stormy orthodox element which would, I am informed, attempt to force the Age Consent affair on the Conference. They want that it should enter its protest against the Bill. I can't accept the Chair where the majority may drive in such a resolution unless I entirely exclude it from the programme."[57] Subsequent events did not alleviate Bombay anxieties concerning the new extremist party or its leader, whom Wacha referred to as a "hot fire-brand."[58] The Bombay leaders were distressed by what they believed to be the irreparable damage done to their cause by the Tilakites. "It is a pity," wrote Wacha in 1899, that "Tilak & his party do not yet perceive the potentiality of the mischief their own rash acts are leading to. Our enemies are waiting to see a big split in our camp ... But Tilak is already spoilt. They have made a hero of him and he has grown giddy. He thinks he is the coming Saviour of India."[59]

[54] Wacha to Naoroji, April 6, 1888.
[55] *Indian Spectator*, September 18, 1892.
[56] *Indu Prakash*, January 2, 1888.
[57] Wacha to Naoroji, May 9, 1891.
[58] *Ibid.*, November 15, 1899.
[59] *Ibid.*, April 15, 1899.

By this time, Pherozeshah Mehta, the acknowledged head of the Bombay Presidency Association, but a man who was sensitive to criticism, was not on speaking terms with Tilak. Communication between the two leaders was accomplished indirectly through Daji Khare and N. M. Samarth.[60] On at least two occasions, in 1898 and in 1905, Mehta stayed away from the annual Congress gatherings because he feared criticism from extremists such as Tilak and wished to disassociate himself from the adulation accorded to these men.[61]

[60] Although Khare was an active member of the Bombay Presidency Association, he remained a close friend of Tilak. They had met at Deccan College in the 1870's. Tilak usually stayed at Khare's house when he visited Bombay.

[61] C. Sankaran Nair to Mehta, December 10, 1898, Mehta Papers; N. V. Gokhle to G. K. Gokhale, December 22, 1905, Gokhale Papers, 205/8.

Chapter VIII

TILAK AND THE BOMBAY PROLETARIAT

> The infamous sentence pronounced by the British jackals against the Indian democrat Tilak ... evoked street demonstrations and a strike in Bombay. In India, too, the proletariat has already developed to conscious political mass struggle.[1]

> I gathered that every Hindu sympathized in his heart with Tilak and has not the slightest idea why ... The mill-hands ... say 'you have taken away our guru,' although they have not the faintest idea who or what Tilak is.[2]

By 1905 Tilak and the Poona politicians were ready to turn to Bombay City for the next mass movement. The mill-hands were a ready-made sphere for the political organizer because of their physical unity and lack of leadership. "If any patriot will make an industrious effort," suggested Paranjpe in 1905, it should not be difficult to "get up a mass meeting of 25,000 mill operatives."[3] Prior to this time, Tilak's interests had been confined to Poona and the Deccan. Since his visits to Bombay City had been few and far between, his knowledge of the Bombay political scene was limited. Although Tilak wrote to Mehta in 1893 that Bombay needed a bold leader to safeguard the rights of Hindus, he was not then prepared to step into the breach, as he was fully occupied organizing the festivals and the famine campaign.

During this period Tilak opposed the factory legislation introduced by the government. The two factory acts of 1881 and 1891 were modest in scope and covered the most basic labour demands such as the fencing of dangerous machinery, the limitations on the working hours of women and children, and the institution of a weekly day of rest.[4]

[1] V. I. Lenin, *The National-Liberation Movement in the East* trans. M. Levin (Moscow, 1957), pp. 14–15, quoted in Reisner and Goldberg, pp. 660–661.
[2] Sir George Clarke to Lord Morley, July 31, 1908, Morley Papers, MSS Eur. D 573/42E, IOL.
[3] *Kal*, October 6, 1905, *BRNP*, 1905, No. 40.
[4] Bipan Chandra, *The Rise and Growth of Economic Nationalism in India* (New Delhi, 1966), pp. 323–352.

Tilak disapproved of factory legislation because he believed, like other nationalists, that it was "basically inspired not by a philanthropic feeling for the oppressed Indian workers but by Lancashire's desire to throttle its Indian rival" and that it would lead to the ruination of Indian industry.[5] Tilak's views were shaped also by his interest in industrial advancement. Partly to add to his income and partly to contribute to Indian industrial development, the young Tilak borrowed 5,000 rupees to establish a cotton-ginning factory at Latur in Hyderabad State.[6] Thus Tilak was more interested in championing the cause of Indian industry than in improving the conditions of the Indian worker. He was not alone in this position; such arguments were enunciated in other circles of Poona. The moderately inclined *Quarterly Journal of the Poona Sarvajanik Sabha* maintained that there was not "the least justification for a legislative enactment to regulate factory labour."[7]

Tilak was more prepared to espouse the cause of labour when it came into conflict with the rulers. A Signallers' Association of the Great Indian Peninsula Railway had been formed in 1897 with the assistance of three Tilakites, N. C. Kelkar, D. R. Bapat, and S. L. Joshi. Kelkar was the legal advisor to the Association. They helped to represent the workers' demands to the company. Because of a stalemate in negotiations the 638 members of the Association decided to go on strike in 1899.[8] Just before the strike the signallers requested the advice and assistance of Tilak and Kelkar, but both refused to act because they feared that if the strike were directed by a Poona Brahman it would be discredited.[9] However, the *Mahratta* and the *Kesari* warmly supported this cause.[10] The strikers then secured the gratuitous services of the Bombay Presidency Association lawyer, Hari Sitaram Dixit. Despite the active financial assistance of members of the Bombay Presidency Association, who subscribed at least 9,000 rupees for the signallers,[11] the strike was eventually defeated.

Tilak turned his attention to Bombay City in 1905 to promote the dual concepts of swadeshi and boycott. The movements had been

---

[5]*Ibid.*; *Mahratta,* March 13, 1881, December 23, 1888.
[6]Keer, *Lokamanya Tilak,* p. 58.
[7]*QJPSS,* IV, No. 1 (July, 1881), p. 39.
[8]Bombay Police Abstracts, May 9, 1899, para. 646, May 16, 1899, para. 679, May 25, 1899, para. 716.
[9]*Ibid.,* June 2, 1899, para. 760.
[10]*Mahratta,* May 7 and 14, 1899; *Kesari,* June 6, 13, and 20, 1899.
[11]Bombay Police Abstracts, June 1, 1899, para. 764.

popularized in Bengal as a means of protest against the partition of the province in 1905. The true patriot was exhorted to buy only swadeshi articles and to boycott foreign goods. The movement was both political, in that it was conceived as a means of protest, and economic, in that it was argued that it would lead to a revival of Indian industry.

The highlight of the western Indian movement was a bonfire in Poona City on October 8, 1905. A crowd of 5,000 listened to speeches by Tilak and Paranjpe on the necessity of the movement and then ceremoniously consigned foreign-made articles of every description— clothes, velvet caps, umbrellas, lead pencils—to the bonfire.[12] When it burst into flame, one Maratha paper suggested that "the eyes of the spectators sparkled with patriotism"; the "prolonged impotency" of the Maratha people had been destroyed and the breasts of the onlookers "throbbed with the hopes of future greatness."[13] Tilak then called the assembled group to walk three times around the fire, to apply ashes to their temples, and to take an oath never to purchase English cloth even at the risk of having to go naked. The occasion ended with three cheers for Shivaji.[14]

For weeks the swadeshi spirit swept through Maharashtra. Students and businessmen rivalled each other in the ingenuity of their swadeshi efforts. Fifty students at the Rajaram High School refused to write examinations because the paper was foreign-made.[15] Businessmen set up swadeshi stores and banks, and planned factories to produce everything from paper to matches. To direct their enthusiasm into proper channels, the *Kesari* published detailed information suggesting how the would-be capitalist could establish a factory. It listed the amount of capital and raw materials required and the most promising locations for production. The *Kesari* advised Indian businessmen to produce goods such as matches, bangles, belts, glass, and cigarettes.[16] A recent commentator, to indicate the extent of the popular feeling for swadeshi, noted that seventy-five prostitutes met at Nasik and resolved to use only swadeshi articles.[17]

However, for the movement to assume significant proportions it was imperative for Tilak to recruit Bombay merchants and manufac-

---

[12] *Source Material BHFM*, II, 609–610.
[13] *Bhala*, October 11, 1905, *BRNP*, 1905, No. 41.
[14] *Ibid.*
[15] *Source Material BHFM*, II, 606–607.
[16] *Kesari*, October 17, 1905.
[17] A note in the records of MHFM.

turers to the cause. To accomplish this, Tilak attempted to persuade Dinshaw Wacha to exert influence on the mill-owners to supply dhotis to the Indian market at moderate rates, but the mill-owners refused to comply with this request.[18]

Dinshaw Wacha, the spokesman for the manufacturers, was critical of the extremist program of boycott and by what he described as the "economic Cheap Jacks who are now vociferously hawking the Swadeshi Shibboleth" in certain parts of the country. Wacha considered that the mill-owners were the true exponents of swadeshi because they had attempted to promote industrial advancement and to improve the material condition of the people for more than thirty years. The weakness of the Poona and Bengal agitation was that it gave swadeshi a "political colour" which jeopardized the support of the government and the European mercantile community. "Swadeshi," according to Wacha, should be a platform on which all can meet, "official and non-official, European and Indian, the political agitator and the quiet worker."[19]

Tilak was not discouraged by the rebuff from the mill-owners and launched a society in Bombay, the *Swadeshi Vastu Prarcharini Sabha* (Society to Promote the Use of Swadeshi Goods), to popularize swadeshi in Bombay. In one year the society held ten public meetings which usually attracted several thousand people.[20] The speakers included Tilak, Paranjpe, the nationalist leader of the Berar, Dada-

---

[18]*Source Material BHFM*, II, 217; A. P. Kannangara, "Indian Millowners and Indian Nationalism," *Past & Present*, No. 40 (July, 1968), pp. 147–164. It was argued in this article that the manufacturers had little to gain from the swadeshi movement and nothing from the boycott program.

[19]*Kaiser-i-Hind*, December 23, 1906; *Gujarati*, June 3, 1906; *Indian Textile Journal*, July, 1908, p. 315.

[20]*Mahratta*, September 23, 1906. The society held the following meetings in the first year of operation:

Date	President	Number Present
August 26, 1905	G. S. Khaparde	1,000
September 1, 1905	M. R. Bodas	1,500
October 15, 1905	B. G. Tilak	8,000
October 25, 1905	Ali Mohammed Bhimji	3,000
November 8, 1905	Daji Khare	3,000
November 18, 1905	Dr. M. G. Deshmukh	4,000
November 26, 1905	C. V. Vaidya	3,000
February 26, 1906	Daji Khare	2,500
March 18, 1906	V. P. Vaidya	2,500
April 1, 1906	Vasanji Khimjee	4,000

saheb Ganesh Shridhar Khaparde, the Khoja, Ali Mohammed Bhimji, a retired chief justice of Gwalior, Rao Bahadur Chintaman Vinayak Vaidya, and the Karhada Brahman editor of the Marathi-language *Bhala*, Bhaskar Balwant Bhopatkar. By the time of the first annual general meeting, forty-four factories and joint stock companies had been set up in the region. This provided proof, according to Kelkar, that the swadeshi movement was "not now a farce, but a reality: the thin end of the wedge of Indian industrial revival has now been successfully driven in."[21]

There was an element of truth in Kelkar's assertion, since some of the leading capitalists of Bombay City associated themselves with the swadeshi cause. The establishment of the Bombay Swadeshi Co-operative Stores Company Limited, with a capital outlay of 250,000 rupees, on December 11, 1905, typified this co-operation. Among its directors were four prominent Bombay mill-owners, Ratanji Tata, Goverhandas Khatau, Manmohandas Ramji, and Dwarkadas Dharamsi, and the Poona politician *Balasaheb* Natu.[22] The support of such leading Parsi and Gujarati business magnates demonstrated Tilak's capacity to transcend regional and community boundaries. However, there were limits to this non-Maharashtrian support. The Bombay mill-owners participated in a program sponsored by Tilak, but they did not join Tilak's party. Tilak's followers included very few Gujaratis and Parsis. None of the lieutenants or secondary leadership were from these groups.

Although many of the smaller enterprises, lacking the necessary capital and technical advice, collapsed after the initial surge of enthusiasm had waned, the swadeshi movement did contribute to Indian economic development. It helped in a modest way to create a larger market for Indian goods, and thus provided an incentive for capitalistic undertakings.

However, the Poona leaders were more interested in forms of political protest than in the slow and unspectacular development of Indian industry. In its political aspects the Bombay boycott movement was a failure. Whereas Bengal could boast of a sizeable decline in Manchester imports for the one year after 1905, Bombay witnessed an increase.[23] Even in Bengal the success of the boycott movement was

[21] *Ibid.*, September 30, 1906.
[22] *Ibid.*, September 23, 1906.
[23] *Kaiser-i-Hind*, February 24, 1907. Statistics of cotton goods (figures in millions) exported from Lancashire to three regions of India in 1905 and 1906 (published by the Manchester Chamber of Commerce).

temporary. By 1908 Manchester had reasserted itself and the imports to India of all the principal articles soared above the 1905 totals.[24]

Owing to the limited political prospects for the swadeshi and boycott movements, Tilak turned to the more promising field of labour. In an attempt "to educate the mill-hands," Tilak addressed a number of labour rallies in Bombay City in 1907 and 1908. He pointed out that the swadeshi movement would benefit not only the Brahmans but the whole of Indian society. The employees would benefit from any general improvement in Indian industry. He also urged the mill-hands to abstain from liquor, because the liquor industry was an important source of revenue for the government.[25]

The dual programs of swadeshi and temperance represented unlikely issues with which to politicize the Bombay proletariat since the workers were not yet imbued with any sense of nationalism or hostility to the colonial government. The mill-hand was fond of toddy and, according to one commission of the day, spent more money on liquor than on food and clothing combined.[26] Swadeshi represented a long-term pious hope in the future of Indian industry. The immediate beneficiaries of a successful movement would be the mill-owners rather than the operatives.

The Poona politicians rested their appeal to labour on surer grounds

Exports to:	1905 Yards	1905 Pounds	1906 Yards	1906 Pounds
Bombay	90.86	8.47	91.01	8.63
Madras	13.14	1.43	14.62	1.64
Bengal	127.96	11.61	120.93	11.20

[24]Statistics indicating the values of the five principal articles imported into India from 1903 to 1908 in millions of rupees.

	1903–04	1904–05	1905–06	1906–07	1907–08
Sugar	59.36	69.03	77.75	87.38	92.27
Hardware, cutlery	23.28	23.80	22.67	26.61	31.65
Apparel	19.96	22.40	22.18	21.12	25.83
Glass	9.92	11.26	11.25	12.11	14.45
Carts, carriages	4.35	5.50	7.68	9.25	11.80
	116.87	131.99	141.53	156.47	176.00

V. G. Kale, *Indian Industrial and Economic Problems* (3d ed., Madras, 1921), p. 123; R. K. Prabhu, "The Breakdown of Boycott—A Reply," *Modern Review*, V (February, 1909), 162–166.

[25]*Source Material BHFM*, II 252–254, 258–259.

[26]*Indian Textile Journal*, XIX (April, 1909), 235.

when they supported an abortive one-week strike of the postal peons for higher wages in 1906. Paranjpe donated twenty-five rupees to the strikers' fund.[27] In supporting the peons, Tilak pointed out that they were only exercising their right of combination and adopting tactics which were regarded as a "legitimate weapon of agitation in Europe." By considering strikes "illegal," the government, the largest employer of labour in India, had deliberately shut its eyes to the plight of the labouring classes.[28] Tilak also suggested that nationalist leaders should consider the feasibility of working within the framework of strikes:

Recently there have been many strikes. Opinions will vary as to whether the leaders should or should not turn to good account this tendency of the people to develop their powers of combination. The Anglo-Indian papers will always criticize us if we support the people. It is unlawful to make strikes. Strikes develop when reason fails. I am extremely sorry that the Bombay people did not help the postmen in their strike in a way in which they should have. Those that strike do not mean disrespect. The Postal Department is in the position of our servant. It is intended to benefit the people only.[29]

The climax of Tilak's mass movements occurred in 1908, in the form of a strike which represented a spontaneous protest against Tilak's arrest, sentence, and deportation to Mandalay. For six days the metropolis was paralyzed. Most of the city mills were forced to close down. The organizers of the grain, cloth, share and freight markets, and the cotton exchange followed suit out of sympathy for Tilak. Because the mill-hands roamed about the city in gangs, the military was called out. In the ensuing battles at least sixteen people were killed. This was the high point of Tilak's popularity. Although he was spirited away to Gujarat, the solid foundations of his mass political agitation had at last appeared to bear worth-while political fruit.

Tilak was arrested on June 24, 1908. He was prosecuted on the basis of several of his articles which seemed to condone revolutionary tactics. They were written at a time of growing ferment in Maharashtra and revolutionary violence in Bengal, which manifested itself in the assassination of two Englishwomen at Muzafferpur on April 30, 1908. By deporting the chief architect of mass political agitation and the foremost exponent of violence, the British hoped to stem the rising tide of extremism.

[27]Bombay Police Abstracts, August 20, 1906, para. 646.
[28]*Kesari*, August 21, 1906.
[29]Bombay Police Abstracts, September 17, 1906, para. 736 (a).

The Bombay Governor, Sir George Clarke (1907–13),[30] did not anticipate that the Tilak conviction would create serious unrest in Bombay City. It was his belief that, "outside of the student class" and "a section of the Brahmins," Tilak's following did not amount to much.[31] The mill-hands were the one uncertain political factor. Because they were gullible and excitable, they could be roused by outside agitators.[32]

Despite his optimism, the Governor took every precaution. During the trial the court was guarded by two hundred European policemen and thirty Indian mounted police. A squadron of Indian cavalry and half a battalion of British troops were called up in readiness. To provide maximum security, Tilak was housed in the High Court for the duration of the ten-day trial. The proceedings began on July 13 and lasted until July 22. For five of the eight days in which the Court was in session, Tilak was permitted to make his own defence—a plea which lasted more than twenty-one hours. Tilak took advantage of the public platform provided by the Court and the "extraordinary latitude" permitted by the Judge and the Advocate General to launch what one official later referred to as "a vehement political attack on British administration."[33] The marathon speech has since been acclaimed, by a more impartial commentator, as "the strongest affirmation of the freedom of the press in the annals of Indian history."[34]

Throughout the trial Bombay City witnessed sporadic violence. On July 17 the mill-hands struck in twenty-eight of the eighty-five mills of the city. They then proceeded to break the windows and furniture of other mills where the operatives were forced to work. On the same day three Europeans, trapped in a partially wrecked liquor store, were rescued from the fury of a mob by the timely intervention of the cavalry.[35] However, by the last day of the trial the mill-hands had resumed work. The Governor, weary after the long trial and relieved by the limited occurrences of violence in Bombay City, commented

[30]Sir George Sydenham Clarke (1843–1933), Royal Military Academy, Lecturer, Royal Engineering College, 1871–80, Secretary to Colonial Defence Committee, 1885–92, member of War Office Reconstruction Committee (1904) and Committee of Imperial Defence, Governor of Victoria, 1901–03, created baron in 1903.
[31]Clarke to Morley, July 10, 1908.
[32]*Ibid.*, July 24, 1908.
[33]*Source Material BHFM*, II, 271.
[34]Wolpert, *Tilak and Gokhale* (Berkeley, 1962), p. 221.
[35]H. G. Gell, Commissioner of Police, Bombay to BG, August 27, 1908, quoted in *Source Material BHFM*, II, 256–275; I. M. Reisner and N. M. Goldberg (eds.), *Tilak and the Struggle for Indian Freedom* (New Delhi, 1966), pp. 545–628.

to the Secretary of State that despite great efforts to induce the mill-hands to riot, they had not exhibited much interest in the Tilak case.[36]

The Governor's assessment proved premature. One day after Tilak's sentence the city came to a standstill and remained so for six days. Work was stopped in the large majority of the eighty-five mills. Gujarati and Parsi businessmen closed their stores for six days out of sympathy for Tilak's six-year imprisonment. The important markets of the city ground to a halt. Whole streets were decorated with black bunting. Tilak's photograph was prominently displayed in store windows throughout the city.

For several days gangs of mill-hands, numbering in the thousands, roamed throughout the city. The objects of their displeasure were predictable: they stoned the police, Europeans, and the establishment of any businessmen who did not observe the six-day strike. The violence was accompanied by the shouts of "Tilak Maharaj-ki-jai, Chhatrapati Tilak Maharaj-ki-jai" (Victory to King Tilak, Victory to King Tilak).[37] In similar vein a Gujarati pamphlet, widely circulated throughout the city, declared that "Mahatma Tilak is our life and soul."[38] It was but a short step to the apotheosis of the politician: some mill-hands declared Tilak to be an incarnation of Vishnu.[39]

It was with extreme difficulty that these gangs were dispersed. The mobs were not daunted by warnings or by the approach of the military, which they greeted with a volley of stones. The mobs retreated when the military opened fire, but frequently regrouped in other areas of the city. The intensity of the strike may be gauged by a *Times of India* report of an encounter on the afternoon of July 24:

... about 2 o'clock in the afternoon at the Currey Road Station ... some Europeans, who happened to pass the road at the time, were followed and stoned by a crowd of mill-hands and for protection they ran to the station. The mob stormed the station and threw stones, smashing glass windows ... All efforts to persuade them to disperse proved futile and the police and volunteers had to open fire ... the rioters dispersed leaving 5 killed and 12 wounded.[40]

In the course of the demonstrations several attempts were made to

[36]Clarke to Morley, July 24, 1908.
[37]Ram Gopal, *Lokamanya Tilak: A Biography* (Bombay, 1956), p. 334.
[38]*Times of India*, August 1, 1908.
[39]Clarke to Morley, July 24, 1908.
[40]*Times of India*, July 25, 1908, quoted in V. B. Karnik, *Strikes in India* (Bombay, 1967), p. 49.

disrupt the transportation of the city. One group placed large slabs of stone on the tram tracks. Another partially wrecked the Currey Road Station and delayed the Poona Mail train, which was carrying reinforcements to the Bombay garrison. The mill-hands were joined by workers from the nearby railway workshops. But by July 29 the strike had spent itself and the city returned to normal. Faced with military reinforcements, heavy rains, and economic deprivation, the mill-hands returned to work.

Assessing the disturbances, the Governor was forced to admit that he was surprised by the extent of support for Tilak within the city. "The conspiracy in this part of India," he added, was "better organized than I thought."[41] To the Governor, the most puzzling aspect of the strike was the sympathy of the wealthy Gujarati and Parsi merchants for Tilak. He concluded that it was due to their timidity and political ignorance. It was paradoxical that, while they recognized the "necessity of our rule," they felt a "sentimental regard for Tilak." The problem, he concluded, was that the leading citizens of Bombay "do not lead" and wielded no significant political influence. Clarke also stated that the moderate party of Bombay was now clearly "intimidated" and its members were "residing in their tents." They had "no platform" and "no propaganda" to match the appeal of the extremists.[42]

In accounting for the demonstrations, officials emphasized the charismatic personality and organizing talent of Tilak. It was considered fortunate that he had been removed from the scene, for he would "no doubt in time have had a large organized body of mill-hands at his disposal." It was the opinion of the same officials that Tilak's lieutenants lacked the talent and ability to continue this work.[43]

Historians have elaborated Tilak's 1908 achievement. It has been argued that the strike indicated the broad support for the Tilak party. It underlined the success of Tilak's attempts to enlist groups outside the Congress. Tilak was able to appeal to both Brahmans and non-Brahmans, capitalists and labourers, Maharashtrians and non-Mahrashtrians.[44] Tilak's Bombay activities have been vigorously applauded by a group of Soviet historians who have developed the myth of the proletarian-minded Tilak. They have amplified the interpretation of Lenin, who hailed the "democrat Tilak" as a leader who contributed

---

[41]Clarke to Morley, July 31, 1908.
[42]*Ibid.*
[43]*Ibid.*; *Source Material BHFM*, II, 259.
[44]For instance, Ram Gopal, pp. 332–340.

to the rising political consciousness of the Indian proletariat.[45] It was their contention that the extremists, by enlisting the Bombay proletariat in the national-liberation movement, helped to awaken the political awareness of labour:

> They [the extremists] organised the first trade unions, led the workers' struggles for their rights and better conditions, at the same time carrying on anti-colonial agitation among them. They also introduced to the Bombay working class certain socialist ideas they had drawn primarily from the experience of the Russian working class. Thus, by some aspects of their activity the Tilakites were objectively instrumental in awakening the class consciousness of the Indian proletariat.[46]

While it is evident that Tilak discredited the Bombay nationalist party in its own territory, it is less clear whether he enlisted labour to the nationalist cause or helped to awaken the class identity of the proletariat. Because he was a Poona politician, Tilak had a limited understanding of urban conditions and the aspirations of labour. Because he wished to build up Indian industry and gain the support of Indian manufacturers, Tilak avoided the important areas of conflict between labour and management. He looked instead for broader issues which would dramatize the conflict between the rulers and the ruled rather than the tensions within Indian society.

But Tilak took a dubious labour stand on the critical question of the day—the legislation of a twelve-hour day. The issue came to a head in 1905 after the introduction of electric lighting in many of the Bombay mills. The mill-owner could now extend the dawn-to-dusk work day to fifteen or sixteen hours. While some of the hardier operatives welcomed the additional wages, the majority opposed the longer hours.[47] Beginning in 1905 there was a rash of strikes against the electric light, the symbol of longer hours. The strikes culminated in a riot in October, 1905, in which "mobs of operatives roamed from one late-working mill to another, calling out workers, throwing rocks, breaking windows and, in one case, destroying the attendance sheets and other records kept by the timekeeper."[48] Sporadic strikes against the hours of work continued until the legislation of the twelve-hour day in 1911.[49]

[45]Lenin pp. 14–15.
[46]Reisner and Goldberg, pp. 660–661.
[47]Karnik, *Strikes in India* (Bombay, 1967), pp. 31–33; Reisner and Goldberg, pp. 538–541.
[48]Morris David Morris, *The Emergence of an Industrial Labor Force in India: A Study of the Bombay Cotton Mills*, 1854–1947 (California, 1965), p. 105.
[49]Karnik, pp. 33–34.

Although some of the mill-owners agreed to the principle of a twelve-hour day, it was not observed in most of the mills. It was left to Lovat Frazer, editor of the *Times of India*, to champion the cause of the "Bombay slaves." In a series of articles in the *Times* of September, 1905, Frazer castigated the mill-owners for their "cold-blooded inhumanity" and their attempts to exploit the mill-hands in the interests of profit.[50] The *Times* campaign received the endorsement of the *Maratha Aikya Icchu Sabha* (Society for the Promotion of Unity among Marathas). Although the primary purpose of the society was to encourage education among the "backward" classes,[51] it organized a meeting of some eight to ten thousand Maratha workers who demanded the legislation of a twelve-hour day.[52] While the *Sabha* did not represent the Bombay proletariat (the working classes had no effective organization or leadership in 1905), it did reflect the prevailing opinion on the question of hours. The Factory Commission of 1907 concluded that the great majority of operatives were in favour of a twelve-hour day.[53]

The Poona reaction to the twelve-hour day was predictable. Since the agitation was championed by Lovat Frazer, a spokesman of Anglo-Indian opinion, and since it was timed to coincide with the inauguration of the swadeshi movement, the *Mahratta* could only ridicule the position of the *Times* as a "hollow ebullition based more on imagination than on facts." It was ironic, argued the *Mahratta*, that the English editor should be attracted by "so-called slavery of the mill-hands, when slavery of a more real and crushing kind is to be met with in so many other walks of Indian life" mainly as a result of foreign rule.[54] Tilak took the argument one step farther when he maintained that government employees in the Postal and Telegraph Departments and labourers in the tea plantations of Assam and Ceylon were "actually in worse conditions" than the Bombay mill-hands.[55] Far from being slaves, the *Mahratta* added, most of the workers were content with their situation and preferred longer hours.[56] The *Times*

[50] *Times of India*, September 13 and 28, 1905.
[51] Reisner and Goldberg, p. 418.
[52] *Times of India*, September 25, 1905. The meeting, chaired by Rao Bahadur Vithalrao Krishnaji Wandekar, included the following speakers: N. G. Powar (Secretary of the *Sabha*), D. B. Pavdar, K. A. Keluskar, Dr. L. B. Dhargalkar, V. D. Bhogle, S. Y. Malwarkar, K. A. Karegaumker.
[53] *Indian Textile Journal*, XIX (August, 1909), 366.
[54] *Mahratta*, October 1, 1905.
[55] Bombay Police Abstracts, October 16, 1905, para. 984 (b).
[56] *Mahratta*, October 1, 15, and 22, 1905. The Indian Factory Commission came to a

of India campaign was a thinly disguised effort launched by interests of the Lancashire cotton manufacturers and designed to undermine the swadeshi movement.[57]

While exposing the contradictions inherent in the position of the *Times of India,* Tilak was revealing the anomalies in his own labour stand. As a democrat and a social reformer, he sympathized with the plight of the non-Brahman peasant and urban masses. But as a nationalist he looked for issues which would dramatize the conflict between the rulers and the ruled. Movements which would disturb relations between labour and management or between Brahmans and non-Brahmans could only impede the progress of the national movement.

The most realistic conclusion concerning the 1908 strike was suggested by a recent commentator who questions Tilak's contribution to the emerging consciousness of labour and casts doubt on the significance of the 1908 strike:

> The strike which shook Bombay was a spontaneous and elemental outburst. It had no organization and no leaders. The conviction of Lokamanya Tilak and the sentence inflicted upon him was merely the spark which lighted the fire. The fire of discontent, anger and resentment was smouldering since long. The strike was not merely a protest against the harsh treatment meted out to an eminent patriot, but it was in essence a revolt against the unbearable conditions of work and life to which labour had been subjected since the beginning of the industrial era. The revolt was, however, a momentary affair. It blazed for a few days and then died without leaving a trace. There was no repetition of that revolutionary action for many years. It left no memories; it left no landmark. Workers were soon back at work as if nothing happened.[58]

Indian communists, unlike their Soviet counterparts, have tended to agree with this assessment. R. Palme Dutt, one of the most prolific of Indian communist writers, has pointed out some of the limitations of the *Lokamanya's* leadership. Although he briefly mentions Lenin's 1908 assessment of the "democrat" Tilak, Dutt stresses the "reactionary" elements af Tilak's leadership. It was a mistake in tactics for "radical nationalists" such as Tilak to align their opposition to imperialism with the "most reactionary forces of Orthodox Hinduism" in the 1890's. Similarly, the revival of Indian nationalism in 1905 was

---

different conclusion. It found that the majority of the operatives were in favour of a twelve-hour day.

[57] *Ibid.*; *Rast Goftar,* September 17, 1905.
[58] Karnik, pp. 52–53.

socially reactionary because the "Orthodox Nationalists, while building on this religious basis for their argument, could derive no weapon or plan of action therefrom save the universal weapon of the desperate, but impotent, petty-bourgeois elements divorced from any mass movement—individual terrorism." The swadeshi and boycott campaigns, while tactically more plausible, were expressions of the "bourgeois character of the movement."[59]

Tilak's activities after his release from prison in 1914 provide further proof of the limited impact of Poona politicians on the Bombay proletariat. The infrequent visits of the *Lokamanya* to Bombay, from 1914–1920, seem to provide an admission that the mass proletariat "base" of 1908 was the most a nationalist could expect from the city. On the one reported occasion in which Tilak again addressed the Bombay mill-hands, on November 25, 1919, he expressed the same ambivalence of a nationalist who sympathized with labour. Tilak advised the Bombay workers to follow the example of English labour and to form trade unions: "the stronger these were, the sooner they would obtain their rights." But he could not hide his nationalistic bias when he suggested that the distinction between men as labourers and as masters was false and had originated in Britain. In fact, all Indians were labourers, or more correctly "Sudras" and "slaves"; the British were the only masters. Tilak finished on the note that the working classes should sink all their differences with Indian management and make a combined effort to emancipate themselves from the "Bureaucrats or white Brahmins."[60]

During the last years of Tilak's life there were some indications that he was moving to the left. On one occasion Tilak suggested to an official that it was the duty of the Government "to make the mill-owners give better wages and to introduce legislation for the purpose, if necessary" and to establish a "profiteering law or real control of prices."[61] This sympathy for labour was further evident in the 1920 Manifesto of the Congress Democratic Party, drafted by Tilak, which advocated "a fair share of the fruits of labour, a fair minimum wage, reasonable hours of work, decent house accommodation" for the working classes.[62] On his 1918–19 visit to Britain, Tilak established

[59] R. Palme Dutt, *India Today* (2d ed., Bombay, 1949), pp. 304–309.
[60] *Source Material BHFM*, II, 317–319.
[61] *Ibid.*, II, 321.
[62] *Mahratta*, August 18, 1920. The Manifesto also called for "nationalisation of railway tariffs by legislation with a view to assist industrial development and to abolish privileges and favouritism in their working."

close links with the leaders of the Labour Party, contributed 2,000 pounds to its coffers, and addressed groups such as the Fabian Society, the Labour Conference, and the Trades Union Conference.[63] Aware of the support of the Labour Party for nationalist movements, Tilak realized the important role which Labour might play in the advancement of the Congress. It is difficult to determine the impact of the Labour Party on Tilak other than to note that the mature Tilak acquired some of the rhetoric of the left, and referred to the British Indian government as "capitalistic."[64]

Tilak's awareness of the left was increased by contact with the Fabian Socialist, Joseph Baptista (1864–1930), who was one of Tilak's chief lieutenants from 1914 to 1920. From the time when Baptista publicly defended Tilak's conduct in the 1907 Surat Congress and assisted him in the 1908 trial, there arose a close friendship between the two which grew over the years. A Goan Christian,[65] Cambridge-educated,[66] a successful lawyer in the Bombay High Court, and a Bombay municipal corporator from 1901, Baptista was an important asset to the Tilak party. Widely travelled in Europe, he was a friend of the influential. Lord Willingdon knew him "quite well" and liked him,[67] while Pherozeshah Mehta hoped that his own "mantle" would fall on Baptista.[68] Unlike many of Tilak's followers, Baptista was more at home in the modern and cosmopolitan city of Bombay than in Poona. One of the oldest members of the Fabian Society (he joined it in Cambridge in 1886), he took a keen interest in trade-union movements in Bombay City and campaigned for an eight-hour work day, increased wages, and improved conditions for labour. He became chairman of the first All India Trade Union Congress of 1921, president of the second Congress in 1922, and by this time was president of "almost all the Trade Unions in Bombay."[69]

But there were limits to Tilak's leftist leanings, as indicated by a 1920 address on the "Bolshevik peril" in which he suggested that

[63] *India*, May 23, September 12 and 19, 1919; *Source Material BHFM*, II, 313.
[64] *Source Material BHFM*, II, 314.
[65] Baptista came from a Maratha family which had been converted by the Portuguese to Christianity in the 16th century. *Mahratta*, September 21, 1930.
[66] L. C. E. (Bombay, 1887); B.A., LL.B. (Cambridge, 1899); Barrister-at-law (1899).
[67] Lord Willingdon to Lord Montagu, July 18, 1917, Montagu Collection, MSS Eur. D 523/18. Lord Willingdon was Liberal member for Hastings (1900–06), Bodwin Division of Cornwall (1906–10), Governor of Bombay (1913–19), Governor of Madras (1919–24), Governor-general of Canada (1926–30), Viceroy of India (1931–36).
[68] A comment made by Mehta in 1913. *Mahratta*, September 16, 1923.
[69] *Ibid*.

"India need have no fears. Bolshevism preaches equality of all and nobleness of manual labour. We already have these doctrines in a more refined and truly spiritual manner. Bolshevism, as it is preached in the West, cannot succeed in India. Let us stick fast to our Vedanta and all our desires shall be fulfilled."[70] However, it is as anachronistic to judge Tilak purely in terms of labour leadership as it is to accept the myth of the proletarian-minded *Lokmanya*. As a nationalist, Tilak was more concerned with the ongoing struggle against the British, as a political realist, he was content to establish the rudiments of a mass political party. Judged in these terms Tilak's Bombay campaign was a success, and 1908 probably represented the high point of the *Lokmanya's* career. He was the master of two cities, the most powerful politician in western India and perhaps in the whole of India. The Bombay moderate leadership, discredited in its own territory, was so disheartened by the signs of extremist support that they did not attempt to organize a provincial conference until 1915, eight years after the previous one.[71]

Tilak's bold siege of Bombay City helped to broaden the basis of his party. During the swadeshi campaign he gained the support of the Surti Bania, Iccharam Surajaram Desai, the influential editor of the weekly newspaper *Gujarati*.[72] Tilak received endorsement from some other non-Maharashtrian quarters, notably the Khoja, Ali Mohammed Bhimji, and Baptista. He also demonstrated that on a particular issue he could appeal to significant Gujarati and Parsi businessmen. Meanwhile Tilak consolidated his strength among the Maharashtrians of Bombay City. An addition to the party was the former Chief Justice of Gwalior, Rao Bahadur Chintaman Vinayak Vaidya (1861–1938), an author and historian.

Within Poona City there was a corresponding expansion of Tilak's political base. Lakshman Balwant Bhopatkar (1880–1960) was, like Baptista, an important asset, and was to become one of Tilak's principal lieutenants after 1914.[73] Following the example of Tilak, Bhopatkar

[70] Keer, *Lokmanya Tilak*, p. 429.

[71] From 1907 to 1915 there were only two provincial conferences, both organized by the extremists, at Dhulia (1908) and Satara (1914). In 1915 the moderates and extremists held separate conferences in Poona.

[72] Although the English columns of the *Gujarati* tended to be moderate in tone, the more important and lengthy Gujarati columns reflected the views of the extremists. "Statement of Anglo-Vernacular Newspapers and Periodicals Published in the Bombay Presidency During the Year 1906."

[73] Bhopatkar began to contribute to the *Mahratta* in 1903; he joined the Congress in 1905.

played numerous sports at college (cricket, tennis, fencing, wrestling) and developed an upright, "well-knit frame" and "Goliath-strength" despite his short (five feet two inches) stature.[74] Throughout his life he was an exponent of the benefits of physical fitness and wrote numerous books on the subject such as *My System of Physical Culture, Exercises for Ladies, Fencing,* and *Wrestling,* together with treatises on law and other subjects. Bhopatkar later became chairman of the Maharastriya *Mandal,* a well-known physical culture institute of Poona. He relished the heroic role of a Kshatriya Brahman with its related attributes of courage and self-discipline. When he was seriously injured by a bomb explosion at a Poona reception to Gandhi in 1934, he refused to leave the assembly in spite of seventy-three splinters and profuse bleeding. Two years previously he had exhibited nerves of steel when he survived a twenty-minute ordeal with a cobra in his jail cell. A lawyer who became one of the leading members of the Poona bar, a journalist, a municipal corporator, an author, Bhopatkar was a versatile man.

Unlike many of Tilak's earlier followers, who were socially conservative, Bhopatkar believed that Hinduism could best be strengthened by reform. He wrote in favour of intercaste marriage, advocated the abolition of untouchability, and had sponsored a resolution in the Poona Municipal Corporation since 1905 to throw open all the tanks of the city to Untouchables.[75] Whereas the older leaders, such as the Natus and Jinsiwale, favoured no tampering with the Hindu social order, Bhopatkar typified the younger leader who advocated some accommodation with modern forces in the interests of preserving tradition. Bhopatkar sometimes wore a *bhagava*-coloured cap and thus identified himself with the militant tradition of Maharashtra.

Tilak's growing status in Maharashtra and the Congress party attracted supporters throughout the Deccan and the satellite regions of the Berar and the Marathi districts of the Central Provinces.[76]

---

[74] Indra Prakash, *Dharamvir Bhopatkar* (New Delhi, 1949), preface, p. i.
[75] *Mahratta,* January 29, 1937.
[76] The Marathi districts of the Central Provinces were Wardha, Nagpur, Chanda, and Bhandara.

	Marathi population (1911)	Per cent of total population	Total population (1911)
Berar	2,400,793	78.5	3,057,162
Central Provinces (Marathi districts)	2,059,696	75.7	2,720,918

He gained the respect of the Deshastha *Dadasaheb* Ganesh Shridhar Khaparde (1854–1938), one of the principal leaders of the Berar. Khaparde publicly praised Tilak in 1907 as "the only man capable of making Government listen" and a "desperate man" who "reckoned not of his life"[77] and privately wrote to Tilak that he could not do without him.[78] From 1891 the careers of Tilak and Khaparde were closely intertwined. The two were ranged on the same side of the Age of Consent controversy, though they were to clash later when Khaparde, president of the 1891 Social Conference, had to settle a vehement debate between Tilak and Ranade.

Khaparde came to support intercaste marriages, temple entry for low castes, and the abolition of untouchability, but he was a conservative by nature who counselled caution in matters of social reform. As a theosophist he had a "patriotic admiration" for the "spiritual wisdom of ancient India" and valued many of the old customs such as *Ayurvedic* medicine.[79] Khaparde's career was further linked with Tilak's when he became one of the five trustees in the protracted Tai Maharaj adoption case. Khaparde was an advocate, a member of the Amraoti Municipal Corporation and its vice-president for seventeen years, and later became a member of the Viceroy's Legislative Council. A witty and eloquent speaker, he set up debating and gymnastic societies to quicken the intellectual and physical development of youth. Khaparde could afford to live and spend "lavishly" and became known as the "Nabob of Berar."[80]

Khaparde's counterpart in the Marathi districts of the Central Provinces was the bearded Deshastha Brahman, Dr. Shivram Balkrishna Munje (1872–1948). A graduate of Grant Medical College of Bombay, Munje became a leading oculist of the Central Provinces, and participated in the Boer War as an officer in the Medical Corps. He first met Tilak at Raigad in 1899.[81] Munje was once described by the *Mahratta* as a "staunch Hindu," committed "to restore Hinduism to its proper place and strength." He attempted to root out those

---

[77] P and J, 1908, 546.
[78] B. G. Khaparde, *Shri Dadasaheb Khaparde Yance Caritra (Life of Mr. Dadasaheb Khaparde)* (1962), p. 10, quoted in G. S. Kashikar, "Political Thought of G. S. Alias Dadasaheb Khaparde" (unpublished paper, Nagpur Conference on modern Maratha history).
[79] Kashikar, pp. 2, 7.
[80] *Ibid.*, p. 1.
[81] Balshastri Haridas, *Dharmavira Do. Balkrishna Shivarama Munje Yance Caritra (Life of Dr. Balkrishna Munje, Protector of Religion)* (Poona, 1966), I, 29.

social forms of Hinduism, such as early marriage and the practice of untouchability, which sapped all the "manhood and energy from the Hindu race."[82] He devoted much of his time and energy to the the founding of Bhonsle Military College (1936), which provided training for Indian youth.

It is more difficult to measure Tilak's impact on a whole generation of students who were to come of age after 1914. They were inspired by the more activist program of Tilak, his 1905 clarion call to self-rule ("Swaraj is my birthright and I will have it"), and the associated revolutionary tradition exemplified by the Savarkar brothers. Although more at home in the cosmopolitan center of Bombay, and a member of the Council of the Bombay Presidency Association, the Pathare Prabhu lawyer, Mukund Ramrao Jayakar (1873–1959), expressed the typical response of the young to Tilak's heroic defence of 1908 when he later wrote that "my contact and my consequent esteem for Tilak increased enormously."[83] Jayakar found Tilak to be less elitist than the Bombay leaders. Whereas Dinshaw Wacha, the Bombay moderate leader, was "livid with rage" when Jayakar visited him without an appointment, Tilak patiently waited outside Jayakar's law offices for three hours, when Jayakar's assistant mistook the *Lokamanya* for an up-country client. Tilak dismissed this "affront" with a good-humoured reply.[84]

Among the students of Nagpur who invited Tilak to their town following the 1901 Calcutta Congress was the Deshastha, Madhao Shrihari Aney (1880–1968), who was to become an influential politician of the Berar.[85] Several years later a young graduate of Deccan College, Pandurang Mahadev Bapat (1880–1967),[86] proceeded to the United Kingdom on a government scholarship to study engineering, but joined up with the Savarkar brothers instead. The young Bapat was a firebrand who once addressed a meeting with a revolver in hand and seriously considered blowing up the Houses of Parliament.[87] On his return to India he disseminated information about the latest techniques of bomb manufacture to revolutionaries throughout

[82] *Mahratta*, September 16, 1923.
[83] M. R. Jayakar, The Story of My Life, 2 vols., *Vol.* 1, 1873–1922 (Bombay, 1958), I, 95.
[84] *Ibid.*, I, 90–91, 210.
[85] Keer, *Lokamanya Tilak*, p. 189.
[86] For his leadership in the Mulshi satyagraha campaign, Bapat acquired the title of *Senapati* (commander).
[87] *Illustrated Weekly*, LXXXVIII, No. 48 (December 31, 1967), pp. 36–37.

India. He was arrested in 1912 after the Alipore bomb incident.[88]

But there was a brittle quality to Tilak's western India party which depended too much on the inspiration of the *Lokamanya*. When he was removed from the scene, the mass party, which he had built over two decades, collapsed. Save for several sparks of revolutionary activity, the fires of organized protest, which had burned brightly for two decades in Maharashtra, were extinguished. The Tilak party had no other leader who could rekindle this spirit.

Prior to 1908 the Tilak party lacked a co-ordinated strategy to attain the goal of swaraj. The party was made up of various factions, each of which viewed its own program as the more viable form of action. The militant extremists, such as the Natus and Paranjpe, saw politics in terms of rousing audiences and blindly striking out against the government at every opportunity: this was "extremism at its purest and most irrational."[89] The revolutionaries, a related faction, were more concerned with acts of terrorism than with demonstrations of political support. Kelkar was a representative of the more "moderate" extremists in that he preferred to work through established channels and institutions, such as the press, the corporation, and the Congress. There were a number of "one-issue" politicians who chose to concentrate on a single aspect of national regeneration, such as temperance, the paisa fund, or national schools. One group attempted to blend militant nationalism with social reform and chose to work for the amelioration of the labouring and depressed classes. The charismatic authority of Tilak was the chief bond which united such diverse groups.

[88] *Mahratta,* November 12, 1937.
[89] Hugh F. Owen, "The Leadership of the Indian National Movement, 1914–20" (unpublished Ph. D. dissertation, Australian National University, 1965), p. 99.

Chapter IX

THE LEGACY OF TILAK

It [Non-co-operation Politics] is a hot-potch of rights and righteousness; of patriotism and piety; of incarceration and incantation; legislation and liturgy and so on.[1]

After Mr. Tilak's death his lieutenants found themselves in a tower of Babel. All of themselves called themselves Mr. Tilak's followers but very few agreed between themselves about Mr. Tilak's teachings.[2]

Released from jail in 1914, Tilak virtually abandoned the tactic of mass movements outside the Congress in favour of more constitutional forms of agitation. Having enunciated the goal of swaraj and having built up a sizeable following, Tilak chose to work within the framework of the Congress and of the legislatures and later to appeal to the British Labour Party. Although some of Tilak's followers regarded the new strategy as a manifestation of caution and compromise,[3] it was born of confidence rather than weakness. With the deaths of Pherozeshah Mehta and Gopal Krishna Gokhale in 1915, Tilak was the pre-eminent leader of western India and one of the most powerful figures in the Congress. His new program was designed to harness the hitherto undirected flow of protest into more constructive channels of political pressure.

Tilak's enhanced status enabled him to move from the restricted sphere of regional politics into the all-India arena. While he retained his regional ties and interests, he modified his policies in the light of the larger perspectives of panregional politics. The recognition of

[1] *BHFM*, III, Part 1, p. 680.
[2] M. J. Kanetkar, *Tilak and Gandhi: A Comparative Character Sketch* (1935), IOL pamphlet, p. 33.
[3] A significant number of Tilak's lieutenants opposed re-entry to the Congress in 1916: they included Bhopatkar, Deshpande, Khadilkar, Munje, and Paranjpe. Gangadhararav Deshpande, *Majhi Jivanakatha (My Life Story)* (Bombay, 1960); V. K. Paranjpe, *Shivrampant Paranjpe: Vyakti Vakravata, Vadmaya (Shivrampant Paranjpe: His Life Speeches and Writings)* (Poona, 1954), p. 68; M. D. Vidwans (ed.), *Letters of Lokamanya Tilak* (Poona, 1966), p. 276.

the demands of the Muslim League and the support of institutional politics in the period after 1914 reflected the attempt of a hitherto regional politician to adopt a more national stance. Tilak's altered positions do not necessarily reflect the frustrations of an extremist, whose back had been broken by an extended imprisonment, or an advancement of age, which blunted the fiery militance of youth. As a mature politician, with an expanding political base and a more national perspective, Tilak saw the need to revise previous strategies to suit changing political circumstances.

A comparison between the membership of the fifteenth Bombay Provincial Conference (moderate) and the seventeenth Bombay Provincial Conference (extremist), both held in Poona in 1915, suggests the broader base of the Tilak party and the net results of two decades of politicization. There were approximately twice as many delegates at the extremist conference (929) as there were at the moderate gathering (571). The extremists attracted some 46 per cent of their delegates from the Deccan (outside of Poona), Konkan, and Karnatak; the moderates drew only 24 per cent. Considering the distance of the Karnatak from Poona (several hundred miles), the Belgaum delegation of 90 members demonstrated the existence of vigorous district groups in the southern extremities of the Bombay Presidency, groups which were replicated in most of the districts of the Deccan, Konkan, and Karnatak. Bombay City, despite Tilak's campaign, still remained a moderate preserve with 134 delegates (23.5 per cent) as against 69 delegates (7.4 per cent) at the extremist meeting. While the moderates could garner a scattering of representatives from the far-flung northern regions of Gujarat and Sind (41 delegates, 7.2 per cent), the Tilakites were virtually unrepresented (4 delegates, 0.5 per cent).

An analysis of the occupations of delegates at the two conferences indicates that the extremists were a more diverse cross-section of the population. The moderate returns suggest a heavy occupational bias in favour of the professions (54.3 per cent), which represented very little advance, in terms of diversification, from the early years of the Congress.[4] By contrast, more than half of the extremist delegates followed occupations connected with trade and the land (58.7 per cent); they outnumbered the professionals (39.3 per cent) by a sizeable

[4]McDonald and Stark, pp. 64–65. The occupations of the Mahrashtrian delegates at the 1889 Congress have been analysed by Stark as follows: professional, 44 per cent; trade, money-lending, 25 per cent; land, 25 per cent; other, 6 per cent.

margin. Unlike the earlier Congresses, which were dominated by lawyers, the largest single occupational category at the extremist conference was the merchant group. The differences between the two conferences can be exaggerated, for, with few exceptions, the delegates came from the professional, mercantile, and landed middle classes. Those who could be classified as urban and rural labour (millhands, artisans, tenants) were few and far between.

When Tilak undertook a campaign to revive local political associations, to gain greater representation at the 1915 Congress, and to organize the Indian Home Rule League in 1916, he could count on the support of influential leaders in most of the major centers of the Marathi-speaking region. The already-strong Poona group was further strengthened by the additions of Lakshman Bhopatkar, the young Chitpavan lawyer, Damodar Vishwanath Gokhale, who joined the staff of the *Kesari* in 1915 and became General Secretary of the Poona *Sarvajanik Sabha* shortly after, and the seasoned revolutionary *Senapati* Bapat, who joined the staff of the *Mahratta* in 1915. The Satara leadership rested in the hands of two experienced lawyers, *Dadasaheb* Raghunath Pandurang Karandikar (1857–1935) and Ganesh Ballal Phansalkar, who had been members of the Congress from the 1890's. Although Karandikar had sided with the moderates in 1907, he was, like Daji Khare, a "connecting link" between the two parties.[5] He was a close friend of Tilak, his legal advisor in the Tai Maharaj case, and joined Tilak's Home Rule League in 1916. Karandikar was elected to the Bombay Legislative Council in 1911. Some other Deccan and Konkan leaders included V. G. Ketkar, a Nasik lawyer and eldest son-in-law of Tilak, Shankarrao Shrikrishna Deo (1871–1958), an advocate of Dhulia; V. R. Lele, a lawyer of Sholapur, and Sadashiv Khando Altekar of Karad, who was municipal chairman of Karad in 1918. Baptista was joined in Bombay City by Dr. Dinkar Dhondo Sathaye, a specialist in ophthalmology with degrees from Edinburgh and Glasgow. Like Baptista, Sathaye took an interest in labour movements and was president of the India Labour League and the Bombay Mill-Hands' Association in 1920.

There was a similar depth of support in the distant centers of Berar, Central Provinces, and Karnatak. Khaparde and Munje were established Congress figures and the young lawyer, Madhao Shrihari Aney, had already launched himself on a long and illustrious

---

[5] Owen, p. 98.

GEOGRAPHICAL DISTRIBUTION OF DELEGATES AT
THE FIFTEENTH AND SEVENTEENTH BOMBAY PROVINCIAL
CONFERENCE (B P C), POONA, 1915

	BPC (moderate)	Per cent	BPC (extremist)	Per cent
POONA	257	45.0	428	46.1
DECCAN, KONKAN (outside Poona)				
Satara	13		96	
Sholapur	13		55	
Ahmednagar	20		35	
Khandesh	21		45	
Thana/Kolaba	21		47	
Nasik	4		12	
Ratnagiri	1		3	
Native States	8		5	
TOTAL	101	17.7	298	32.0
KARNATAK				
Belgaum	21		90	
Bijapur	3		16	
Dharwar	14		24	
TOTAL	38	6.6	130	14.0
BOMBAY CITY	134	23.5	69	7.4
GUJARAT AND SINDH				
Surat	10		2	
Broach	4			
Kaira	2			
Ahmedabad	14		2	
Sind	11			
TOTAL	41	7.2	4	0.5
TOTAL	571		929	

Occupations of Delegates at the Fifteenth and Seventeenth B P C, Poona, 1915[a]

	B P C (moderate)	Per cent	B P C (extremist)	Per cent
PROFESSIONAL				
Law	151		248	
Medicine	13		53	
Journalism	20		33	
Other	86		32	
TOTAL	270	54.3	366	39.3
TRADE				
Merchant	120		283	
Sawkar	2		20	
Other	53		32	
TOTAL	175	35.2	335	35.8
LAND				
Landlord/proprietor	37		153	
Inamdar/sardar	8		26	
Farmer/agriculturalist	4		33	
Other	2		—	
TOTAL	41	8.3	212	22.9
MISCELLANEOUS				
Private service	9		13	
Other	2		6	
TOTAL	11	2.2	19	2.0
TOTAL	497		932	

[a] This table is incomplete since the occupations of some delegates are not listed. In addition, some delegates are listed under two occupations.

career. Aney established an association to represent the Yeotmal district of the Berar in 1916. The principal center in the Kanarese-speaking Karnatak[6] was Belgaum, where the leadership was shared by two lawyers, Dattatraya Venkatesh Belvi and Gangadharrao

[6] Within Bombay there were three Kanarese districts (Belgaum, Bijapur, and Dharwar) in the south of the presidency.

Balkrishna Deshpande (1871–1960). Belvi was a leading member of the local bar, a president of the municipality, a member of the Bombay Legislative Council (1911–20), and a member of the Congress from the 1890's. Deshpande, who first came into contact with Tilak while a student at Deccan College, helped to organize the Belgaum celebrations of the Ganapati and Shivaji festivals and to establish swadeshi concerns, the Swadeshi Clothing Store and the Deccan Store.[7] After 1914 Deshpande emerged as one of the most important figures of the Karnatak, later referred to as "the soul of Karnatak nationaalism."[8] The foremost politician at Bijapur was the Kannada lawyer, Shrinivas Venkatesh Kowjalgi, who was a member of the municipal corporation for twenty-one years from 1897 and chairman for several years. Vinayak B. Joshi, a pensioner in the Educational Department, was a significant figure in Dharwar politics.

In terms of educational qualifications and political experience, Tilak's post-1914 lieutenants and associates reflected the growing status of his party. Many of them were the established leaders of their districts, elected to positions of influence in the municipalities and the provincial legislative councils. Within Tilak's lifetime and shortly thereafter, nine of his assistants (Kelkar, Khaparde, Munje, Karandikar, Belvi, Baptista, Bhopatkar, Khare, and Deo) were elected to provincial legislative councils. Having gained depth in his secondary leadership, Tilak could now consider the feasibility of working within the legislatures, an option which was not available in the 1890's.

Among Tilak's chief deputies there was greater social diversification after 1914 than before. Whereas the principal lieutenants in the 1890's were Chitpavan (Kelkar, Khadilkar, Paranjpe), those who now joined Tilak came from other Brahman communities: Khaparde, Munje, Deshpande, and Aney were Deshastha; Bhopatkar was a Karhada. However, there were limits to this heterogeneity, for, with the exception of Baptista, all the dominant figures of the Tilak party were Brahman.

While Poona provided the model and inspiration for this network of mofussil groups, district associations were shaped and spawned by local politicians. As in the famine campaign of 1896–97, the Poona leaders played a co-ordinating role, linking themselves with established district *sabhas* and local leadership. It was not until 1905, in connection

[7]Deshpande, pp. 109–111, 116–118.
[8]*Mahratta*, December 7, 1930.

with the swadeshi movement, that Tilak, Kelkar, and Paranjpe made any concerted effort to consolidate their influence throughout the region. The formal organization of a Maharashtra party did not take place until 1916 with the establishment of the Indian Home Rule League.

Since Tilak's last mass movement, the organization of the League, has recently been described by Hugh Owen,[9] it will suffice to suggest some comparisons with earlier campaigns. Established in Belgaum on April 28, 1916, Tilak's League represented a concerted effort to capture the Congress and to apply pressure on the government to grant Home Rule. Whereas Tilak's previous efforts were loosely structured programs designed to sow the seed of unrest, the League was an attempt to reap the political harvest of two decades of protest.

To further this purpose, the Indian Home Rule League established a broad-based committee with representatives from all the important towns of the region.[10] Six branches were established at the following centers: Central Maharashtra, the Karnatak, the Berar (two branches), Central Provinces, and Bombay City. The League carried out a vigourous campaign of recruitment which included whirlwind tours throughout the districts. In two weeks of 1918, Tilak covered more than 2,000 miles (1,000 by rail and 1,200 by motor), and delivered thirty-five lectures to some 300,000 people.[11] To explain its purposes the League published six books in Marathi and two in English, with translations in Gujarati and Kannada.[12] The League made a determined effort to interest groups, such as the Marwadis and non-Brahman agriculturalists, hitherto unrepresented in national politics. Membership entailed the small annual sum of one rupee and an entry fee of two rupees. The latter fee was subsequently dropped.

The Home Rule movement might be considered Tilak's first attempt to initiate a national campaign. It was an advance on the

---

[9]Keer, *Lokamanya Tilak*, pp. 350–367; Hugh Owen, "Towards Nation-Wide Agitation and Organisation: The Home Rule Leagues, 1915–18," in D. A. Low (ed.), *Sounding in Modern South Asian History* (California, 1968), pp. 159–195; T. V. Parvate, *Bal Gangadhar Tilak* (Ahmedabad, 1958), pp. 334–371.

[10]Those comprising the executive Central Committee included Tilak, Khaparde, Kelkar, Baptista, Munje, Aney, Karandikar, G. B. Phansalkar (Satara), and D. V. Belvi (Belgaum). Added to the Central Committee were Dr. Sathaye (Bombay), Dr. R. G. Vaze, C. V. Vaidya (Kalyan), V. R. Patwardhan (Poona), N. R. Alekar (Nagpur), and V. R. Lele (Sholapur). Owen, "The Leadership of the Indian National Movement," p. 182.

[11]*India*, March 18, 1918.

[12]Parvate, pp. 363–364; *Mahratta*, November 5, 1916.

mass movements of the 1890's which had limited appeal outside of Maharashtra since they were couched in regional terms and centered on local issues. Although the swadeshi-boycott movement crossed presidency boundaries, Maharashtrians played a supporting role to the main Bengali thrust. But even in 1916 there were provincial limitations to Tilak's Home Rule League. Shackled by a regional identification and following, Tilak confined his espousal of a national issue to those Marathi-speaking areas where he could count on assured support: Maharashtra, the Karnatak, the Berar, and the Central Provinces.

It is ironic that a relative newcomer to Indian politics, Annie Besant, could weld together a more national organization. Her associated All-Indian Home Rule League, also founded in 1916, attracted support in South India, United Provinces, Gujarat, Sind, Bihar, and Bombay City.[13] With her India-wide organization, Annie Besant represented a new type of politician and foreshadowed the role of Gandhi. Like C. R. Das of Bengal and Lala Lajpatrai of the Punjab, Tilak epitomized the older regional leader who acquired national influence by virtue of alignments with like-minded power-brokers of other regions.

Measured against the previous mass movements, Tilak's League was a striking success in terms of response and recruitment. By the time he left for England in 1918, nearly 300,000 rupees had been subscribed to the League.[14] The membership rose from 1,000 in 1916 to over 14,000 in 1917, 32,000 in 1918, and over 40,000 by 1921. Of the 14,128 members in April, 1917, the League claimed 42 per cent to be Brahman, 43 per cent non-Brahman, and two per cent Muslim.[15]

If the League membership figures can be accepted as a valid indicator of non-Brahman commitment to the Home Rule program,[16] they represent substantial gains for the Tilak party. There were very few non-Brahmans at the 1914 extremist meeting of the Bombay Provincial Conference, held just three years previously at Satara. Despite two decades of active recruitment, there had been only twelve non-Brahmans out of a total of 231 delegates. Approximately 90 per cent of the delegates were listed as Brahman.[17]

[13]Owen, "The Leadership of the Indian National Movement," p. 171.
[14]*India*, April 26, 1918.
[15]*Times of India*, May 18, 1917.
[16]The discussion below seems to suggest that non-Brahman involvement in League activities was peripheral.
[17]*Report of the Sixteenth Bombay Provincial Conference* (Satara, 1914).

An analysis of the leadership of the League and the newly revived Managing Committee of the Poona *Sarvajanik Sabha* indicates that, if there was a substantial increase in non-Brahman membership in Tilak's organizations, the non-Brahman recruits played a secondary role in the leadership of his party. There was only one non-Brahman member of the Managing Committee for the years 1916–21. Baburao Bhaurao Phule, a descendant of *Mahatma* Jotiba Phule and a member of the Poona Municipal Corporation, was elected to the committee in 1920. In terms of the social diversification of leadership, the revived *Sabha* of 1916 represented very little advance on the caste composition of the old body, as analysed by Gordon Johnson for the years 1878–97.[18] Close to 90 per cent of Tilak's top Poona echelon continued to be drawn from the Brahman communities.

MANAGING COMMITTEE OF THE POONA *Sarvajanik Sabha*, 1916–21 COMMUNITY

Year	Chitpavan	Deshastha	Karhada	Brahman	Gujarati/ Marwadi	Non-Brahman	Unidentified
1916–17	18	8	2	2	4	—	3
1917–18	18	7	2	2	4	—	3
1918–19	17	6	2	2	2	—	4
1919–20	21	5	2	2	2	—	4
1920–21	22	6	2	5	2	1	4

In an attempt to attract non-Brahmans to the League, Tilak found a useful ally in the Maratha, Vithal Ramji Shinde. Having completed his studies in sociology and comparative religion at Oxford, Shinde devoted his life to the amelioration of Untouchables and formed the Depressed Classes Mission Society in 1905. While not a member of Tilak's party, Shinde was prepared to support the Home Rule platform and formed the Nationalist League of Marathas to encourage non-Brahmans to support the League.[19] Like Bhopatkar, Shinde believed in the compatability of social reform and nationalist agitation. He was disappointed when Tilak stopped short of a commitment to the

[18] Gordon Johnson, "Chitpavan Brahmins and Politics in Western India in the Late Nineteenth and Early Twentieth Centuries," in Edmund Leach and S. N. Mukherjee (eds.), *Elites in South Asia* (Cambridge, 1970), p. 109.

[19] S. L. Karandikar, *Lokamanya Bal Gangadhar Tilak: The Hercules & Prometheus of Modern India* (Poona, 1957), pp. 473–474; Owen, "The Leadership of the Indian National Movement," p. 255.

abolition of untouchability at the 1918 All-India Depressed Classes Conference. Tilak also cultivated the support of the Bombay non-Brahman lawyer M. R. Jayakar, whom he persuaded to be president of the Poona District Conference of 1918.[20]

The more influential non-Brahman leaders regarded Tilak's League with suspicion and doubted whether "justice and fair play" might be meted out by a body "dominated by the Brahmin Extremist Party."[21] Bhaskarao Vithojeerao Jadhav, "Shahu Maharaj's man," saw greater prospect in separatist organizations. He founded the Maratha Educational Conference in 1907 and revived the *Satyashodak Samaj* in 1914. He was supported by the Kolhapur Jain, A. B. Latthe, and the young Poona Maratha, Keshavrao Marutirao Jedhe, who came into prominence in 1918. Jedhe was critical of the legacy of the *Lokamanya*. He opposed the presentation of an address of welcome to Tilak, on his return from England in 1919, and opposed the erection of a memorial statue to Tilak after his death. During the 1920's the *Satyashodak Samaj* non-Brahmans linked Tilak with Chiplunkar and branded both as "enemies of the country."[22]

As on many other social questions, Tilak took an ambiguous stand on the non-Brahman issue. While the *Mahratta* "heartily supported" the demand for special electorates for Lingayats, Marathas, and Jains following the Montagu Declaration of 1917,[23] Tilak could not resist several publicized remarks which suggested a differing attitude. On one occasion he advised artisans to stick to their trades and to leave politics to the Brahmans;[24] on another he sarcastically asked whether non-Brahmans planned "to handle the plough or hold the grocer's pair of scales in the Legislative Councils."[25]

In order to mollify non-Brahman criticism of such remarks, Tilak made a formal speech at Poona in which he blamed the British for the problem: it was "British policy and not the influence of Brahmins that has thrown the non-Brahmins into the background." "Nothing

[20]Owen, "The Leadership of the Indian National Movement," p. 251.

[21]A statement made by G. D. Naik, President, Bombay Provincial Conference of the Backward Classes, 1918, *Times of India*, April 29, 1918.

[22]Gail Omvedt, "The Non-Brahman Challenge in Poona, 1922–26" (unpublished, Maharashtra Study Group, May, 1971), p. 1.

[23]*Mahratta*, October 7, 1917, quoted in Owen, "The Leadership of the Indian National Movement," p. 259.

[24]J. E. Sanjana, *Caste and Outcaste* (Bombay, 1946), p. 75, quoted in Maureen L. P. Patterson, "A Preliminary Study of Brahman versus Non-Brahman Conflict in Maharashtra" (unpublished M. A. thesis, University of Pennsylvania, 1952), p. 97.

[25]Keer, *Lokamanya Tilak*, pp. 429–430.

short of Self-Government," Tilak maintained, "would mend matters."[26] This was an evasive reply which was hardly calculated to satisfy non-Brahman leaders, since it exonerated the Brahmans and failed to recognize the need for special treatment for non-Brahmans. Tilak's non-Brahman stance was hampered by unwillingness or inability to clarify the ambiguities of his position. He was once asked by a prominent non-Brahman leader, S. K. Bole, to explain his position on a 1901 *Kesari* article which argued that it was improper for Marathas to insist upon the right of performing their religious rites with Vedic hymns. Tilak avoided the question by telling Bole that the article had been written by one of his lieutenants.[27] Tilak thus failed to disassociate himself from a remark which linked him with the advocates of Brahmanical supremacy. Tilak's ambiguous remarks about non-Brahmans and the legislatures occurred at a critical juncture in the history of modern Mahrashtra. As in South India, the Montagu Declaration of 1917 provided a fillip for concerted non-Brahman political organization. The Tilak legacy provided one branch of non-Brahmans with an additional incentive for separatist organizations.

At the height of Tilak's influence and popularity Gandhi appeared on the political scene and began to make his presence felt in Mahrashtra as in the rest of India. He formed a close friendship with Gangadharrao Deshpande, who invited Gandhi to the Belgaum Conference of 1916. At the request of Gandhi, Deshpande later sent two young workers, *Babasaheb* Soman and *Pundalik* N. T. Katagade to labour in the ashrams in Bihar.[28] Shankarrao Dattatreya Deo (b. 1894) also travelled to Bihar to participate in the Champaran satyagraha at the suggestion of Deshpande. Although still loyal followers of Tilak, Deshpande, S. M. Paranjpe, and Dr. D. D. Sathaye joined in the Rowlatt satyagraha of 1919.[29] They were attracted to Gandhi's militant program, which seemed more in harmony with Tilak's earlier mass movements than the more recent strategy of working within the legislatures.

Tilak adopted a cautious and wary attitude toward the rising new

[26] *Ibid.*, pp. 430–431.
[27] *Ibid.*, p. 172.
[28] D. D. Karve (ed.), *The New Brahmans: Five Maharashtrian Families* (Calcutta, 1963), pp. 231–234.
[29] Hugh Owen, "Organising for the Rowlatt Satyagraha of 1919," in R. Kumar, (ed.), *Essays on Gandhian Politics: the Rowlatt Satyagraha of* 1919 (Oxford, 1971), p. 72.

star in the Indian political firmament. When asked by Deshpande to give his opinion on Gandhi at the 1916 Belgaum Conference, Tilak was interrupted by Khaparde who stated that "He does not belong to our Party."[30] Tilak refrained from comment. In the next few years Tilak and Gandhi engaged in much publicized verbal jousts concerning their respective theories of politics and interpretations of the *Gita*. Of the debate Gandhi once concluded, "My method is not Tilak's method."[31] But behind this war of rhetoric and tactical differences there were many shared common aims and a "mutual respect for each other's dedication and influence" which "provided a basis for joint effort" in several political conferences of 1917 and 1918.[32]

One reason for Tilak's wary policy toward Gandhi was his absence from the Indian political scene during the critical months from September, 1918, to November, 1919. Tilak was in England when the Rowlatt legislation was framed and passed and when Gandhi organized a nation-wide satyagraha movement in protest. By the time Tilak returned, Gandhi was a force to be reckoned with and an established Congress leader. Tilak's absence may help to explain the uncertain response of the *Mahratta* and the *Kesari* to the announcement of passive resistance in March, 1919. In the following months the *Mahratta* wavered between cautious acceptance of Gandhi's program, reserving the "liberty to settle the details," and positive endorsement of "soul-force" which it regarded as "superior to brute-force."[33] The vacillations of the Poona press reflected a division among Tilak's lieutenants as to how they should respond to this new political movement. Gangadharrao Deshpande, the designated leader of the Tilak forces while the *Lokamanya* was in England, advocated participation in the Rowlatt satyagraha. He was joined by the Bombay leader Dr. D. D. Sathaye and the Poona lieutenant S. M. Paranjpe. Sathaye was a member of the Executive Committee of the Satyagraha Sabha.[34] Participation was strenuously opposed by Khaparde and Dr. Munje who publicly critized the Gandhian campaign. With the exception of one Berar "convert" to Gandhi, Waman Rao Joshi, who was a leader of Amravati, Khaparde and Munje were able to obtain only a limited response to satyagraha in the Berar and Central Provinces.[35]

[30] Keer, *Lokamanya Tilak*, p. 351.
[31] *Ibid.*, p. 425.
[32] Masselos, "Gandhi and Tilak," p. 93.
[33] *Mahratta*, March 9 and April 13, 1919.
[34] Owen, "Organising for the Rowlatt Satyagraha," p. 77.
[35] D. E. U. Baker, "The Rowlatt Satyagraha in the Central Provinces and Berar,"

Because of the divisions within the Poona, Bombay, and Karnatak leadership, there was no effective opposition front to Gandhi in Maharashtra.

Those Tilakites who joined Gandhi in 1919 did not see participation in the Rowlatt satyagraha as inconsistent with their loyalty to Tilak. Waman Rao Joshi addressed one meeting in April, 1919, in which the photographs of both Tilak and Gandhi were garlanded.[36] Together with Deshpande, Paranjpe, and Sathaye, Joshi favoured co-operation with Gandhi as the best strategy for the Tilak forces. Thus when Tilak returned from England in November, 1919, he was confronted by a split in his party on the question of Gandhi.

Antagonism surfaced at the 1919 Congress when Gandhi favoured acceptance and sincerity in working the proposed reforms, whereas Tilak advocated "responsive co-operation." A compromise resolution was agreed upon.[37] Shortly after this Congress, Gandhi reversed his strategy in favour of non-co-operation and within nine months had persuaded the Congress to accept this position at the special session of September 1920, at Calcutta.

Tilak had failed to take a definite stand on non-co-operation since the 1919 Congress. During the first months of 1920 he gave a half-hearted endorsement of non-co-operation ("I will do nothing to hinder the progress of the movement"),[38] but remained sceptical concerning its potentiality for success. Uncertain as to the strength of Gandhi in the country and in the Congress, Tilak probably followed a wary policy of observing the political winds.

Tilak had reservations also concerning the Khilafat movement. Tilak believed that Muslims should be drawn to the Congress on the basis of the national issue of swaraj rather than on the basis of sectarian and foreign policy issues. In a seeming reversal of his 1896 position on religion and nationalism, he advised the Congress, "Never seek to introduce theology into our politics."[39] Tilak declined an invitation of Shaukat Ali to attend a meeting of the Council of the All-India Muslim League in May, 1920, to discuss the Khilafat question on the grounds that this was an issue for separate consideration by the Muslim leadership.[40]

---

in R. Kumar, *Essays on Gandhian Politics*, pp. 118–121.
[36] *Ibid.*, p. 121.
[37] Masselos, "Gandhi and Tilak," pp. 93–94.
[38] Keer, *Lokamanya Tilak*, p. 426.
[39] *Ibid.*, pp. 425–426.
[40] *Ibid.*, p. 423.

Tilak's death in August, 1920, removed the one possible obstacle to the acceptance of non-co-operation by the Congress. Tilak was the only man who might have marshalled the opposition to Gandhi's program and might have forced Gandhi to modify it. But Tilak's positions on the Montagu reforms and his publicized opposition to Gandhian strategies do not provide any sure indicator as to how he might have acted. Because he was a pragmatic and flexible politician, who quickly perceived shifts in the political winds, there is no certainty that he might have opposed Gandhi. Tilak's opposition to Gandhi was strategical rather than ideological; he was not yet convinced, at the time of his death, that the program of non-co-operation was a viable one and that Gandhi had a sufficient following to capture the Congress.

It is the view of Professor N. R. Phatak, author of a recent Marathi biography of Tilak, that the *Lokamanya* would have made common cause with Gandhi had he lived longer. To support this contention Professor Phatak cites a London letter from Tilak to Dr. Sathaye, dated May 15, 1919, in which Tilak wrote, "I have already *written before* that we should fully support Mr. Gandhi. It is impossible to give you any more detailed advice from here; for by the time it reaches India it is stale & useless."[41] When Tilak returned to Bombay on November 27, 1919, he publicly stated that "he wished he had been in Bombay when Mr. Gandhi began Satyagraha. He would have borne the difficulties with him and undergone the hardships."[42] The argument of Professor Phatak is a convincing one. Tilak was too strong a nationalist and a centrist not to have come to terms with Gandhi.

It was left to Tilak's lieutenants to interpret the political legacy of the *Lokamanya* in September, 1920. They were severely handicapped by fate, which gave them with too little time to galvanize the Maharashtrian party and find an alternative to the Gandhian strategy, which was fully developed at the Calcutta Congress, just one month after Tilak's death. Moreover, the four potential heirs to the mantle of the *Lokamanya*—Kelkar, Baptista, Khaparde, and Deshpande—lacked the charismatic authority or the desire to take over the Maharashtra party and to establish their leadership. Unlike Gandhi, who later hand-picked Nehru as a successor, Tilak failed to designate an heir-apparent who might have made possible a smoother transfer of power.

Of the four lieutenants, Kelkar was the most likely leader of

[41] Narhar Raghunath Phatak, *Lokmanya* (Bombay, 1972), frontpiece.
[42] *Bombay Chronicle*, November 28, 1919.

the Maharashtra party. The senior associate of Tilak and located in Poona, he inherited the *Kesari-Mahratta* newspapers and the Poona organization. But Kelkar was not equipped to lead, for he lacked the "driving power" of Tilak and the ability to impose his will on the diverse elements of the Tilak party. "Well known for his sobriety of judgment," respected by "all sections of political thought," and "quietly persuasive and coldly logical,"[43] Kelkar was a less imaginative politician than Tilak. As a journalist, an author, and a parliamentarian, Kelkar was an interpreter rather than an innovator of policy.

Based in Bombay, Baptista was handicapped by geographical disadvantages. Like Kelkar, he was an eloquent rather than a powerful speaker, and a "victim of alliterative phrases."[44] He did not seriously covet the mantle of the *Lokamanya* and gradually retired from national politics to concentrate on local concerns during the 1920's.

An established Congress leader and the undisputed head of the Berar branch of Tilak's party, Khaparde was the one lieutenant who might have regrouped the Maharashtra party. But, like Baptista, he was hampered by his geographical base together with the indecisiveness of the Poona politicians and their inability to hold the front lines of the party firm in the Deccan and Karnatak.

The position of Kelkar and Khaparde was undercut by a series of defections to Gandhi which took place in the last four months of 1920. Gandhi's greatest prize was the "conversion" of Gangadharrao Deshpande, although Deshpande had long been sympathetic to Gandhian programs. Appointed to head the Tilak party when Tilak and Kelkar went overseas in 1918–19, Deshpande was a fourth possible heir to the Tilak legacy. As one of the most influential politicians in the Karnatak, he soon created a broad Gandhian wedge in the flank of Maharashtra.[45] "Conversions" were not limited to the Karnatak, and many younger men such as *Senapati* Bapat and Shankarrao Dattatreya Deo were attracted to the "revolutionary" program of swaraj within one year. Gandhi's appeal above the heads of the established regional parties also secured some more seasoned politicians such as S. M. Paranjpe, who voted for Gandhi at Nagpur, and Khadilkar, who became an "out and out follower" of Gandhi.[46] What happened in Maharashtra was symptomatic of what was occurring

---

[43] Jayakar, I, 401.
[44] *Ibid.*
[45] *Ibid.*, I, 376–377.
[46] *Mahratta*, April 23, 1922.

in other provinces such as Bengal. Gandhi's new ideas were spreading like a "prairie fire" and consuming the constituencies of regional leaders. They were thus faced with the dilemma in 1920 of whether they could afford to oppose Gandhi and still retain "their position in public life."[47]

The "conversions" within Maharashtra and the Karnatak had been preceded by Gandhi's 1919 capture of Bombay City, which represented an additional wedge in the flank of the Maharashtra party. While never master of the city, Tilak had considered Bombay City to be within the Maharashtrian sphere of influence, and had established a branch of the Home Rule League there. But Tilak was hampered by the class composition of the Marathi-speaking population and the paucity of Maharashtrian middle-class leadership. His Bombay branch was overshadowed by the more vigorous and more influential Home Rule League branch, set up by Annie Besant, which attracted the significant Muslim leader Mohammed Ali Jinnah, and drew support from the powerful Gujarati middle class. Gandhi benefited most from the burgeoning Gujarati activity and consciousness. It was in Bombay City that he drew greatest support for the Rowlatt satyagraha of 1919—support which came largely from the Gujarati leaders of the Besant Home Rule League branch.[48]

Faced with the rapid turn of events in September, 1920, Kelkar and Baptista "sat on the fence trying to find out 'which way the cat would jump.'" During August and September they "vacillated with timidity" and failed to develop a consistent policy toward Gandhi and non-co-operation.[49] As a result they failed to control the Congress vote of the Bombay delegation or to develop an effective challenge to Gandhi. At the September Congress more than two-thirds of the Bombay delegates supported Gandhi's non-co-operation resolution in preference to B. C. Pal's amendment which would have removed the Council boycott from the Gandhian proposal.[50]

Of the Tilakites only Khaparde took a bold stand against Gandhi in 1920. He published a short memorandum pointing out that the non-co-operation resolution would "divert the energies of the Congress

[47]Jayakar, I, 372, 375–376.
[48]J. Masselos, "Some Aspects of Bombay City Politics in 1919," in R. Kumar, *Essays on Gandhian Politics,* pp. 145–188.
[49]Jayakar, I, 372, 375.
[50]Despite the opposition of Kelkar, Baptista, Jayakar, Jinnah, and V. J. Patel, the Bombay Presidency delegates favoured Gandhi's resolution to B. C. Pal's amendment by 243 to 93 votes. *Times of India,* September 11, 1920.

into directions of attaining soul force and moral excellence, and lose sight of the political aspect of affairs."[51] Khaparde was able to control the Berar delegation, which was one of two provinces to vote against Gandhi in September, 1920, by twenty-three votes to six. The other region to oppose Gandhi was the neighbouring Central Provinces which favoured Pal's amendment by thirty-three votes to thirty.

Unlike Khaparde, who expressed his opposition to Gandhi openly, the Poona leaders adopted a hesitant approach of lukewarm support for non-co-operation. Commenting on the September decision of the Congress, the *Mahratta* accepted it as the "verdict of the Nation" which was now "a *fait accompli*", but could not resist criticism of the decision to boycott the councils.[52] Gandhi was never much impressed by this "conversion of Maharashtra" and doubted the "sincerity of the Maratha allegiance."[53] During the next few years Gandhi publicly chastised the Maharashtra leadership and once commented that "Maharashtra in spite of its capabilities had no faith."[54] Maharashtra acquired the reputation of being a "slacker" in the Congress movement and some of its leaders "earned the unenviable reputation of the movement, wolves in sheep's disguise, who had entered into the fold with the view ... of weakening the strength of the movement."[55]

This charge was aired publicly in 1922 when Kelkar resigned as president of the Maharashtra Provincial Congress Committee as a protest against *Bombay Chronicle* criticisms of the Maharashtrian nationalist effort. Kelkar questioned the "supposed backwardness" of Maharashtra in terms of non-co-operation activities and denied that there was any "want of faith in N. C. O. itself."[56] There was some point to Kelkar's contention, for, despite their differences with Gandhi, the leading Tilakites had attempted to implement the official Congress policy from 1920 until its suspension in 1922. During this period they had accepted the boycott of the councils. Some of the leading figures of the region, such as Bhopatkar, had suspended their law practices. More significantly, both the older Tilakites, such as Kelkar and Paranjpe, and the younger leaders, such as Bapat and Deo, had participated with "great enthusiasm" in the local

[51] R. C. Majumdar, *History of the Freedom Movement in India* (Calcutta, 1963), III, 98–99.
[52] *Mahratta*, September 12, 1920.
[53] Jayakar, I, 377.
[54] *BHFM*, III, Part 2, p. 314.
[55] Jayakar, I, 377.
[56] N. C. Kelkar, A. *Passing Phase of Politics* (Poona, 1925), p. 64.

CONGRESS MEMBERSHIP BY REGION, 1921[a]
(LEADING EIGHT PROVINCES)

	Congress Membership
Bihar	350,000
United Provinces	328,000
Andhra	188,599
Bengal	172,098
Gujarat	169,113
Central Provinces (Hindi)	149,065
Punjab and N. W. F. P.	102,307
Maharashtra	79,489

LAWYERS WHO SUSPENDED PRACTICE IN 1920–21 BY REGION
(LEADING TEN PROVINCES)

Bengal	300
United Provinces	116
Andhra	108
Karnatak	53
Punjab	50
Central Provinces (Hindi)	45
Central Provinces (Marathi)	45
Madras	34
Berar	16
Maharashtra	15

NUMBERS OF CHARKAS RECORDED IN 1921 BY REGION
(FIGURE IN THOUSANDS)
(LEADING NINE PROVINCES)

	(Figure in Thousands)
United Provinces	386,000
Bengal	300,000
Bihar	200,000
Andhra	180,000
Utkal	36,000
Central Provinces (Hindi)	25,000
Madras	25,000
Karnatak	22,000
Maharashtra	14,000

[a] Gopal Krishna, "The Development of the Indian National Congress as a Mass Organization, 1918–1923," in Thomas R. Metcalf, ed., *Modern India: An Interpretative Anthology*, California, 1971, p. 262; *Mahratta*, January 21, 1923.

Mulshi satyagraha. They had championed the interests of the Mavala-Maratha peasants of Mulshi against the Tata Company, which had been authorized by the government to acquire land for a dam and hydroelectric works.[57]

While it is true that the established Congress leaders of Maharashtra supported the Gandhian program in 1920-22, they failed to generate the enthusiasm evident in some other regions. By the end of 1921 Maharashtra, together with some of the senior nationalist provinces of Bengal and Madras, had been outstripped in terms of membership by the burgeoning nationalist regions of Bihar, the United Provinces, Andhra, and Gujarat. The tables below suggest that in terms of Congress membership and participation in non-co-operation, Maharashtra had failed to keep pace with the spectacular growth within other regions.

At the first opportunity to implement an alternative strategy to the Congress program, a sizeable proportion of Maharashtrian leaders broke ranks with the Gandhian majority. After the suspension of non-co-operation in 1922 the Congress set up a committee to consider future strategy. In the course of the inquiry a cleavage emerged between the "no-changers," those who favoured the continuation of the present program, and the "pro-changers," those who wished to remove the boycott of the councils from the Congress strategy.[58] While the "no-changers" carried the vote within the country, with an approximate two-thirds majority,[59] within Maharashtra and its satellite regions the vote was in favour of the "pro-changers." The vote in Maharashtra was particularly interesting since it underlined the growing disunity of the Tilak forces. The table classifies this vote by local regions:[60]

	"No-change"	"Pro-change"	No-opinion
Maharashtra	25	18	2
Northern Karnatak	11	5	2
(Belgaum, Bijapur, Dharwar)			
Berar	4	21	1
Central Provinces	9	14	4
(Marathi)			
Total	49	58	9

[57]Indira Rothermund, "Gandhi and Maharashtra, Nationalism and the National Response," *South Asia: Journal of South Asian Studies*, No. 1 (August, 1971), pp. 61-62.
[58]*Report of the Civil Disobedience Enquiry Committee, Appointed by the All India Congress Committee*, 1922 (Allahabad, 1922).
[59]While 302 Congressmen voted for a "no-change" policy, 155 favoured one of the

The senior Poona leaders, such as Kelkar and Bhopatkar, advocated a "pro-change" policy, but many of the younger Poona leaders, such as S. D. Deo and V. V. Dastane, broke ranks to support the Gandhian majority. While Deshpande could deliver a "no-change" vote in the Karnatak, and Khaparde a "pro-change" vote in the Berar, Kelkar could no longer control the Congress vote in Maharashtra. The vote thus marked the diminished influence of the established Tilakites within the Congress and the region. It also underlined the split between some of the older Tilakites and the younger Brahmans who joined Gandhi. It indicated the growing influence of mofussil towns such as Belgaum, and satellite regions such as the Karnatak. Poona no longer enjoyed unquestioned political hegemony over the Marathi-speaking region.

The 1922 cleavage marked the beginning of a formal rift between the older Tilakites and the Congress. During the 1920's differences, which were initially strategical, broadened to become ideological. The most powerful remnants of the Tilak party, Kelkar and Bhopatkar, drifted toward the Hindu Mahasabha and eventually severed ties with the Congress in the 1930's. They were joined by Dr. Munje and Veer Savarkar, the former revolutionary.

According to M. R. Jayakar, one of the primary reasons for the defections of these prominent leaders from the Congress was the "essential incompatibility between the Maratha mind as moulded by Tilak's doctrines and Gandhi's teachings."[61] The argument that the martial tradition of Maharashtra did not harmonize with the non-violent values of Gandhi has been further suggested by the biographer of Bhopatkar, who has argued that the "programme of Ahimsa and Satyagraha failed to capture the Mahratta imagination for long because it neither fully utilised Mahratta energy nor appealed to their national trait of ever being on the offensive in warfare."[62] The differences between the "gujarati-bania concept of satyagraha"[63] and the martial style of politics of Maharashtra could be elaborated at length. There was great disparity between the aristocratic and ostentatious life style of Khaparde and that of the self-effacing *Mahatma*. There was a similar difference between Bhopatkar's emphasis on

---

"pro-change" alternatives.
[60]*Report of the Civil Disobedience Enquiry Committee.*
[61]Jayakar, I, 378.
[62]Prakash, p. 37.
[63]Baker, p. 122.

physical and mental training and Gandhi's stress on moral preparation.

The argument concerning values can be exaggerated for two of the most militant followers of Tilak, Paranjpe and Bapat, succeeded in transferring their loyalties from Tilak to Gandhi. A persistent critic of the moderate elements within Tilak's group and of the decision to re-enter the Congress in 1916, Paranjpe viewed non-co-operation as the logical extension of Tilak's earlier campaigns to organize mass agitation outside the Congress in order to apply maximum pressure on the government. Although critical of some aspects of Gandhian methods, such as the program of spinning and emphasis on ahimsa, Paranjpe accepted Gandhi as the political heir to Tilak.[64]

The younger *Senapati* Bapat made an even greater transition than Paranjpe. As a follower of Savarkar, Bapat addressed public meetings "spitting brimstone and fire," participated in revolutionary activities, and believed the "bomb and broom" to be the most effective instruments of social and political change. Attracted to the militant program of Gandhi, Bapat took a vow of non-voilence but "did not make a fetish of it." As the commander of the Mulshi satyagraha he followed non-violent tactics when it suited his purposes, but did not hesitate to use a revolver when the need arose and, as a result, received a jail sentence of seven years.[65] Both Paranjpe and Bapat worked effectively within the framework of Congress organizations, although they did not accept all the Gandhian values.

The argument concerning the differing regional values and styles of politics ignores the many tactics shared by Tilak and Gandhi. The older Tilakites could support many elements of Gandhi's program, such as swadeshi, temperance, the boycott of foreign cloth, and peasant campaigns, for these were established Tilak procedures. They could also participate in movements to break a particular law or policy, considered immoral, because this practice had been initiated by Tilak in 1896. Some of the older Tilakites, including Kelkar, Bhopatkar, and Munje, courted arrest in the 1930 civil disobedience movement to protest against the salt and forest laws.[66]

It was only when Gandhian tactics conflicted with established Tilak policies that the older Tilakites baulked in their support of non-co-operation. The boycott of educational institutions ran counter to

---

[64]Paranjpe, p. 68.

[65]M. P. Shikhare, "Senapati Bapat," *Illustrated Weekly*, LXXXVIII (December 31, 1967), 36–37.

[66]*Mahratta*, August 3, 1930, and January 10, 1932.

Tilak's plan to promote national education. The boycott of the councils was diametrically opposed to the strategy of responsive co-operation. Gandhi's support for the Khilafat movement ignored Tilak's warning about the danger of Congress espousal of Pan-Islamism.

Bereft of the political leadership and inspiration of Tilak, the older Tilakites adhered steadfastly to the established political formulas. Stripped of their accustomed authority with the national and regional Congress and, eventually, within their own city, they clung to the trappings of remaining power, the legacy of the *Lokamanya*. But their loyalty was to a legend, to a static vision of the past which distorted the traditon of the *Lokamanya*. Tilak himself was a flexible politician who refused to be bound by previous strategies and revised his tactics according to changing political realities. The older Tilakites lacked the ability or authority to reinterpret effectively the tradition of Tilak.

Of the differences between Gandhi and the older Tilakites the most critical one was the Muslim question. The disputes over the various boycotts related to tactical issues, but the Congress relationship to the Muslim League concerned both tactics and a perception of society desired by the nationalists. The older Tilakites criticized the Khilafat movement because they believed it was "overtainted with the spirit of Pan-Islamism." The linking of this issue with the Congress program was an unfortunate policy, since it was introducing "religious matters in the Congress which is a national body composed of people of different religions." Behind these criticisms was a belief that it was dangerous to play "the game in order to please the Muhammedans," for it was argued that this community placed its sectional interests above national commitment.[67]

Both Kelkar and Munje condemned the response of the Muslim leadership to the Moplah riots of Malabar in 1921, in which Hindu temples were desecrated and Hindus forcibly converted to Islam. Kelkar complained that the reaction of leading Muslims was not as "full throated and did not ring as true as it should in these days of Hindu-Muslim unity."[68] Analysing the Hindu-Muslim question in retrospect, Bhopatkar claimed that there was a "culpable ignorance of the Muslim mind on the part of the Congress leaders" which was a dangerous predicament since "the Muslim mind is never satisfied with what it demands." In the opinion of Bhopatkar, the "greatest

---

[67] Kelkar, pp. 103, 119, 123.
[68] *Ibid.*, p. 103.

blunder" of the Congress was the acceptance of the Communal Award in 1932 which provided a permanent statutory Muslim majority in the Punjab and Bengal Legislative Council.[69] The Khilafat issue coupled with the Communal Award provided important reasons for the defections of the older Tilakites from the Congress.

By closely adhering to the principles of Tilak's Khilafat policy, the older Tilakites chose to ignore Tilak's alternative Muslim policy enunciated in 1916. Tilak was an enthusiastic backer of the Lucknow Pact, and the agreement between the Congress and the Muslim League granting separate electorates for Muslims. Tilak thus accepted the participation of a separate body, the Muslim League, in the national movement, together with the principle of special treatment for minorities. He also exhibited faith in the national interests of the 1916 Muslim leadership. When Tilak was criticized by Munje and members of the Hindu Sabha for conceding too much to the Muslims, he countered this criticism by suggesting that "we [the Hindus] could not have yielded too much" to the Muslims.[70] This suggests that Tilak was far more flexible about the Muslim question than many of his followers. Tilak's 1916 vision of a modern plural society, in which the respective interests of Hindus and Muslims would be represented, was not substantially different from that of Gandhi and the principle elaborated in the 1932 Communal Award. But, as on many social questions, Tilak's liberal aims were obscured by his operation within the framework of a traditional idiom. Because he sometimes spoke the language of Brahmanical and Hindu interests and adopted some of the symbols of orthodox society, many of his followers regarded the *Lokamanya* as a liberal defender of Hindu values. This suggests that, while tradition may provide a vehicle for modern ideas, this medium may hamper the diffusion of modernity.

Within Maharashtra the political eclipse of the older Tilakites was a relatively rapid process. After the suspension of non-co-operation in 1922, they played a role in the foundation of the Swaraj Party and enjoyed a temporary political revival in the council elections. In 1923 the Swaraj Party was the largest group in the Bombay Provincial Council: Many of the older Tilakites, including Kelkar, Bhopatkar, Jayakar, Karandikar, and Belvi, were successful at the polls. Bhopatkar was the elected member for Poona City.[71] But with the emergence of

[69]Prakash, pp. 62–63.
[70]Keer, *Lokamanya Tilak*, pp. 365–366.
[71]*Mahratta*, November 18, 1923.

a new Gandhian leadership, coupled with the greater political organization of the non-Brahmans during the 1920's, the electoral authority of the older Tilakites was progressively undermined. After the extension of the franchise in 1935, the Democratic Swarajya Party, the local successor of the Swaraj Party, could secure only five of the 156 seats in the Bombay Assembly elections of 1937.[72] Bhopatkar was defeated in the Poona City contest.[73] The once powerful Poona-based leaders could no longer control the vote of their own city.

The political rout of the older Tilakites in the 1930's was caused by a coalition of the younger generation of Brahman leaders, such as S. D. Deo and N. V. Gadgil, and the non-Brahman leaders, such as Jedhe. During the 1930's they wrested control of the Maharashtra Provincial Congress from the older Tilakites who withdrew to the Hindu Mahasabha. While the leadership of the Congress remained largely in the hands of the younger Brahmans for the next decade, non-Brahmans freely joined the Congress and secured many subordinate positions.[74] The co-operation of liberal Brahmans and non-Brahmans provided a broad and stable base for the Congress party in Maharashtra.

Born in the last decade of the nineteenth century, Deo and Gadgil made an easy transition from Tilak to Gandhi. They perceived both to be liberal Hindus who represented a centrist position within the Congress, avoiding the extremes of socialism on the left and the Hindu Mahasabha on the right. They appear, in retrospect, to be the more legitimate interpreters of the legacy of the *Lokamanya* since Tilak believed that issues of social and economic reform and communal organization should be subservient to the overriding question of swaraj.

It is interesting to speculate why the non-Brahman leaders accepted a coalition with the younger Brahmans, in view of the previous connections of Brahmans with the Tilak party and the narrow interpretation of the Tilak legacy by the older Tilakites. The issue raises the larger question of why Maharashtra, with a history of Brahman domination of the early nationalist associations similar to Madras, avoided the extreme Brahman–non-Brahman conflict which emerged in the south. While there was an eruption of anti-Braham sentiment in

---

[72]*Ibid.*, February 26, 1937

[73]Bhopatkar was defeated by the Congress candidate, B. M. Gupte. Bhopatkar received 11,695 votes and Gupte 15,939 votes.

[74]Patterson, p. 121.

1948, after the assassination of Gandhi by a Chitpavan Brahman (a manifestation of a long-term simmering conflict),[75] it did not prevent caste co-operation within the Congress during the 1930's and 1940's. This bears on the larger issue of why the legacy of the *Lokamanya* does not appear to have been divisive within Maharashtra.

The fate of the Tilak party after 1920 provides a possible answer to this question. The political eclipse of the older Tilakites in the 1930's removed the one significant obstacle to non-Brahman participation in the Congress, since many of the senior followers of Tilak had opposed the non-Brahman challenge of Brahman political and social authority. The younger Brahman leaders took a more liberal stance on the non-Brahman question.

The culture of the region may provide a more significant reason for the relative absence of caste conflict in modern Maharashtra. The Brahman–non-Brahman conflict in Madras was heightened by a cultural cleavage between the Aryan upper caste and the Dravidian non-Brahman groups.[76] There was no such division in Maharashtra; all segments of society shared common myths and traditions based on a blending of the culture of the Aryan north and the Dravidian south. The early Brahman nationalists furthered this sense of Maharashtrian solidarity by emphasizing traditions which had broad appeal: chiefly Shivaji, the bhakti saints, and popular deities such as Ganesha. They ignored symbols such as the Peshwas, which could have been divisive.[77] Tilak's modern reputation is firmly grounded on the inauguration of the Shivaji movement and on the support for the popular culture of the region. In retrospect, Tilak's identification with the syncretistic tradition of Shivaji looms larger than his criticisms of the incipient non-Brahman movement and the interpretation of the legacy of the *Lokamanya* by his senior lieutenants. This may explain why criticism of the *Lokamanya* has been muted in modern Maharashtra.[78]

---

[75]*Ibid.*

[76]Eugene F. Irschick, *Politics and Social Conflict in South India* (California, 1969).

[77]*Vishnushastri* Chiplunkar was an exception. He glorified the Peshwa period of Maratha history.

[78]Dhananjay Keer has written the only non-Brahman biography of Tilak (in English). Although he is more critical than many of Tilak's Brahman biographers, his approach is sympathetic to the *Lokamanya*. Tilak has received more criticism in Marathi-language material such as V. Ghate, *Divasa Ase Hote*. Most of the non-Brahman writers seek to expose certain limitations of the Tilak party rather than to make a frontal attack on the *Lokamanya*.

During his lifetime Tilak spoke in the many voices of a transitional leader who reflected the uncertainties and ambiguities of a society involved in rapid change. He attracted to the Maharashtrian nationalist party a diverse group of individuals with varying commitments to traditional and to modern values. It is not surprising that after Tilak's death there was a dispersion which reflects the divided loyalties of the *Lokamanya* himself. Unlike the senior Poona lieutenants and the younger Brahman leaders, Baptista chose to retire from national politics in order to concentrate on civic and labour problems within Bombay City and on the political organization of the East Indian community.[79] Another important lieutenant of Tilak, Khadilkar, followed suit in the 1930's. An enthusiastic Gandhian during the 1920's, Khadilkar gradually retired from politics to become one of the leading dramatists of the region.[80] One of Tilak's own sons, Shridharpant, became an admirer of Dr. Ambedkar and participated in the reformist Social Equality League, a group which stressed inter-caste activities, before he took his own life in 1928.[81] The son of Shridharpant, Jayantrao, following in his grandfather's footsteps, became editor of the *Mahratta* and *Kesari* newspapers.

The majority of Tilak's follower chose to interpret his legacy in centrist or right-wing terms. With the exception of Baptista and Sathaye, the Maharashtra party produced very few left-inclined nationalists. In part this was a reflection of Tilak's limited exposure to socialist ideas until the last years of his life. But, more significantly, it reflects the *Lokamanya's* pragmatic proclivities, his belief that detailed ideological programs should be subservient to the broad goal of nationalism. Tilak had a limited interest in defining the future shape of Indian society; he preferred to concentrate on the immediate realities of attaining swaraj. While Tilak helped to develop a sense of regional consciousness and, to a lesser extent, national consciousness, he failed to define the goal of this consciousness. It is ironic that many intellectuals of contemporary Maharashtra look to Shivaji rather than to Tilak, for the social and political experiments of the seventeenth century seem to provide a clearer vision of the type of society which is to be desired.

[79] *Mahratta*, September 21, 1930.
[80] *Ibid.*, August 12, 1934.
[81] Zelliot, p. 130.

CONCLUSION: THE *LOKAMANYA* AS MYTH

"Myths are what's left over from everyday life. Some area that is not completely resolved."[1]

The dispersion of the Maharashtrian party after 1920 occurred because the myth of the *Lokamanya* was focussed on the personality of one man, Tilak. Without the presence of the dynamic mythmaker his lieutenants inherited a static tradition. This situation had been foreshadowed on two previous occasions when, with Tilak in jail, his party lacked a sure sense of direction.

The success of Tilak was due to an ability both to understand the traditions of his society and to epitomize them. He was the heroic leader cast in the mould of Shivaji who, by his reorganization of the Ganapati festival, linked himself with the popular religious tradition of Maharashtra. In his writings and speeches he drew upon his familiarity with mass culture to introduce humour, sarcasm, and various dramatic techniques; by re-interpreting and disseminating Vedic knowledge he established a connection with the high Sanskritic tradition. He was a unique individual who symbolized the range of Maharashtrian experience.

During his career Tilak demonstrated the capacity to define myths in a creative fashion. By an imaginative revitalization of existing traditions, such as those of Ganesha and Shivaji, he attempted to redirect the goals of his society. He also popularized new symbols, such as swadeshi, to introduce modern concepts. His seminal phrase of 1905, "Swaraj is my birthright and I will have it," ranks with Gandhi's concept of satyagraha as a significant symbol of the nationalist movement.

While myths provided a stimulus to political activity, they also hampered Tilak's efforts. The modern and liberal Tilak was often shackled by traditional interpretations of myths. His followers and political audience did not always fully comprehend the purport of his symbols or concentrated on one segment of them. The traditional

[1]Sidney Nolan, quoted in the *Sydney Morning Herald*, July 7, 1973.

CONCLUSION : *Lokamanya* AS MYTH   219

medium sometimes obscured the modern content. The many ambiguities of Tilak's political life reflected the difficult role he chose to play—one which attempted to appease modern, traditional, and charismatic authority. In many respects Tilak was a prisoner of his own myths.

Another work viewed the four mass movements of Tilak largely in terms of failure.[2] Although the *Lokamanya* achieved a measure of success in politicization, he failed, mainly because of the inadequacy of his mythmaking, to bridge the gap between Brahmans and non-Brahmans, Hindus and Muslims, and to establish himself as a truly national leader. It was difficult for a Chitpavan Brahman to develop myths which would transcend caste, sectarian, and regional boundaries. Implicit in this approach was the assumption that Gandhi succeeded because of a greater mythmaking capacity. Coming from a non-Brahman community and from a region which had no recent record of territorial expansion, Gandhi could elaborate myths which were national in character.

There are a number of conceptual flaws in this interpretation. The success of a politician cannot be measured solely by numbers or by the failure to achieve immediate stated goals. A mass movement which is nipped in the bud by government repression may fail in an immediate sense but provide a long-term stimulus for politicization. A second weakness of the previous work is its sectarian approach to Indian history and its tacit acceptance of the usurper theory, promoted by the British, which held that the Brahmans had usurped power which rightly should be the preserve of the non-Brahmans and implied that the interests of Brahmans and non-Brahmans were incompatible. Although the communal and Brahman–non-Brahman conflicts did hamper Tilak's efforts, it is not correct to suggest that they alone account for the extent of his achievement. Any balanced assessment must include reference to class interests (capital versus labour and landlord versus peasant) and the uneven rate of modernization at this time. The values of modernity created new allegiances which modified caste and religious differences. A final limitation of the thesis is the implication that local traditions, whether based on caste, on religion, or on region, cannot be nationalized. While some myths are more susceptible of nationalization than others, the successful adapta-

[2]Richard Ian Cashman, "The Politics of Mass Recruitment: Attempts to Organize Popular Movements in Maharashtra, 1891–1908" (unpublished Ph.D. dissertation, Duke University, 1968), pp. 212–218.

tion of the initially parochial Gujarati-Bania concept of satyagraha seems to dispell this notion.

There is no certain basis to the argument that Tilak was a less creative mythmaker or political tactician than Gandhi. Tilak was aware of the dynamic role which tradition could play. He demonstrated that civil disobedience on selected issues was a potent political weapon. His experiments with mass politics, which involved groups outside the sphere of elite politics, provided a blueprint for Gandhi's later campaigns.

A recent study of Gandhi has stressed the significance of political timing as a factor in explaining Gandhi's dramatic rise to power as the leader of the Congress. Gandhi benefited from political circumstances, "the policies of the raj at war," which thrust him "out of the restricted world of local grievances into the all-India political arena."[3] The war helped to create a greater reservoir of dissatisfaction which prompted "cultivators, industrial workers and businessmen to seek new means of redress" and focussed "the discontent of all groups on the raj."[4] Put in the language of myth, the post-war political conditions created a situation in which a national leader could give a plausible general explanation of those uncertain areas "left over from everyday life." Significant segments of Indian society agreed that there was a common national solution to many local and sectional problems. As a shrewd politician Gandhi recognized the potential of the myth and succeeded in capturing it. But it was not Gandhi who created the myth; it was the myth and the circumstances that produced it, which established Gandhi as the *Mahatma*, the chief symbol of the nationalist movement. Recent studies of Jinnah have suggested a similar process. Jinnah's Partition destiny was created by the political events which led to the development of a new Muslim identity in the 1930's.[5]

There was no consensus in Tilak's time. The areas "left over from everyday life" were too broad and too unresolved to permit the development of a myth of resolution. The transitional state of society, the uneven rates of modernization, and the ambiguous attitudes toward tradition and modernity prevented the emergence of common areas of agreement in which sectional interests would be submerged in the pursuit of some larger goal. The myth of the *Lokamanya* was a bold

[3] Judith M. Brown, *Gandhi's Rise to Power: Indian Politics* 1915–1922 (Cambridge, 1972), p. 159.
[4] *Ibid.*, p. 358.
[5] C. H. Philips and M. D. Wainwright (eds.), *The Partition of India* (London, 1970).

attempt to define a new consensus, but it only reflected the extent of unresolved areas within Maharashtrian and Indian society. For, while the myth created some new areas of caste and class co-operation, it also exposed some existing sectional conflicts and exacerbated them. Tilak symbolized the uncertain striving of his society for a new goal, the nature of which was yet to be made manifest.

After 1920 the myth of the *Lokamanya* soon became obsolete. With the changed conditions after the war and the new direction under Gandhi the myth was no longer relevant. Since it represented an "unresolved" myth of a society in transition, it had little appeal to a society with a more certain explanation of its areas of darkness. Tilak's lieutenants were not sufficiently imaginative to re-define the myth to apply to a new situation. Overwhelmed by the new myth of resolution, the myth of the *Mahatma,* they could only cling to the static transitional myth of the *Lokamanya.*

APPENDIX 1

SOCIAL BACKGROUND OF SOME PROMINENT FIGURES OF THE POONA BRAHMAN ELITE, 1880–1920

	Caste	Place of birth	Father's occupation
Gopal Ganesh Agarkar (1856–1895)	Chitpavan	Village of Tembhu, Satara dist.	Clerk
Waman Shivram Apte (1858–1892)	Chitpavan	Asolipal, Sawantwadi State	Braham pandit
Dr. Ramkrishna Gopal Bhandarkar (1837–1925)	Saraswat	Malvan, Ratnagiri dist.	Landowner
Chintaman Gangadhar Bhanu (1856–1929)	Chitpavan	Dahivadi, Satara dist.	Clerk
Lakshman Balwant Bhopatkar (1880–1960)	Karhada	Thana	*Shirastedar* (chief clerk of court)
Vishnushastri Vishnu Krishna Chiplunkar (1850–1882)	Chitpavan	Poona	Government reporter
Gopal Krishna Gokhale (1866–1915)	Chitpavan	Kotaluk, Ratnagiri dist.	Clerk, Kagal State
Wasukaka Wasudeo Ganesh Joshi (1856–1944)	Chitpavan	Dhom, near Wai, Satara dist.	Money-lender
Dhondo Keshav Karve (1858–1962)	Chitpavan	Sheravli, Ratnagiri dist.	Clerk
Narsinh Chintaman Kelkar (1872–1947)	Chitpavan	Village of Modlimb, Miraj State	Clerk, *Mamlatdar*
Krishnaji Prabhakar Khadilkar (1872–1948)	Chitpavan	Sangli State	Money-lender, *Mamlatdar*
Mahadev Ballal Namjoshi (1853–1896)	Chitpavan	Beerwadi, Kolaba dist.	Merchant
Balasaheb Balwant	Chitpavan	Poona	Sardar,

Name	Caste	Place	Occupation
Ramchandra Natu (1855–1914)			landowner
Shivram Mahadev Paranjpe (1864–1929)	Chitpavan	Mahad, Kolaba dist.	Money-lender
Raghunath Purushottam Paranjpye (1876–1966)	Chitpavan	Murdi, Ratnagiri dist.	Farmer
Annasaheb Vinayak Ramchandra Patwardhan (1847–1917)	Chitpavan	Poona	Lawyer
Mahadev Govind Ranade (1842–1901)	Chitpavan	Niphad, Nasik dist.	Private secretary, Kolhapur State Service
Bal Gangadhar Tilak (1856–1920)	Chitpavan	Chikalgaon, Ratnagiri dist.	School-master, *Khot*

	Family's economic status	*Generation which migrated to Poona*
Agarkar	Extremely poor	First
Apte	Father "well-to-do" but wealth lost in Waman's childhood	First
Bhandarkar	Wealthy	First
Bhanu	Small income. At the time of the Peshwas it had been well connected	First
Bhopatkar	Moderate income; father "not a rich man"	First
Chiplunkar	Wealthy	Several generations; family migrated during Peshwa times
Gokhale	"Poor but respectable"	First
Joshi	Estate valued at 2,000 rupees; suggests that he lived comfortably	First
Karve	Poor	First
Kelkar	Large landowners: they lived comfortably	First
Khadilkar	Poor	First
Namjoshi	Poor. Namjoshi was a self-made man	First
Natu	Wealthy, aristocratic. Assets valued at 24,997 rupees in 1897	At least several generations

Paranjpe	Property valued at 150 rupees	First
Paranjpye	Moderate means; owned small estate	First
Patwardhan	Wealthy; father a successful lawyer	Second?
Ranade	Moderate income	First
Tilak	Moderate means; suffered from lengthy lawsuits concerning their landed rights	First

	Level of education	College(s) Attended	Occupation(s)
Agarkar	M.A.	Deccan	Journalist, professor
Apte	M.A.	Deccan	College principal
Bhandarkar	M.A., Hon. LL.D.	Elphinstone, Deccan	Professor, Sanskritist
Bhanu	B.A.	Deccan	Writer, professor
Bhopatkar	M.A., LL.B.	Fergusson	Teacher, writer, politician, journalist
Chiplunkar	B.A.	Poona (Deccan)	Journalist, writer
Gokhale	B.A.	Rajaram, Elphinstone, Deccan	Journalist, professor, politician
Joshi	Matriculate	None	Publisher, entrepreneur
Karve	B.A.	Wilson, Elphinstone	Professor, social worker
Kelkar	B.A., LL.B.	Deccan	Journalist, politician
Khadilkar	B.A.	Deccan, Fergusson	Journalist, politician, dramatist
Namjoshi	Matriculate	None	Journalist, educator
Natu	High school	None	Property owner
Paranjpe	M.A.	Deccan	Journalist, educator, politician
Paranjpye	D.Sc., M.A.	Fergusson,	Educator,

		Cambridge, Paris, Göttingen	Minister, Ambassador
Patwardhan	B.A., LL.B., L.C.E., L.M.S.	Deccan, Elphinstone	Doctor, lawyer
Ranade	M.A., LL.B.	Elphinstone	Judge, writer, politician, social reformer
Tilak	B.A., L.L.B.	Deccan	Journalist, politician

APPENDIX 2

NUMBER OF *MELAS* IN SOME IMPORTANT TOWNS OF THE REGION FOR SELECTED YEARS, 1894–1910[a]

Poona : 70–75 (1894), 90–100 (1895), 66 (1899), 25–30 (1900), 44 (1907), 43 (1908)
Bombay : 35 (1895), 68 (1896), 40–44 (1900), 45 (1906) 46 (1908) 29 (1910)
Ahmednagar: 49 (1908), 27 (1900)
Belgaum : 5–6 (1906)
Dhulia : 28 (1896), 14 (1899), 14–15 (1900), 13 (1901)
Kolhapur : 5 (1903), 5 (1906), 1 (1908), 2 (1909)
Nagpur : 4–5 (1901), 4–5 (1903)
Ratnagiri : 5 (1908), 2 (1909)
Satara : 15 (1900)
Sholapur : 18–19 (1906), 12 (1909)

[a] Based on J. S. Karandikar, *Shriganeshotsavaci,* newspaper and police reports.

APPENDIX 3

SELECTIONS FROM THE SONGS OF THE *Sanmitra Samaj Mela*[b]

Verse 9

Mother [British administration] look at my Bal [Tilak] and look at your Gopal [Gokhale].
Old woman your head has become bald and you have lost your mind;
Forsaking Bal, you have married Gopal a second time.
Bal has large, spirited and attractive eyes.
Why are you fond of this ill-starred paramour?
Look at Bal's bearing and royal luster,
Look at your silly lover and throw him out,
Bal is a Maratha hero.

You may have deemed Bal arrogant, but he is hardy and has received wounds on the battle-field.
The other man is a flatterer and he is a moderate because he is a eunuch in a harem.
Bal is a person of good character, Gopal is the dirt of the gutter.

Gopal made you believe that Bal did not love you,
Under his influence, you deported Bal.
This man Gopal has murdered his own brother,
To please you he had Bal deported,
His cheeks are stained with his brother's blood.

Verse 11.
SONG OF GOPAL

Beat up the drums, beat up the drums!
I an a magician,
I am a great success (refrain)
I have seen four continents,
I am a graduate,
I was born a Brahman, then I forgot about my community,
Next I took a vacation from my caste.
If someone tries to challenge me, then I will have him arrested,
This is the way in which I remove thorns from my side

I am a very lonely man, but the whole world is in my hand,
Who knows when I'll sacrifice myself?
I will dance to the tune of my master,
I will lose at sport for the sake of my master.
But I'm capable of winning one game;
I will string a rope around Bal's neck
And enjoy myself as he swings.

[b] Printed in 1909. Phatak, *Adarsh Bharatasevak*, pp. 392–394. This represents a free translation of some of the more important lines of the song.

APPENDIX 4

ACTIVE MEMBERS OF THE COUNCIL OF
THE BOMBAY PRESIDENCY ASSOCIATION, 1885–1909[a]

Listed as follows: (1) number of meetings attended; (2) name; (3) years of active association with the Council; (4) community; (5) occupation(s).

- (191) Dinshaw Edulji Wacha (1885–1909), Parsi, journalist, mill agent.
- (124) Pherozeshah Merwanji Mehta (1885–1909), Parsi, lawyer.
- (98) Chimanlal Setalvad (1892–1909), Gujarati Hindu (Brahma-Kshatriya),[b] lawyer.
- (97) Narayan Vishnu Gokhle (1892–1909), Maharashtrian Brahman (Chitpavan), lawyer.
- (68) Balchandra Krishna Bhatwadekar (1893–1909), Maharashtrian Brahman, doctor.
- (66) Narayan Ganesh Chandavarkar (1885–1899), Maharashtrian Brahman (Saraswat), lawyer.
- (64) Goculdas Kahandas Parekh (1886–1909), Gujarati Brahman, lawyer.
- (63) Lulubhai Asharam Shah (1899–1909), Gujarati Hindu, lawyer.
- (63) Damodar G. Padhya (1897–1909), Maharashtrian Brahman, schoolteacher.
- (60) Nanabhoy Rustomjee Ranina (1885–1899), Parsi.
- (57) Javerilal Umiashankar Yajnik (1885–1896), Gujarati Brahman (Nagar), author, journalist.
- (55) Daji Abaji Khare (1890–1909), Maharashtrian Brahman (Chitpavan), lawyer.
- (55) Rustom K. R. Kama (1892–1909), Parsi, lawyer.
- (55) Rustom N. R. Ranina (1898–1909), Parsi, doctor.
- (51) Vijbhookhundas Atmaran (1885–1905), Gujarati Hindu (Modli Bania), merchant.
- (50) William A. Chambers (1893–1909), Englishman, engineer.
- (48) Atmaram Pandurang (1885–1898), Maharashtrian Brahman (Gaud Saraswat), doctor.
- (45) Tribhovandas Mangaldas Nathubhai (1885–1909), Gujarati Hindu (Kapole Bania), merchant, landlord.

(44) Vundrovandas Purshotumdas (1885–1893), Gujarati Hindu (Bhunsaly Kshatriya), merchant, landed proprietor.
(44) Narayan Madhav Samarth (1885–1909), Maharashtrian Hindu (Chandrasenya Kayastha Prabhu), lawyer.
(41) Kashinath Trimbak Telang (1885–1889), Maharashtrian Brahman (Gaud Saraswat), lawyer.
(39) Balkrishna Narayan Bhajekar (1893–1909), Maharashtrian Brahman, lawyer.
(39) Cowasji Hormusji (1885–1896), Parsi, doctor.
(39) Sorabjee Eduljee Warden (1894–1908), Parsi, merchant.
(38) Gansham Nilkanth Nadkarni (1885–1901), Maharashtrian Brahman (Gaud Saraswat), lawyer.
(35) Vishnu Krishna Bhatwadekar (1887–1909), Maharashtrian Brahman, lawyer.
(34) Ganesh R. Kirloskar (1885–1891), Maharashtrian Brahman, lawyer.
(34) Amiruddin Tyabji (1892–1909), Muslim (Suleiman Bohra), merchant.
(31) Hari Sitaram Dixit (1901–1909), Gujarati Brahman (Vadnagara Nagar), lawyer.
(31) Manekshah Jehangirshah Taleyarkhan (1885–1899), Parsi, lawyer.
(29) Shapoorshah Hormusji Hodiwala (1897–1905), Parsi, merchant, schoolteacher.
(28) Shrinivas Aiengar S. Setlur (1894–1907), South Indian Brahman, lawyer.
(27) Kazi Kaburudin (1899–1909), Muslim, lawyer.
(22) Abdulla Meherali Dharamsi (1885–1897), Muslim (Khoja), lawyer.
(22) R. K. Tarachund (1903–1909), Parsi, lawyer.
(21) Manubhai Nanabhai Haridas (1903–1909), Gujarati Hindu (Kayastha), lawyer.
(21) Mohamed Ali Jinnah (1903–1909), Muslim, lawyer.
(21) Dinsha P. Kanga (1885–1886), Parsi, lawyer.
(21) Shamrao Vithal Kaikini (1885–1886), Maharashtrian Brahman (Saraswat), lawyer.
(20) Hormusji Ardeseer Wadya (1897–1909), Parsi, lawyer.
(20) Khurshedji Rustomji Kama (1885–1909), Parsi, mill-owner, journalist.
(20) Jijibhoy E. Mody (1892–1899), Parsi, lawyer.

[a]Compiled form the "Minutes of the Council of the Bombay Presidency Association," Vols. I–III.
[b]A Gujarati community which appears to be of the same stock as the Khatris of the Punjab.

GLOSSARY

abhang, *abhanga*	Devotional verse
ahimsa	Non-violence
Bania	Merchant, trading caste
bhagava	Ochre color
bhakti	Devotion; the devotional tradition
Bhatia	Trading caste from Gujarat and Sind
Brahmachari	One who has taken a vow of sexual abstinence; one who is in the first (celibate) of the four stages which constitute the Hindu model of life
chatri	An awning or parasol which covers a throne, an image or some other significant object or person
deshmukh	Landed aristocrat of Maharashtra
Dharma	Hindu concepts of law, individual and group duty, cosmic order
gunda	Criminal, gangster
inam	Land grant in perpetuity which is rent free; *inamdar*, the holder of an *inam*
jagir	Originally a temporary land grant in lieu of salary which became hereditary in British times. A *jagir* was usually larger than an *inam*; *jagirdar*, the holder of a *jagir*
jati	A kinship group based on endogamy
Khatri	Weaver caste
khot	Hereditary village revenue officer of the Konkan; *khoti*, the system of revenue collection of the Konkan
kirtan	Devotional sermon with songs
kulkarni	Village accountant
Kunbi, *kunbi*	Cultivator; cultivator caste
lawnie	Bawdy song
Lokahitawadi	Title: "Adviser of What is Good for the People"
Lokamanya	Title: "One who is Revered by the People"
Mahatma	Title: "Great Soul"
mamlatdar	Revenue officer in charge of a sub-district
mandal	A society; *mitra mandal*, a friendly society
mandap	Decorated pavilion

GLOSSARY

Maratha	A caste cluster members of whom were traditionally soldiers and cultivators; an inhabitant of Maharashtra
math	Monastery
mela	A singing party which takes part in a festival; a religious fair
mofussil	The country areas as distinct from the town; in Maharashtra it usually refers to those areas other than Bombay and Poona
Muharram	Muslim festival to venerate the martyrdom of Hasan and Hasain
peth	Ward
prakrit	Vernacular language
Prarthana Samaj	Prayer Society; a western Indian variant of the *Brahmo Samaj*
prayascita	Penance, expiation
ryot, *rayat*	Peasant, cultivator
sabha	A society
sadhu	Monk, holy man
samadhi	A state of deep meditation or a devotional act of self-immolation; the place where an important figure is cremated and where some of the remains are buried
Samyukta Maharashtra	United Maharashtra; the movement for a unilingual state of Maharashtra
sannyasi	Wandering religious ascetic
sardar	A landed aristocrat of Maharashtra who performed military services for the state in pre-British times
sarvajanik	Public
satyagraha	A term coined by Gandhi to refer to a campaign of non-violent resistance
Satyashodak Samaj	Truth-Seeking Society founded by *Mahatma* Jotiba Phule
sawkar	Money-lender
shastri	Scholar learned in the Sanskrit classics
swadeshi	Of one's own country
Swadeshi Vastu Prarcharini Sabha	Society to Promote the Use of Indigenous Goods
swaraj	Self-rule
tabut	Emblem of Muslim martyrs used in the *Muharram* festival
taluka	Sub-district
tamasha	A dance-drama, popular in rural areas, which involves earthy humor; a form of entertainment
vani	Village money-lender
wada	Compound
zamindar	Hereditary landholder

INDEX

Abhangs, 14
Abhinav Bharat, 91
Abkhari, 130, 135
Acworth, H. A., 68
Advocate General, Bombay, 143, 179
Afghan war, first 29
Agarkar, Gopal Ganesh, 52, 222, 223, 224; conflict with Tilak in DES, 49–51
Age of Consent Bill, 52, 189; support of, 56, 57–58, 57n; Tilak's campaign against, 56, 57–58, 57n, 61n, 62, 94, 170
Ahimsa, 1, 10, 211. See also Non-violence
Ahmedabad, 161n, 195
Ahmednagar, 23, 57n, 136, 195; and mela movement, 81, 226
Akalkot, Chief of, 102, 112n
Ali, Shaukat, 204
Alibag Taluka (Kolaba), 135, 158; Association of, 134; Alibag Revision Settlement, 134, 134n
Alienation, land, 124; Bombay Government and, 144, 145, 146; in Kolaba and Thana, 135, 145n. See also Punjab Land Alienation Act
Alipore, bomb incident, 191
Allahabad, 57, 126
Altekar, Sadashiv Khando, 194
Amalner Taluka (Khandesh), 136
Ambedkar, Dr. B. R., 217
Amraoti, 189, 203
Andhra region, 209, 210
Aney, Madhao Shrihari, 190, 194, 196, 197, 198n
Anjanvel Taluka (Ratnagiri), 46
Anjuman-i-Islam, 57
Apte, Govind Vinayak, 130, 131, 133
Apte, Hari Narayan, 89
Apte, Waman Shivram, 49, 222, 223, 224
Arya Bhushan Press, 49
Aryans, 83, 84, 216
Asceticism, 10, 12, 14, 15, 75
Assam, 183
Atmaran, Vijbhookhundas, 158, 158n, 229
Aundh, Chief of, 100, 102
Aurangzeb, 15
Ayerst, Lieutenant, 114
Ayurvedic medicine, 189

Baji Rao I, 8
Baji Rao II, 9
Banias, 125, 135, 142, 154, 211, 220; and *mela* movement, 85; Modli, 158; Surti, 187
Banks: agricultural, 148; swadeshi, 174
Bapat, D. R., 173
Bapat, *Senapati* Pandurang Mahadev: a revolutionary, 190–191, 212; and Mulshi satyagraha, 190n, 208, 210; joins Tilak, 194; follower of Gandhi, 206, 212
Baptista, Joseph, 186n, 187, 194, 197, 198n; lieutenant of Tilak, 186, 205, 206, 207, 207n; a socialist, 186; retires, 217
Baroda, 28, 76, 99, 99n. See also Gaekwar of Baroda
Barve, Narayan Shivram, 126–127, 137
Bassein (Thana), 136
Belgaum, 161n, 193, 195, 196, 196n, 197, 198, 198n, 210, 211, 226; leaders of, 196–197; Conference, 202, 203
Belvi, Dattatraya Venkatesh, 196–197, 198n, 214
Benares, 59, 120; Raja of, 102
Bengal, 11, 140, 160n, 161n, 169, 178, 199, 207, 209, 210, 214; Bengali culture, 6; Bengalis, 6, 121; politicians of, 149–150; and swadeshi movement, 173, 174, 175, 176, 177, 177n
Berar, 175, 188n, 198, 203, 209; support for Tilak in, 188, 189, 194, 196, 199, 206; opposition to Gandhi in, 208; "pro-change" vote in, 210, 211
Besant, Annie, 199, 207
Bhagavad Gita: Tilak on, 12, 55, 114; Tilak and Gandhi disagree on, 203
Bhairav, 76
Bhakti tradition, 75; and poet-saints, 6, 9, 10, 43, 101, 103, 216; and Kshatriya tradition, 9–10, 12, 14, 15; and regional nationalism, 9–10, 13, 14, 15, 43, 101, 103
Bhala, 87, 176
Bhandarkar, Dr. Ramkrishna Gopal, 70, 222, 223, 224
Bhanu, Professor Chintaman Gangadhar, 113, 114, 222, 223, 224
Bharucha, Shapurji, 165

233

Bhatias, 67, 68, 157, 157n, 158, 158n
Bhatwadekar, Sir Balchandra Krishna, 147, 161n, 229
Bhavani, 10, 12, 76, 104
Bhavnagar, Chief of, 100n, 102, 112n
Bhide, Nilkanth Waman, 88, 89, 90
Bhimji, Ali Mohammed, 175n, 176, 187
Bhonsle Military College, 190
Bhopatkar, Bhaskar Balwant, 176
Bhopatkar, Lakshman Balwant, 187n, 197, 200, 222, 223, 224; lieutenant of Tilak, 187–188, 192n, 194; participates in satyagraha, 208, 212; leaves Congress, 211; on communal question, 213–214; and Swaraj Party, 214; and Democratic Swarajya Party, 215, 215n
Bhor, Chief of, 100n, 102
Bhownuggree, Sir Muncherjee Merwanji, 165, 165n
Bihar, 67, 199, 202, 210
Bijapur, 113, 137, 195, 196n, 197, 210
Bodas, Mahadev Rajaram, 91, 137, 175n
Bohras, Suleiman, 157, 167
Bole, S. K., 202
Bolshevism: Tilak on, 186, 187
Bombay Assembly, 215
Bombay Chamber of Commerce, 64
Bombay City, 40, 57, 64, 94, 95, 107, 204, 205; Tilak's campaign in, 4, 150, 151, 168, 172–191; nationality of, 6; elites of, 18, 19, 27, 28, 41, 134, 152–171, 174–175, 176, 178; moderate leaders of, 69, 70, 135, 136, 147, 148, 160–171, 181, 182, 190, 193, 195, 229–230; communal riot in, 66, 67, 70, 71, 75; cow protection in, 67, 68, 70; Ganapati movement in, 76, 78, 81, 84, 85, 90–91, 226; plague in, 112, 113n; Shiv Sena, 120; press of, 149, 164–165, 168, 169, 187; society of, 151–156; Bombay-Poona rivalry, 168–171; swadeshi movement in, 173, 174–176, 177; postal strike in, 177–178; 1908 strike in, 178–184; Tilak's lieutenants in, 186, 187, 194, 206, 207; Home Rule movement in, 198, 199, 198n, 207. *See also* Bombay Presidency Association; Capitalists; Millhands, Millowners; Mills; Non-Brahmans
Bombay Gazette: critical of Bhahmans, 31, 35
Bombay Government, 36n, 45, 62, 99, 135, 156; elites in, 17, 19; policy towards Brahmans, 17, 18, 20, 23–32, 35–37, 38, 39, 44, 73–74; as mythmaker, 34–35, 44, 118–119; policies on caste, 37–39; policies on Muslims, 38, 39, 79; criticized by Brahmans, 43, 44, 68, 69, 70, 71, 72, 74; legislative council reforms and, 63–66; reaction to communal riots, 68, 69, 70, 71, 73, 74; and the Ganapati movement, 84–85, 88, 93; support of Shivaji memorial, 112; plague policies, 112–113, 113n; and Kolhapur, 117–118, 119; famine policies, 123, 125–126, 132, 138, 139, 140, 141, 144, 148; land policies, 124, 138–141, 143, 144–150; and no-rent campaign, 131, 137–138, 141–143, 149; reaction to 1908 strike, 179, 180, 181. *See also* Myths
Bombay High Court, 117, 156, 160, 179, 186
Bombay Land Revenue Amendment Bill, 87, 146–149
Bombay Legislative Council, 134, 146, 147, 194; reforms and, 63–66
Bombay Mill-Owners' Association, 65
Bombay Municipal Corporation, 37, 64, 165n
Bombay Native Piece-Goods Merchants' Association, 65
Bombay Native Share and Stockbrokers' Association, 165
Bombay Presidency, 18, 66, 99, 141, 146, 160, 193
Bombay Presidency Association, 129, 135, 148, 171, 171n, 173; Council of, 147, 153, 157, 158, 161–163, 165, 168, 190, 229–230; social background of, 153, 156–158, 160, 167–168; declining elite support, 161–163, 164–165, 166–167
Bombay Provincial Conference, 52, 62, 65, 69, 161, 161n, 169, 170, 187, 187n, 199; comparison between the 1915 moderate and extremist conferences, 193–196
Bombay Provincial Council, 214
Bombay Samachar, 164
Bombay University, Fellows of, 64
Bombay Workers' Conference, 156
Boycott: of British goods, 165, 173, 174, 175, 185, 199, 212; impact on imports and exports, 176–177, 177n; of councils, 207, 208, 210, 213
Brahmans, of Maharashtra, historians, 4, 216n; communities of, 7, 17–19; Kshatriya role of, 8, 9, 90, 188; British policy towards, 17, 18, 20, 23–32, 35–37, 38, 39, 44, 73–74; social and political dominance, 20, 20n, 37–38, 39, 62, 140, 152, 153; sexual perceptions of, 26, 90; response to British rule, 32–34, 39–40, 42–43, 44; myths of, 34–35, 39, 43, 44; alienation of, 37, 38, 39, 45–46, 74; occupations of, 41, 154; criticism of Bombay Government, 43, 44, 68, 69, 70, 71, 72, 74; language of Brahmanical interest, 56, 214; attempts to politicize non-Brahmans, 75, 80, 80n, 85, 86, 97, 104, 109, 200; conflict with Kolhapur, 116–118, 119; and Tilak party, 197; liberals, 215,

216, 217. *See also* Chitpavans; Deshasthas; Militant tradition; Myths; Peshwas
Brewin, Mr., 56–57
Brown, Judith M., 220, 220n
Buddha, 51, 119; Buddhists, 53
Budhwar *Peth* (Poona), 77

Calcutta, 6, 27, 161n, 190, 204, 205
Capitalists, 169, 174; of Bombay City, 135, 176, 181; British, 153; British rule described as, 186
Cashman, Richard Ian, 219, 219n
Caste, 103, 116, 117, 164, 168, 219; and Tilak, 53–55, 56–57, 169; communities in politics, 57, 57n; and Ganapati movement, 81, 85. *See also* Brahmans; Non-Brahmans; Untouchables; and individual castes by name
Catanach, I. J., 41
Central Division, 37, 64, 65, 65n, 73, 136
Central Provinces, 161n, 189, 194, 198, 199, 203, 208; Marathi districts of, 188, 188n, 209; Hindi districts of, 209
Ceylon, 183
Chambers, W. A., 168, 229
Champion, 168
Chandavarkar, Narayan Ganesh, 160n, 161n, 162, 164, 170, 229
Chapekar, brothers, 91, 114; and Natu group, 59
Chapekar, Damodar Hari, 114; and the Ganapati movement, 91
Charismatic authority, 120, 205; of Tilak, 181, 191
Chhatre, Professor, 47
Chichgur, Hormusji, 165
Chiefs, 29, 30; and Shivaji movement, 100–101, 102, 105, 106, 109, 111, 122. *See also* Princes; *Sardars*
China, 62, 157
Chiplunkar, *Krishnashastri* Hari, 40
Chiplunkar, *Vishnushastri* Vishnu Krishna, 45, 49, 61, 201, 222, 223, 224; on Kshatriya role of Brahmans, 8; on Peshwas, 8, 40, 216n; criticism of liberals, 40; nationalist protest, 44
Chirol Valentine: on Brahmans, 32
Chitpavans, 47, 61, 89, 90, 115, 216, 219, 222, 223; description of, 18, 21, 34; dominant position of, 18, 19, 22, 152, 200; response to British rule, 19, 32–34, 43; political activism of, 27, 32; and conspiracy theory, 29–30; and Ganapati movement, 76, 85, 91; in Tilak party, 95, 126, 127, 147, 197. *See also* Brahmans
Chitrashala Press, 61, 129
Christian, 22, 152n, 186

Civil disobedience. *See* Non-cooperation
Civilians (of ICS), 26, 82; hostility to Brahmans, 23, 36, 36n; and Bombay *rayats*, 138–139, 140, 141
Civil Service: Indian (ICS), 20; Uncovenanted, Bombay, 19; Covenanted, Bombay, 20
Clarke, Sir George, 110, 179n; and 1908 strike, 179–180, 181
Collectors, 129, 133, 137, 138; Assistant, 130
Commons, House of, 63, 64, 165, 165n, 190
Communal Award, 1932, 214
Communal riots, 62; in Bombay City, 56 66–71, 75, 156, 167; in Poona City, 60, 72–73, 74, 92–93; in the Deccan, 66, 70–71, 72, 73, 74, 87; at Prabhas Patan (Junagadh), 66; at Yeola (Nasik), 70, 72, 73; at Dhulia (Khandesh), 71. *See also* Cow protection
Communications: of elite and society, 61; between rulers and elite, 72, 73, 74
Communists: on Shivaji, 119; on Tilak, 184–185. *See also* Lenin; Soviet historians
Congress, Indian National, 119, 120, 121, 147, 161, 169, 171 188, 191, 192, 194, 198, 203, 204, 206, 207, 220; Lord Reay on, 37; attempts to broaden base of, 45, 46, 56, 75, 79, 80, 84, 96, 97, 98, 105, 106, 111, 125, 181; Poona circle of, 52; princes and, 110, 111; Bombay branch of, 151, 153, 159, 160, 164, 165, 166, 168; presidents of, 157, 160, 160n; opposition to, 165; Muslims and, 167, 213, 214; at Surat (1907), 186; at Calcutta (1901), 190; re-entry of Tilak group (1916), 192n, 212; membership of, 193, 193n, 209; at Calcutta (1920), 204, 205; and non-cooperation, 207, 207n, 208, 209; and Maharashtra, 208, 209, 215, 216. *See also* Bombay Presidency Association; Bombay Provincial Conference, Non-cooperation, *PSS*
Congress Democratic Party, Manifesto, 185, 185n
Conspiracy, 181; theory, 17, 23–24, 29–32, 73; limitations of theory, 32–34; no-rent, 137, 143. *See also* Myth
Constitutional politics, 123, 161; and Tilak, 192, 193
Cornwallis, Lord, 149
Cow protection, 59, 107, 119, 126–127, 136, 145; in Bombay City, 67–68; and communal riots, 68, 70; in Deccan, 67, 68; *Gaupalan Upadeshak Mandali*, Bombay, 67; *Gorakshak Mandali*, Bombay, 67, 67n; Gujaratis and, 67n, 68; society in Poona, 60, 67

INDEX

Cultivators, 133, 135, 149, 150. See also Rayats
Curzon, Lord, 86, 87, 88, 110; critic of Bombay famine and land policies, 138, 139–140, 141, 146, 147, 149 150
Cutch, 99; Maharaja of, 100n, 102

Dahanu Taluka (Kolaba), 135
Dantra, Pestonji Behramji, 135
Darjis, 85
Daruwalla bridge (Poona), communal riot, 92
Das, C. R., 199
Dastane, V. V., 211
Davakinandan, Maharaj, 57
Deccan, 6, 8, 11, 19, 38, 41, 69, 103, 167, 172, 195; Brahmans of, 17, 18, 19, 61, 79; *PSS* branches, 27; famine in, 28; 112, 123; riots, 1875, 28, 41, 144; aristocracy of, 64, 99–100, 115, 122; cow protection in, 67; Ganapati movement in, 76, 78, 81, 82; press of, 82; and Shivaji movement, 107, 115; *rayats* of, 124, 145, 150, 151; no-rent campaign in, 126, 127, 129; Congress in, 188, 206. *See also* under individual towns
Deccan Agriculturalists' Relief Act, 41, 144; support of, 124; opposition to extension in 1891, 148, 149
Deccan Association, 38, 62, 62n; supported by princes, 110, 111, 116
Deccan Bank, 111
Deccan College, 96, 190; enrollments, 19, 19n, 41n; Tilak attends, 47, 48, 171n, 197
Deccan Education Society, 48; disputes within, 49–51, 52; princely support of, 100, 102, 110, 111, 160; support from Bombay and Poona, 159–160
Deccan *Sabha*, 126n, 129
Deepchund, Veerchund, 158, 158n
Democrat, Tilak as, 181, 184
Democratic Swarajya Party, 215
Deo, Shankarrao Dattatreya, 215; participates in satyagraha, 202, 208; joins Gandhi, 206, 211
Deo, Shankar Shrikrishna, 15, 194, 197
Depressed Classes: All-India Conference, 1918 and Tilak, 54–55, 200–201; Mission Society, 200. *See also* Scheduled Castes; Untouchables
Desai, Iccharam, 165, 187
Deshasthas, 22, 137, 189, 190 200; social and economic status, 19, 21, 34; and Tilak, 197
Deshmukh, Dr. Moreshwar Ganesh, 91, 175n

Deshmukh, *Lokahitawadi Sardar* Gopal Hari, 62n, 161n; social critic, 33, 40
Deshpande, Gangadharrao Balkrishna; lieutenant of Tilak, 192n, 196, 197, 202, 203, 204, 205, 206; Joins Gandhi, 202, 203, 204, 205, 206
Desphande, Keshav Ganesh, 110
Dharamsi, Dwarkadas, 154n, 158, 176
Dharwar, 57n, 67, 123n, 161n, 195, 196n, 197, 210; no-rent movement in, 132, 133
Dhulia (Khandesh), 35, 71, 136, 194, 226
Din Bandhu, 156, 156n
District Magistrate, Kolaba, 130, 134
Dixit, Hari Sitaram, 173, 230
Dravidian, 216
Dufferin, Lord, 45, 45n, 46
Durga, (Kali), 1
Dutt, R. C. 139
Dutt, R. Palme, 184
Dvar celebration, Wai, 82

East Indian Community, 217
Education, 157, 159; impact of western, 30, 39–40, 41; encouragement of Maratha, 110, 115–116, 116n, 117, 183; national, 191, 213; boycott of, 212
Education Department, 37–38, 197
Eknath, 11
Eksambekar, Anantrao Joshi, 131, 137
Elective principle, Bombay Legislative Council, 63–66
Electorates, separate, 201, 214
Elites, 100, 118; and colonial society, 17, 44; Deccan, 17–18; Bombay City, 18, 19, 27, 28, 41, 134, 152–171, 174–175, 176, 178; Poona, 27, 42–43, 64–66, 104, 152, 168–171; professional, 27, 42–43, 63, 64n, 79, 152, 153, 158, 159, 193, 194, 196; business, 158, 159, 159n, 193, 194, 196; landed, 193, 194, 196. *See also* Landowners; Merchants; Mill-owners
Elphinstone, Mountstuart, 23–24
England, 54, 63, 64, 143, 199, 201, 203, 204
Erandol Taluka (Khandesh), 136
Erotic tradition, 12, 13, 14, 15, 89
Europeans, 108, 153, 179, 180; and business, 154, 155, 175
Extremists, 170, 178, 181, 187; ideology of, 46, 115, 178; and Brahmans, 80, 168, 199, 200; programme of, 86, 87, 88, 91, 165, 166, 175, 182; and revolutionary movement, 91, 91n; factions within, 96n, 191; and princes, 115, 122; and press, 164, 187n; social background of, 193–196; and non-Brahmans, 199, 200. *See also* Brahmans; Chitpavans; Mass politics; Non-Brahmans; Tilak

INDEX

Fabian socialist, 168, 186
Factory Commission, 1907, 183, 184–185n
Factory legislation, 148, 156; Tilak against, 125, 172–173
Famine: (1876–77), 28, 123; (1896–97), 109–110, 112, 123ff.
Famine campaign, 4, 123–150, 151, 197. *See also* No-rent campaign
Famine Committee, 126; secretaries of, 126, 127n
Famine commissions: (1898), 138, 139, 141, 142; (1901), 138, 140, 141, 144–145
"Famine Narratives," 28, 124
Famine Relief Code, 123, 125, 126, 129, 141, 143
Fergusson, Sir James, 36, 36n
Fergusson College, 41n, 49, 61, 113; social background of students, 22, 24
Ferris, Colonel, 118
Festivals, political rationale of, 78–79. *See also* Ganapati and Shivaji Festivals
Forest laws, opposition to, 130, 136, 145, 212
Forster, E. M., portrayal of Brahmans, 26–27
Frazer, Lovat, 183
Friendly societies (*mitra mandalis*), 157

Gadgil, N. V., 215
Gaekwar of Baroda, 28; Sayaji Rao, 62n, 99, 100n, 112n; political perspective of, 110–111
Ganapati (Ganesha, Gajanan, Chintamani), 13n, 75ff, 114, 216; sexual character of, 13–14
Ganapati festival, 3, 4, 61, 75–97, 98, 106, 109, 144, 145, 150, 151, 197, 218. *See also Mela* movement; Mass politics; Tilak
Ganapati songs, 13–14, 61n, 78, 83–84, 87–88, 89, 227–228
Gandhi, *Mahatma* Mohandas Karamchand, 94, 188, 199, 213; and myths, 2, 219–220, 221; and Tilak, 47, 48, 51, 55–56, 61, 202–203, 204, 205, 207, 212–213, 214, 220, 221; and non-cooperation, 62, 204, 207, 207n, 208, 212; on Shivaji, 121–122; and Maharashtra, 202, 203, 204, 205–208, 209, 210–216, 217, 221
Ganesh *Mandal:* Bombay, 91; Poona, 81–82, 94, 94n, 96
Gazetteer, Poona, on Brahmans, 31–32
Gharat, Ramchandra Lakshman, 134, 134n, 158
Ghate, V., 216n
Ghatis, 155
Ghose, Aurobindo, 110
Ghose, Motilal, 54
Ghotwadekar, Ganesh Narayan, 60, 94n

Girgaum (Bombay), 91
Gita Rahasya, 55, 95n
Gokhale, Damodar Vishwanath, 194
Gokhale, Gopal Krishna, 4, 105, 160n, 192, 222, 223, 224; and Tilak, 49–50, 52; and Ranade, 52, 147, 148; criticized by Bhide, 88–89, 227–228
Gokhle, Narayan Vishnu, 163, 165, 229
Gondal, Maharaja of, 100n, 102
Government of India, 56, 123, 123n, 143, 145, 146. *See also* individual viceroys
Grant Duff, James, 25, 101
Grant Medical College, 189
Great Tradition, 1, 12, 13, 75
Gubernatis, Count, 76, 83
Gujarat, 99, 178, 193, 195, 199, 209, 210
Gujarati, 57n, 164, 168, 169; supports Tilak, 165, 187, 187n
Gujarati, 152n, 198
Gujaratis, 7, 20, 22, 69, 154n, 168, 200; and communal riots, 66, 67, 68; and cow protection, 67, 67n, 68; and Ganapati movement, 85, 90; and Shivaji, 121; in Bombay elites, 153, 154, 157, 160; press of, 164; and Tilak, 176, 180, 181, 187; and Gandhi, 207, 211, 220
Gunda (criminal)-style politics, 96
Gupte, B. A., 50
Gwalior, 76, 99, 99n, 176, 187

Hamilton, Lord, 110, 118; and Bombay land revenue policies, 139, 140, 141, 146, 147–148
Hanuman (Maruti), 15, 76, 78
Harris, Lord, 45, 45n, 62–63, 107, 111; and legislative council reforms, 63–65, 65n, 66; and communal riots, 66, 70, 71, 74; critical of Brahmans, 74; and Ganapati movement, 84–85
Hindoo College, 24
Hinduism, 4, 12, 40, 77, 78, 88, 152, 188, 189, 190
Hindu Mahasabha, 119, 120, 211, 214, 215
Hindu Punch, 90
Hindus, 43, 63, 103, 152n, 167, 213, 219; and communal riots, 66, 68, 69, 71, 72, 73, 92, 93; and Ganapati movement, 78, 79, 80, 83, 84, 85, 87, 90, 91; and Shivaji movement, 105, 106, 114, 119; in Bombay City, 153, 154, 156, 157, 168, 172
Historiography: of Tilak, 3–5; of 1908 strike, 181–185
Hitler, 121
Holi, 14
Holkar, *See* Indore
Home Rule: All-Indian Home Rule League

(Besant), 199, 207; Indian Home Rule League (Tilak), 194, 197, 198n, 199, 199n, 200, 207
Hubli (Dharwar), 67, 123n
Hume, A. O., 167
Hyderabad State, 173

Ichalkaranji, Chief of, 102, 112n, 147; and Shivaji movement, 105, 105n, 106; and Tilak, 115
Inamdars, 105
Indebtedness, peasant, 144, 146, 148
India Labour League, 194
Indian history, 179, 219
Indian Home Rule League. *See* Home Rule
Indian Spectator, 57n, 84, 90, 100, 111, 164, 168
Indore, 99, 99n,; Maharaja of (Holkar), 50, 51, 100n, 102
Indu of Bombay, 86
Indu Prakash, 57n, 164
Industrial advancement, 87, 164, 169, 173, 174, 175, 176, 177, 182, 185n
Industrial Conference, 1892, 53–54, 169, 170
Ireland, 143; Land League of, 123, 143; political styles of, 140. *See also* Parnell

Jagirdars, 99, 106
Jagirs, 99
Jains, 22, 68, 121, 152n, 158, 201
Jame Jamshed, 164
Jamkhandi, Chief of, 100n, 102, 112n,
Japan, 62
Jathar, 105
Jati, 18, 152
Jats, 7
Jawhar, Raja of, 102
Jayakar, Mukund Ramrao, 207n, 211, 214; and Tilak, 190, 201
Jedhe, Keshavrao Marutirao, 94, 201, 215
Jeejeebhoy, Sir Jamsetjee, 163
Jejuri, 11, 104
Jews (Bene Israel), 154, 160
Jinnah, Mohammed Ali, 207, 207n, 220, 230
Jinsiwale, Professor Ganesh Shridhar, 95, 188
Jnaneshwar, 11, 12
Johnson, Gordon, 200
Joshi, S. L., 173
Joshi, Vinayak B., 197
Joshi, Waman Rao, 203, 204
Joshi, *Wasukoka* Wasudeo Ganesh, 129, 222, 223, 224; and Tilak, 59, 61–62
Juma Masjid, 57, 68
Junagadh, 66; Nawab of, 102

Kabraji, K. N., 164
Kagal, Chief of, 102, 106, (Junior), 112n

Kaira, 195
Kaiser-i-Hind, 57n, 149, 164, 168, 169
Kal, 90, 96
Kale, Antaji Damodar, 91
Kalyan (Thana), 142, 198n
Kama, Khurshedji Rustomji, 158, 230
Kamathi, 85
Kanara, 138
Kanarese (Kannada), 152n, 196, 196n, 198
Kapole Banias, 157, 158
Karachi, 64, 157, 161, 161n; Chamber of Commerce, 64, 66
Karad (Satara), 123n, 194
Karaka, Dosabhoy Framjee, 163
Karandikar, J. S., 15
Karandikar, *Dadasaheb* Raghunath Pandurang, 194, 197, 198n, 214
Karhadas, 22, 176, 197, 200
Karma Yoga, Tilak on, 55
Karnatak, Bombay, 196; and Tilak, 193, 194, 196, 197, 198, 199; and Gandhi, 204, 206, 207; and Civil Disobedience Enquiry Committee, 210, 211
Karve, Professor Dhondo Keshav, 89, 222, 223, 224
Katagade, *Pundalik* N. T., 202
Kathiawar, 99
Kayastha Prabhu, 115
Keer, Dhananjay, 216n
Kelkar, Narsinh Chintaman, 197, 198, 198n, 222, 223, 224; on bhakti tradition, 11–12; on Tilak, 47; and factions within Tilak party, 89, 90, 96, 96n; "moderate" extremist, 90, 95–96, 191; as author and journalist, 95; and no-rent campaign, 126, 137–138; and Signallers' Association, 173; and swadeshi, 176; heir of Tilak, 205–206; and Gandhi, 207, 207n; defends Maharashtra non-cooperation effort, 208; and Gandhian Congress, 211, 212; on Muslims, 213; and Swaraj Party, 214
Kelve-Mahim (Thana), 123n, 136
Kesari, 49, 57n, 78, 80, 85–86, 95; in Deccan, 82; factions within, 90, 96; and Shivaji fund, 106–107; and Shivaji tradition, 108, 109, 113–114; critical of Bombay famine policy, 125–126, 129, 138, 141; on Signallers' strike, 173; on swadeshi, 174; staff of, 194, 206, 217; on non-Brahmans, 202; and Gandhi, 203
Ketkar, V. G., 194
Khadilkar, Krishnaji Prabhakar, 222, 223, 224; lieutenant of Tilak, 95, 192n, 197, 217; differences with Kelkar, 96, 96n; supporter of Gandhi, 206, 217; retires, 217
Khan, Afzal, 104, 113, 114, 122

INDEX

Khandesh, 71, 123n, 195; and no-rent campaign, 133, 136, 142
Khandoba, 11, 12, 76
Kharparde, *Dadasaheb* Ganesh Shridhar: and swadeshi, 175–176, 175n; and Tilak, 189, 194, 197, 203, 205, 206; and Home Rule, 198n; critic of Gandhi, 203, 207–208; and Civil Disobedience Enquiry Committee, 211
Khare, Daji Abaji, 147, 161n, 175n, 197; and Tilak, 91, 171, 171n; and forest rules, 136; and *khots*, 137; and BPA, 163, 171, 171n; a "connecting link," 171, 194
Khasgiwale, *Sardar Tatyasaheb* Krishnaji Kashinath, 94n, 105; and Natus, 60
Khatalvad (Kolaba), 130
Khatau, Goverhandas, 154n, 157–158n, 176; and Mulraj, 154n, 157–158n
Khatris, 85, 134
Khilafat movement, and Tilak, 204, 213, 214
Khimjee, Lakhmidas, 67, 72, 159
Khojas, 176, 187
Khoti tenure, 41–42; Tilak against *khoti* bill, 42
Khots, 25, 41, 42; association of Ratnagiri, 137
Kolaba, 18, 195; and no-rent campaign, 127n, 130, 133, 134, 135, 137
Kolhapur, 24, 94, 99, 99n, 115, 116, 119, 123n, 201; Regent of, 101; Shivaji Club, 114; state service, 116, 116n; Darbar, 117; *melas* in, 226
Kolhapur, Maharaja of (Shahu), 62n, 86–87, 100n, 112n; and non-Brahmans, 94, 115, 116, 116n, 117; and DES, 102; and Shivaji movement, 105, 106, 111, 114; conflict with Tilak, 115–119
Kolis, 22, 32
Konkan 18, 29, 46, 76, 147, 155, 193, 194, 195; *khots* of, 25, 41, 137; and no-rent campaign, 126, 127, 137
Kowjalgi, Shrinivas Venkatesh, 197
Kridabhuvan (Poona), 58, 61
Krishna, 13, 51, 114
Krishnaswamy, S., on communal riots, 71–72
Kshatriya, Bhunsalay, 158
Kshatriya tradition, 8, 13; and Shivaji, 7, 8, 10, 11, 98, 103; and bhakti, 7, 10, 11, 14, 16, 103; and Brahmans, 8, 27, 40, 188; and other traditions, 15; and Tilak, 48
Kumar, Ravinder, 41; on Tilak, 52
Kunbis, 22, 124. *See also* Marathas
Kurundwad, Chief of, 100n; (Junior), 99, 105; (Senior), 105, 106

Labour, 172, 178, 182, 184, 185, 187, 194, 217, 219; force of Bombay, 151, 152, 155, 156, 157, 177, 181, 186, 191. *See also* Millhands; Trade unions
Labour Conference (British). 186
Labour Party (British), and Tilak, 186, 192
Laissez-faire policy, of Bombay elites, 148
Lajpatrai, Lala, 199
Lamington, Lord, 149, 149n
Lancashire manufacturers, 173, 176n, 184
Landlords (landowners), 119, 140, 141, 146, 148, 149, 158, 219; and no-rent campaign, 124, 124n, 133, 134, 135, 137, 142. *See also* Alienation (land); Elites; No-rent campaign; *Rayats*; *Sardars*
Land revenue policies (Bombay Government), 124, 138–141, 143, 144–150
Lanowli, 67
Lansdowne, Lord, 64
Latthe, A. B., 201
Latur (Hyderabad), 173
Lawate, Shankar Ganesh, 91, 126
Lawyers, 148, 186, 188, 189, 194; and Bombay elites, 154, 158, 159, 160, 173, 201; and non-cooperation, 208; 209
Leach, Edmund, 13
Lee-Warner, Sir William, 20n, 84; critic of Brahmans, 20, 23, 26
Legislative council reforms, 63–66, 100
Lele, V. R. 194, 198n
Lenin, 172n, 181–182, 184
Lieutenants of Tilak, 59–62, 94–96, 126–127, 186–191, 192, 192n, 194, 196–197, 202–203, 204–209, 210–215, 216, 217, 218, 221
Lingayats, 22, 201
Lingam, 11
Liquor: propaganda against, 87, 136, 177; lobby, 135. *See also* Temperance, Toddy
Little Tradition, 12, 75; and Shivaji, 103–104, 104n, 105
Local boards (Southern Division), 64, 65, 65n
Local government: Brahmans and, 20; Ripon reforms, 23
Lohanas, 68
Lokahitawadi.See Deshmukh; *Sardar* Gopal Hari
Lokamanya. *See* Tilak
Lokhande, Narayan Meghaji, 156
London, 157
Lucknow Pact, 214
Lyall, Sir A. L. and 1898 famine commission, 138, 139, 142

McDonald, Ellen E. and Craig M. Stark, 34, 42
Macdonnell, Sir A. P., famine commission (1901), 138, 139, 140, 144, 146

Madhavrao, 8-9, 76
Madhva, 55
Madras, 95, 139, 160n, 161n, 169, 177n, 210, 216
Mahableshwar, 118
Mahad, 57n, 109
Maharaj, Baba, alias Shrimant Wasudeo Harihar Pandit, 94, 94n, 95, 105, 117
Maharashtra, 93, 154, 154n; Tilak and, 3, 188, 198, 199, 202, 217, 218, 221; culture of, 6-7, 152, 216, 217, 218; traditions of, 6-16; and Shivaji, 6-7, 9, 10, 104, 109, 119, 121; nationalism of, 9-10, 12; and Ganapati, 13-14, 90; and cow protection, 68; and Shiv Sena, 120; and swadeshi, 174; and Gandhi, 202, 203, 204, 205-208, 209, 210-216, 217, 221. *See also* Bhakti tradition; Kshatriya tradition
Maharashtra Provincial Congress Committee, 208
Maharashtrians, 141, 153, 155, 159, 160, 181
Mahavira, 1
Mahim (Bombay), 85
Mahratta, 45, 48, 57n, 59, 66, 68, 74, 97, 105, 107, 110, 111, 116, 117, 121, 169, 173, 183, 201, 203, 208; staff of, 95, 95n, 96, 194, 206, 217
Malabar, 213
Malabari, Behramji Merwanji, 163-164, 164n
Malis, 156
Mamlatdars, 23, 129, 142
Manchester, imports from, 176, 176n, 177
Mandalay, 178
Manufacturers, 182, 184; in Bombay City, 155, 158, 159, 159n; and swadeshi, 174-175, 175n. *See also* Mill-owners; Mills
Maratha Aikya Icchu Sabha, 183
Maratha Brahmans, 17, 18, 24, 54, 140, 154. *See also* Brahmans; Chitpavans
Maratha Educational Conference, 201
Marathas: (non-Brahmans), 200, 201; society of, 6-7; and regional culture, 7; and education, 22, 62n, 110, 117; princes, 28, 99, 99n, 102; and Ganapati movement, 85; and Kolhapur, 117-118; of Bombay, 183; (inhabitants of Maharashtra), 29, 41, 83, 98, 101, 113, 114, 121, 152, 174, 211; and nationalism, 10, 14, 24, 43, 103; (Raj of), 28, 39, 99, 100, 101, 104
Marathi, 89, 126, 152, 152n; and bhakti movement, 13; literature, 34; —speaking region, 90, 188, 188n, 194, 199, 211; press, 95, 96, 164, 168, 176; propaganda in, 129, 198
Markets: Poona, 19, 77, 80; Bombay, 178, 180

Martial: "races," 26; arts, 15-16, 59, 60, 77-80, 114; tradition, 120, 121, 211
Marwadis, 7, 85, 125, 142, 198, 200
Mass politics, 74, 75, 124-125, 164, 167, 172, 185, 192, 198-199, 202, 212; and myths, 44, 97, 122, 220, 221; theory of, 46, 79-80; results of, 97-98, 99, 122, 138, 150, 178, 187, 191, 193, 219. *See also* Myths; individual mass movements
Matheran, 157
Maths, 15-16
Mazzini, 91
Mehta, Pherozeshah, 156-157, 159, 160n, 161n, 170, 186, 192, 229; and Tilak, 70, 171, 172; leader of Bombay, 147, 163, 166
Mela movement, songs of, 13-14, 61n, 78, 83-84, 87-88, 89, 227-228; description of, 77-78; and communal relations, 78, 79, 92-93; spread of, 80-84, 226; and non-Brahmans, 80n, 85-86, 94; and society, 80n, 85-86, 90-91; organization of, 81-83; reaction to, 84-85, 88-89; and politicization, 86, 91, 97; *Sanmitra Samaj Mela*, 86, 87n, 88-89, 227-228; *Bhor Vakil's Mela*, 86; *Shur Maratha Mela*, 86; *Sahakhari Shetaki Mela*, 86; *Chatrapati Sambhaji Mela*, 86; *Namdev Shimpi Mela*, 87; *Nasik Mitra Mela*, 91; contemporary, 93; *Chatrapati Mela*, 94. *See also* Ganapati festival
Merchants, 123, 125; of Bombay, 148, 150, 154, 155, 157, 158, 159, 159n, 174, 181
Mhaske, Gangaram Bhau, 62, 105, 116
Middle class, 194, 207
Militant: politics, 59, 60, 61, 115, 165, 166, 167, 191, 202, 212; tradition, 16, 108, 188; nationalism, 165, 191
Military, 119, 120, 121-122; British, 72, 178, 179, 180, 181; Bombay army, 155
Mill-hands, 150; and communal riots (1893), 69, 156; and Ganapati movement, 85; description of, 155-156, 183; and Tilak, 172, 177, 178-181, 183; and twelve-hour day, 182. *See also* Strikes; Trade unions
Mill-Hands' Association, Bombay, 156, 194
Mill-owners, 67, 148, 153, 159, 165, 182, 183; and BPA, 154, 157, 158; and swadeshi, 175, 176, 177
Mills, 153, 154, 158; Indian and European cooperation in, 155; strike in Bombay, 178, 179, 180; conditions in, 182, 183
Miraj, chiefs of, 102, 112n
Mission house, Poona, 54, 60
Moderates, 96, 173, 181, 187, 187n, 190; and Ranade, 35, 170; reaction to communal riots, 69; 71; criticized by extremists, 87, 88, 89, 90, 96n; comparison with

INDEX 241

extremist provincial conference (1915), 193, 194, 195, 196. *See also* Gokhale
Modernity, 56; authority of, 219
Modernization, 66, 66n, 73, 220
Mofussil, 61, 64, 127, 133, 157, 197, 211
Money-lenders (*sawkars*), 42, 88, 124, 142, 144; and Tilak party, 148
Montagu: Declaration (1917), 201, 202; reforms, 205
Moolji, Damodurdas Thackersey, 158, 158n, 159
Moplah riots, 213
Mosques, 73; music before, 71, 72, 73
Moulvis, against social reform, 56, 57
Mudhol, Raja of, 102
Mudliar, Coopuswamy, 77
Mughals, 120, 121
Maharram, 73, 78, 86, 93
Mulshi satyagraha, 190n, 208, 210, 212
Municipalities, Northern Division, 64, 65n
Munje, Dr. Shivram Balkrishna, 189–190, 197, 198n; and Tilak, 189, 214; lieutenant of Tilak, 192n, 194; and Gandhi, 203; leaves Congress, 211; and civil disobedience, 212; on Muslims, 213, 214
Muslim League, 213; Tilak and, 193, 204 213, 214
Muslims, 29, 43, 63, 152n, 213, 220; of region, 7, 18; and education, 22, 38–39; and Age of Consent, 57; elite, 57, 153, 154, 157, 167; and communal riots, 66–67, 68, 68n, 69, 72–73, 156; and Ganapati festival, 78, 79, 84, 90, 91, 92, 93; and Shivaji movement, 103, 104, 105, 106, 108, 113, 114; and Congress, 167; and Home Rule, 190, 207; and Tilak, 204, 214, 219
Muzafferpur, 178
Mysticism, 10
Myths: definition of, 1, 218; of *Lokamanya*, 2–4, 181, 187, 219, 221; of *Mahatma*, 2; Brahman, 34–35, 39; and politics, 44; Tilak's use of, 97, 218; British, 34–35, 118–119; of Maharashtra, 216; nationalization of, 219–220; of resolution, 220–221. *See also* Conspiracy theory: Symbol; Usurper theory

Nagaon *Sabha*, 134
Nagoba procession, 73
Nagpur, 127, 188n, 190, 206; and *mela* movement, 226
Nagpurkar, 117
Namjoshi, Mahadev Ballal, 49, 70, 106, 222, 223, 224; lieutenant of Tilak, 61, 75
Nana Saheb, 33; (Balaji), 9
Naoroji, Dadabhai, 165, 165n, 166; Harris on, 63

Narotumdas, Harkisondas, 158, 158n
Nasik, 57n, 70, 174, 194, 195; and Ganapati movement, 81, 85; and no-rent movement, 136
Nathubhai, Tribhovandas Mangaldas, 157, 157n, 158, 158n, 229
Nationalism, 35, 53, 177, 182, 184, 197, 204; and festivals, 79, 85; and Maharashtra, 98, 103, 105, 106; Indian, 111; militant, 165; Bombay definition of, 167. *See also* Congress, Indian National
Nationalist League, of Marathas, 200
Native Opinion, 43, 57n, 164
Natu, *Balasaheb* Balwant Ramchandra, 59, 70, 94n, 105, 105n, 113n, 126n, 176; style of politics, 59, 60, 191; defender of orthodoxy, 59, 60, 188; followers of, 60, 94, 108, 126n; and Tilak, 60–61, 94
Natu, *Tatyasaheb* Hari Ramchandra: described as "sepoy," 59; followers of, 60; *mela* of, 92
Natu brothers, 59, 59n, 94
Nehru, Jawaharlal, 205; on Shivaji, 122
New English school, 48–49, 52, 61, 96
Nibandhmala, 61
Nizam state, 117
Non-Brahmans, 37, 43, 63; and Tilak, 4, 75, 181, 184, 200, 201, 202, 216n, 219; of region, 6–7, 76, 216; and education, 38, 62n, 105, 115–116; in PSS, 62, 200; and *mela* movement, 80, 80n, 85–86, 87, 94, 96, 97, 151; Kolhapur, 94, 115–116, 116n; *Satyashodak Samaj,* 94, 201; criticism of Tilak, 94, 201, 202; and Shivaji movement, 98, 99, 104, 105, 109, 151; of Poona, 152; of Bombay City, 153, 155; and Home Rule, 198, 199, 199n, 200; and extremists, 199, 200; and Congress, 215, 216; conflict with Brahmans, 215, 216, 219. *See also* Marathas
Non-cooperation, 192, 207n, 209; and Tilak, 204, 205; and Maharashtra, 208–209, 210, 212, 214; and Civil Disobedience Enquiry Committee, 210, 211, 210–211n. *See also* Satyagraha
Non-violence, 103, 211, 212
No-rent campaigns: (1873), 28, 124; (1896–97), 124n; organization of, 126–133; results of, 133–138, 141–143, 144, 149–150; (Oudh), 143. *See also* Bombay Government land policies; Peasants; *Rayats*
Northcote, Lord, 117n; and Kolhapur, 117, 118; land policies of, 140, 141, 146, 147
Northern Division, municipalities, 64, 65n
Northern India, 141, 143
North-West Frontier Provinces, 67, 139, 209

Olympic festivals, 78
Oral tradition, 14
Orion or Researches into the Antiquity of the Vedas, 55; orthodox, 56, 67, 97, 108, 170, 214; opinion against social reform, 57; defence of tradition, 59, 60, 95, 188; opinion against plague measures, 113; Hinduism, 184
Oudh, 143
Owen, Hugh, 198

Padamjee, Dorabjee, 20, 65
Paisa Fund, 87, 191; Committee, 91; *mela* of, 91
Pakistan, 120
Pal, B. C., amendment of, 207, 207n, 208
Pandharpur, 14
Pandits, 57
Pan-Islamism, 213
Panse, G. D., 137
Panvel, 57n, 127n; Taluka (Thana), 134, 135
Paranjpe, Shivram Mahadev, 109n, 198, 223, 224; and Ganapati movement, 94n; conflict with Kelkar, 95–96; 96n; and plague administration, 113n; and famine campaign, 126, 127n; and labour, 172, 178; and swadeshi, 174, 175, 175n; a militant extremist, 191; lieutenant of Tilak, 197; and Gandhi, 202, 203, 204, 206, 212; and Mulshi satyagraha, 208
Paranjpye, Raghunath Purushottam, 223, 224
Pardeshis, *mela* of, 85
Parekh, Goculdas Kahandas, 161, 161n, 229
Parnell, 35, 143; followers of, 123, 144
Parsis, 63, 65, 67, 90, 149; and Bombay Government, 18, 19; and education, 22; occupations, 41, 43, 154; and politics, 43, 163–164, 165–166, 165n; liquor lobby, 134–135; in Bombay City, 152n; in BPA, 153, 154, 158, 163–164, 165–166, 168; and philanthropy, 159–160; and Tilak, 176, 180, 181, 187
Parvati, 10
Pathans, 7
Patwardhan, *Annasaheb* Dr. Vinayak Ramchandra, 94n, 198n, 223, 224, 225; orthodox figurehead, 94–95, 95n
Patwardhan families, 76, 85
Peasants, 31, 129, 219; condition of, 27, 119, 144, 149; Civilians and, 140; indebtedness of, 146, 148; Tilak and, 150, 151, 184, 212; Mulshi Mavala-Maratha, 210. *See also* No-rent campaigns; *Rayats*
Penal Code, Indian 113, 143
Permanent settlement, 149

Peshwas, 18, 32, 33, 41, 46, 59, 60, 120, 152, 216; as Kshatriya Brahmans, 8–9; and Ganapati, 13, 76, 83; and usurper theory, 25; praised by *Vishnushastri* Chiplunkar, 40, 216n
Peths and Ganapati movement, 77, 81
Petit, Sir Dinshaw, 67, 163
Petitions, 147; no-rent, 129, 137
Petty-bourgeois, 185
Phadke, Vasudeo Balwant, raids of, 28–29; and *PSS*, 30, 35,
Phansalkar, Ganesh Ballal, 194, 198n
Phatak, Professor N. R., 86n, 95n; on Ramdas, 16; on Tilak, 95n, 205
Phule, Baburoa Bhaurao, 200
Phule, *Mahatma* Jotiba Govind, 40, 156, 200
Phulmali community, 156
Physical culture, 15–16, 188; and gymnasiums, 59, 189; *My System of Physical Culture*, and *Exercises for Ladies* by Lakshman Bhopatkar), 188
Plague (1897), 87; administration, 112–113, 113n, 145
Police, 58, 60, 91, 92, 93, 130, 136, 179, 180; Commissioner of, 68, 84, 88; force of Bombay, 155
Political Agent, Kolhapur, 118
Political timing, concept of, 220
Politicization, 75, 80, 80n, 85, 86, 97, 104, 109, 199, 219
Politics, all-India, 192, 193, 220. *See also* Region
Poona, 101, 120, 137, 160, 161n, 172, 173, 183, 186, 198n, 201, 204, 214, 215, 215n; description of, 6; society of, 19, 151–152; education in, 24, 54; revolts in, 29, 32, 35; Brahmans of, 33, 35, 39–40, 71–72, 73–74, 79, 85, 116, 117, 118, 144, 170, 222–225; politicians of, 43, 45, 50, 69, 70, 75, 82–83, 90, 94, 95, 96, 109n, 168, 176, 177, 182, 185, 197, 206, 208, 211; Congress circle of, 52; mission house of, 54; shastris of, 57; and Age of Consent Bill, 57–59; communal riots, 60, 67, 69, 71, 72–73, 74, 92–93; Tilak's support in, 61, 187–188, 194; and legislative council reforms, 64–66; and Ganapati movement, 76, 77, 79, 80–81, 85–86, 87, 88, 90, 92, 94, 226; non-Brahmans, 86, 94, 201; Muslims, 92, 93; Hindus, 93; and Shivaji movement, 105, 108, 113, 114; press of, 108, 116, 117; plague in, 113, 113n; conflict with Kolhapur, 117; "Irreconcilables," 123, 140, 143–144; famine, 125; elites of, 126, 150, 154, 159, 222–225; famine agents, 134, 136, 138, 141; famine campaign, 135, 139, 142, 145; rivalry with Bombay, 168–

171; swadeshi in, 174, 175; provincial conferences, 193, 195, 196. *See also* Deccan College; DES; *DS*; Fergusson College; PSS
Poona Association, 27
Poona Court of Sessions, 60
Poona District: 18, 133, 136; Court, 92; Conference, 201
Poona Mail train, 181
Poona Municipal Corporation, 37, 59, 61, 63, 94, 152n, 188, 200; Brahman dominance of, 20, 20n; Muslim boycott of, 93; plague administration, 113, 113n
Poona *Sarvajanik Sabha*, 52, 161n, 194; constitution of, 27; in 1870s, 28, 124; and Temple, 30, 31; denigrated, 35; and princes, 62, 100, 100n, 106, 115; and Ranade, 62, 106; and legislative council reforms, 65; on Harris, 71; and Shivaji movement, 104; captured by Tilak forces, 115, 126n; and famine campaign, 125, 126, 127, 129, 130, 131, 132, 133, 137, 138, 142, 145; non-recognition of, 132; Managing Committee, composition of, 200
Postal Department, 178, 183
Postal strike, support of, 178
Prabhas Patan, communal riot, 66
Prabhus, 22; Pathare, 190
Prarthana Samaj, 30, 88, 164; criticized, 40, 79
Prayascita, 54
Presidents: INC, 157, 160, 160n; BPC, 161, 161n
Press, 191; Deccan, 28; Anglo-Indian, 29, 31, 68, 69, 72, 178; Indian, 73; Poona Brahman, 116, 117, 203; disloyal, 141; of Bombay, 164, 168, 169, 170; freedom of, 179. *See also Kesari*; *Mahratta*; and other individual newspapers
Price control, Tilak on, 185
Prime minister, 122; Kolhapur, 115
Princely states, 99, 99n
Princes: and *PSS*, 62, 100, 100n, 106, 115; and Shivaji movement, 101, 110, 112, 115, 118, 124, 151; and DES, 102, 160; and social reform, 110-111. *See also* Chiefs; Gaekwar of Baroda; Maharaja of Kolhapur; *Sardars*; and other individual princes
Profiteering law, Tilak on, 185
Proletariat: Bombay, 4, 172, 177, 183, 185; Indian, 182 Prosecution, of Tilak, 178
Public Instruction, Director of, 39, 41
Public Service Commission (1886-87), 19
Punjab, 36n, 139, 161n, 199, 209
Punjab Land Alienation Act (1901), 145, 146, 148, 150
Punjab Legislative Council, 214

Puritan tradition, 68
Purshotumdas, Vundrovandas, 158, 158n, 230

Quarterly Journal of the Poona Sarvajanik Sabha, 173
Queen Empress, 70, 108

Raigad, 189; neglect of memorial at, 101; repair of memorial, 105, 106, 112; festival at, 105, 106, 107, 108-109, 109n
Rajaram, 101
Rajaram High School, 174
Rajasthanis, 20, 154n
Rajputs, 7, 100
Rajwade, V. K., 126; and Ramdas cult, 14-15
Rama, 15, 93
Ramanuja, 55
Ramayana, 15
Ramdas, 79, 91, 101, 109; cult of, 14-15; *Dasabodha* of, 79
Ramji, Manmohandas, 176
Ranade, Mahadev Govind, 65, 95, 223, 224, 225; on Maratha nationality, 9-10, 43-44, 103; famine and land policies of, 35, 124, 125, 147, 148, 148n, 150; denigrated, 35; counters usurper theory, 43-44; and protege, Gokhale, 52; and mission house incident, 54; and Tilak, 55-56, 70, 106, 151, 189; on religion, 56; party of, 62, 62n, 133, 170; and Shivaji, 101, 103-104, 105, 121; memorial fund, 112, 112n. *See also* Moderates
Rand, W. C., 114; plague administration of, 113, 113n
Rangari, Bhau, alias Bhau Lakshman Javle, 60, 94n
Rangaris, *mela* of, 85
Rao, Trimbak, 50
Rast Goftar, 57n, 164, 165
Ratnagiri, 18, 46, 57n, 109, 195; and Ganapati movement, 85, 226; non-rent movement of, 127, 133; *khoti* association of, 137
Ravana, 15
Rayats, 30, 87-88, 108, 143; and moneylenders, 42, 144, 148; and Tilak, 124, 125, 150, 151; and no-rent campaign, 133, 142. *See also* Peasants
Reay, Lord, 63, 101; sympathy for Brahmans, 36, 36n; support of Congress, 37
Reay Market (Poona), 19, 80
Reformation, 103
Region, 209, 210, 219; chauvinism of, 4, 121; politics of, 168, 192, 199, 212; and

244   INDEX

Gandhi, 206–207; culture of, 216
Religion, 158, 168, 185, 200; Tilak on, 55–56, 204
"Responsive co-operation," 204, 213
Revdanda (Kolaba), 57n, 127n, 134
Revivalism, Hindu, 67, 83
Revolutionary movements, 91–92n, 95, 206; and *melas*, 91; and Shivaji movement, 114, 115; Savarkar and, 119; in Bengal, 178; Bapat and, 190–191, 194, 212. *See also* Terrorism
Riots: Deccan (1875), 28, 41, 144; Age of Consent, 58; *mela*, 94; grain, 123; toddy, 136; mill-hands', 179–181, 182; Moplah, 213. *See also* Communal riots
Ripon, Lord, 23, 36
Rivalry, Bombay-Poona, 168–171
Rowlatt satyagraha, 202, 203, 204, 207
Rudolph, Lloyd and Susanne, 26
Rukhmini, 11
Russians, 108; working class of, 182

Sadashivrao Bhau Peshwa, 120
Sadhu, 94
Sahyadri mountains, 101
Saints. *See* Bhakti tradition
Saivite, 12, 68
Salis, and *mela* movement, 85
Salisbury, Lord, 64
Salt laws, 212
Samadhi, 11, 11n, 101, 105
Samarth, Narayan Madhav, 171, 230
Samkara, 55
Samyukta Maharashtra, 119
Sandhurst, Lord, 66, 66n; and land legislation, 145, 146
Sangli, Chief of, 99, 100n, 102
Sanmitra Samaj Mela. See *Mela* movement
Sanskrit, 13, 55; tradition, 218
Saraswati, Dayananda, 58
Saraswats, 22
Sardars, 59, 60, 94, 96, 99–100, 100n, 104, 147; and *PSS*, 62; enfranchised, 64, 65, 66; Agent for, 65; and Shivaji movement, 101, 105, 106, 111, 124
Sarvajanik ganapatis, 77, 80, 81, 82
Sarvajanik Sabha. *See* Poona *Sarvajanik Sabha*
Satara, 26, 57n, 62, 194, 195, 198n; plot in, 32; *mela* movement at, 81, 82, 226; and no-rent movement, 136, 137–138; provincial conference of, 161, 161n, 199
Sathaye, Dr. Dinkar Dhondo, 198; and labour, 194, 217; joins Gandhi, 202, 203, 204, 205; and Tilak, 205
Sathe, Achyut, famine agent, 126, 127, 127n, 130–131, 133
Satyagraha, 62, 205, 211, 218, 220; Mulshi,

190n, 208, 210, 212; Champaran, 202; Rowlatt, 202, 203, 204, 207. *See also* Non-cooperation
Satyagraha Sabha, Executive Committee of, 203
Satyashodak Samaj, 94, 201
Savarkar, brothers, 91, 190
Savarkar, Veer, 119, 211, 212
Sayani, Rahimtoola M., 69, 160n, 161n
Scheduled Castes, 7. *See also* Depressed Classes; Untouchables
Secretary of State, 118, 139, 141, 143, 180
Self-Government, 202
Setalvad, Chimanlal, 161n, 163, 229
Sexual perceptions: of Brahmans, 26, 90; of Hindus, 190
Shahu. *See* Maharaja of Kolhapur
Shanwar *Wada* (Poona), 58n, 70
Shastris, 56, 57
Shepherd community, 11
Shinde, Vithal Ramji, 55, 200
Shiva, 1, 13, 75, 78, 103, 120
Shivaji, 3, 24, 29, 77, 91, 94, 99, 104n, 107, 108, 109, 113, 151, 174, 217; and Kshatriya tradition, 7, 8; as symbol, 8, 98, 106, 119, 216, 218; and Maratha nationality, 9–10, 43–44, 101, 103, 216; and Ramdas, 14, 16; and Brahmans, 104, 118; Gandhi on, 121–122; Nehru on, 122
Shivaji Club, Kolhapur, 114
Shivaji festival, 4, 98–122, 144, 145, 150, 197, 216
Shivaji Fund, 106, 107, 111, 111n, 115, 115n, 122, 124; Committee, 106, 112
Shiv Sena, 120
Sholapur, 57n, 161n, 194, 195, 198n; and no-rent movement, 136; People's Association, 147n; and *mela* movement, 226
Sidapur Taluka (Kanara), 138
Signallers' Association, 173
Sikhs, 7
Sind, 20, 39, 193, 195
Sindhi, 22, 152n
Singh, Ranjit, Pratap and Govind, 122
Sirsi Taluka (Kanara), 138
Slaves, 185
Smritis, 113
Social Conference, 189
Social Equality League, 217
Socialism, 182, 217
Social reform, 157, 191, 200; criticism of, 40, 60; Tilak on, 52–54, 184, 215; advocates of, 53, 57, 58, 59, 164; Gaekwar and, 110–111; Bhopatkar and, 188; Khaparde and, 189; Munje and, 190
Soman, *Babasaheb*, 202
Somnath, 66

INDEX   245

Sonars, 22; *mela* of, 85
South India, 199, 202, 216; languages of, 152n
South Indians, 20, 153
Southern Division, 37, 64, 65, 65n, 137
Southern Maratha Country, 61, 136
Soviet: historians (Reisner and Goldberg), 4, 181–182; Communist writers, 184
Strikes, 149; of signallers, 173; Tilak and, 173, 178; postal, 178; of mill-hands, 172, 178, 179–181, 182; historiography of 1908 strike, 181–182, 184–185
Students, 159; and Tilak, 61, 126, 179, 190; and swadeshi, 174
Subodha Patrika, 57n, 88, 164
Sudharak, 57n, 87, 90, 106
Sudras, 185
Surat, 121, 161n, 186, 195
Survey: Department, 46; settlements, 134, 139
Swadeshi: Co-operative Stores Company Limited, Bombay, 176; Clothing Store, 197
Swadeshi movement, 110, 121, 136, 165, 184, 185, 198, 199, 212, 218; in 1870s, 27; and Ganapati movement, 87, 88; of Tilak, 173–176; results of Tilak's, 176–177, 177n, 187. *See also* Boycott
Swadeshi Vastu Pracharini Sabha, 175, 175n, 176
Swaraj, Tilak on, 190, 191, 192, 204, 215, 217, 218
Swaraj Party, 214, 215
Symbols: and politics, 98–99, 122; Shivaji as, 8, 98, 106, 119, 216, 218. *See also* Myths

Tabuts, 78, 83, 93
Tai Maharaj adoption case, 117, 117n; and Tilak, 47, 117, 189, 194
Taleyarkhan, Manekshah Jehangirshah, 134–135, 158, 230
Tamasha, 9, 13; tactics disapproved, 90, 96
Tantric, 11
Tata, Jamshedji Nasserwanji, 158
Tata, Ratanji 176
Tata Company, 210
Telang, Kashinath Trimbak, 170, 230
Telegraph Department, 183
Telegus, *melas* of, 85
Temperance, 91, 126, 191, 212; and Tilak, 177. *See also* Liquor; Toddy
Temple, Sir Richard, 29n; and Brahmans, 29–31, 74; and Ranade, 35
Temples, 108, 112; Tulsibag, 58n; Parvati Hill, 59; and communal riots, 66, 72; entry of, 189
Terrorism, 185. *See also* Revolutionary movements
Thackeray, Bal, 120–121
Thackersey, Vithaldas Damodar, 154n, 157, 157n, 158
Thakurdwar (Bombay), 91
Thana, 57n, 123n, 195; and no-rent movement, 127n, 129, 133, 134, 135, 137, 142
Theism, 164
Theosophy, 168, 189
Tilak, Jayantrao, 217
Tilak, *Lokamanya* Bal Gangadhar, 175n, 224, 225; myth of, 2–4, 181, 187, 219, 220, 221; and mass politics, 2–4, 46, 78–79, 78n, 87, 97, 109, 124, 138, 144, 150, 161, 166, 176, 178, 191, 192, 198, 199, 202; historiography of, 3–5, 216n; and peasants, 3, 150, 151, 184, 212; and Ganapati festival, 4, 75, 77–79, 78n, 80; and Shivaji festival, 4, 105–107, 109–110, 112, 113–114, 119, 120, 121, 124; and peasant campaign, 4, 125–126, 129–130, 138, 143, 144, 150, 151; and Bombay City, 4, 150, 151, 167, 168, 172–191; and non-Brahmans, 4, 75, 80, 87, 151, 181, 184, 199, 200, 201–202, 219; and proletariat, 4, 177; on *Bhagavad Gita,* 12, 55, 115; on Ramdas cult, 14–15; apotheosis of, 33n, 180; and *khoti* bill, 42; disciple of Chiplunka, 45–46; ancestors, 46–47; parents, 47; personality, 47–48, 49–52; and Gandhi, 47, 48, 51, 55–56, 61, 202–203, 204, 205, 207, 212–213, 214, 220, 221; and Tai Maharaj adoption case, 47, 189, 194; oratory, 48; editor, 48–49, 61, 74, 106–107; conflict in DES, 48–51; and Kshatriya tradition, 48; and Gokhale, 49–50, 52, 89–90, 227–228; on politics, 51; on social reform, 52–54, 55, 56, 80, 184, 215; a liberal, 52, 55, 60; and caste, 53–55, 56–57, 169; and orthodox society, 54, 56–57, 60, 94–95, 95n, 97; on untouchability, 54–55, 200–201; on religion, 55–56, 204; and Ranade, 55–56, 70, 105, 106, 124, 151, 189; lieutenants of, 55, 59–62, 91, 94–96, 126–127, 156, 171n, 186–191, 192, 192n, 194, 196–197, 202–203, 204–209, 210–215, 216, 217, 218, 221; *Gita Rahasya,* 55, 95n; *Orion,* 55; Age of Consent campaign, 56, 57–61, 57n, 61n, 62, 94, 170; charisma of, 56, 181, 191; party of, 56, 61, 62, 94, 98, 110, 124–125, 151, 161, 166, 170, 187–188, 189, 191; on tradition and modernity, 56, 61; and violence, 58–59, 61, 108, 113–114; and Brahmans, 61, 74, 79, 80, 179, 197, 199, 219; and students, 61, 126, 179, 190; in Poona, 61, 187–188, 194; and communal riots, 62, 69–71; and Mehta, 70, 171,

172; and Harris, 71, 74; imprisonment, 88, 180, 185, 192, 193; and tamasha tactics, 89–90; criticism of 94, 170, 184–185, 201, 202; use of myths, 97, 218; and symbols, 109; and princes, 109–110, 124; conflict with Kolhapur, 115–119; captures *PSS*, 115, 126n; and *rayats*, 124, 125, 144, 150, 151; a conservative, 125; and fair price grain shops, 125; on land policies, 148, 150; and Bombay elites, 167, 168, 174–175; Wacha and, 170, 175; and mill-hands, 172, 177, 178–181, 183; and strikes, 173, 178; and swadeshi, 173–177, 177n, 187; on factory legislation, 173; and temperance, 177; a democrat, 172, 181, 184; historiography of 1908 strike, 181–185; Communists on, 181–182, 184–185; on labour issues, 182–184, 185; prosecution of, 182; moves to left, 185–187; on price control, 185; on profiteering law, 185; and Labour Party, 185–186, 192; on swaraj, 190, 191, 192, 204, 215, 217, 218; and constitutional politics, 192, 202; a regional politician, 192–193, 199; and all-India politics, 192–193, 198–199; and Congress, 192n, 194, 212; and Muslim League, 193, 204, 214; and Muslims, 204, 214, 219; "responsive co-operation," 204, 213; and Khilafat movement, 204, 213, 214; death of, 205; legacy of, 215–216

Tilak, Shridharpant, 217
Times of India, 58, 78, 107, 127, 134, 180; and communal riots, 68, 70, 92–93; on labour force, 155, 156, 183–184
Toddy, 130, 136, 177; support for, 135, 135n, 158. *See also* Liquor; Temperance
Trade Union Conference: British, 186; All-India, 186
Trade unions; in Bombay City, 156, 183; and extremists, 182, 185, 186. *See also* Labour; Mill-hands
Trading groups: European, 64, 65; in Bombay City, 153, 154, 157, 158, 168, 180, 187; and swadeshi, 174
Tradition, 61, 168, 188; language of, 56; and modernity, 214, 218–219, 220
Transitional society, 220; myth of, 221
Tribals, 133, 135, 136
Troops, European, 113, 113n. *See also* Military
Tukaram, 11
Tyabji, Amiruddin, 157, 159, 230
Tyabji, Badruddin, 37, 157, 159, 160n, 167
Tyabji, Camiruddin, 157
Tyabji brothers, 157, 167

Umbargaon Taluka, 135

United Provinces, 161n, 199, 209, 210
Unrest, political, 33, 33n; and economic conditions, 42. *See also* Conspiracy theory; Riots; Strikes
Untouchables, 188; Tilak on, 54–55, 200 201; Gaekwar on, 111; abolition of status of, 189, 190. *See also* Depressed Classes; Scheduled Castes
Upanishads, 1
Usurper theory, 24–26, 30–31, 219; countered by Ranade, 43–44. *See also* Myths
Utkal, 209

Vaidya, Rao Bahadur Chintaman Vinayak, 175n, 176, 187, 198n
Vaishnava, 10; tradition, 11, 12–13, 15, 68
Vaishnawas, Vallabha, 57
Vaishyas, 7, 154
Vanis, *mela* of, 85
Vedanta, 187
Vedic ritual (Vedokta question), 116, 202
Vigilante group (Natus), 60
Vincent, R. H., 68, 70
Violence: and Tilak, 58–59; and Natus, 59–60, 92; and *melas*, 92; and Shivaji movement, 103, 107, 112, 113–114, 122; and mill-hands, 178–180. *See also* Non-violence
Vishalgad, Chief of, 112n, 115
Vishnu, 180
Vithoba (Vithal), 10, 15, 75, 180

Wacha, Dinshaw Edulji, 155, 157, 158, 160n, 161n, 190, 229; and toddy, 135; on land legislation, 149; on BPA, 162, 163, 164–165, 166; on Tilak, 170; on swadeshi, 175
Wadas, and *mela* movement, 77
Wadia, N. N., 165
Wai (Satara), 82
Wedderburn, William, 62n
Western India, 67, 151, 155, 174, 187, 192
Widows' Home, 89
Willingdon, Lord, 186, 186n
Wilson, Reverend John, 25
Wilson College, 95
Wolpert, Stanley A., 95n, 114
Working classes, 156, 181, 182, 183, 184; Tilak and 173, 177, 185

Yajnik, Javerilal, 69, 161n, 229
Yeola (Nasik): communal riot in, 70–71, 72, 73; and *mela* movement, 85
Yeotmal, 196
Young India, 122

Zamindars, 64, 140

www.ingramcontent.com/pod-product-compliance
Lightning Source LLC
Chambersburg PA
CBHW021701230426
43668CB00008B/691